MW01602060

I AM + AI

= A BETTER LIFE STORY

HENRY JAMESON

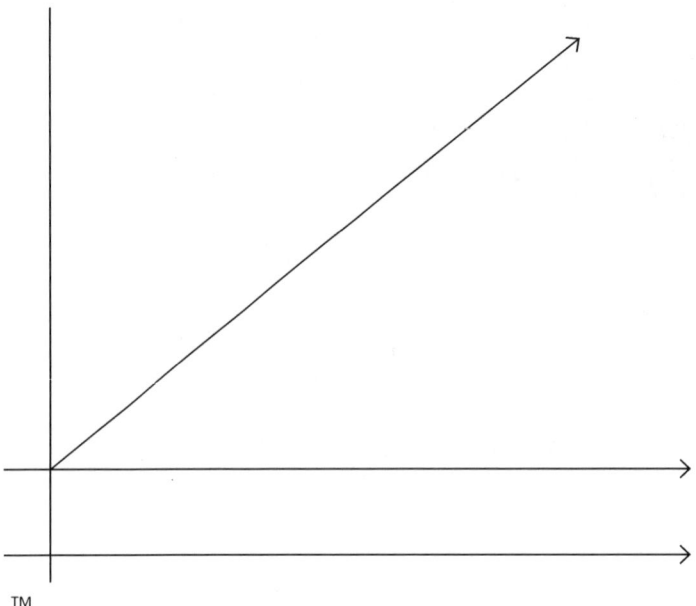

TM

ISBN: 9798303531758

DISCLAIMER

This book is a personal exploration of life improvement. My hope is to offer you ideas, opinions, encouragement, and practical tips to guide your own journey. However, it's important to clarify both what this book is meant to do and what it isn't meant to do.

What This Book Is

- This book is a collection of personal insights, observations, strategies, and explorations into the potential of life enhancing AI that I've found helpful in my pursuit of a better life story. It's about sharing tools that may inspire you to take meaningful action in your own life.

- The intention is to foster self-awareness, motivate positive changes, and provide a framework for personal reflection. My aim is to encourage you to take charge of your choices and use this content as a starting point for your own exploration.

- Consider this book a source of ideas, not prescriptions. Each chapter is designed to offer perspectives that may resonate with your unique experiences and circumstances.

What This Book Is Not

- This is not professional advice. I am not a licensed professional in mental health, medicine, finance, or any other regulated field. Please seek professional guidance when making important choices in these areas.

- This book does not promise guaranteed results. While the concepts discussed have been beneficial to me, they may not be universally applicable. Everyone's path is different, and your outcomes may vary.

It is not a substitute for professional care. If you have concerns that require expert advice, please consult a qualified practitioner in the appropriate field.

CONTENTS

FOREWORD

In a world where complexity grows with each passing moment, tools that distill clarity from chaos are invaluable. This book stands out as a pioneering resource for anyone seeking to enhance their life through purposeful action, self-improvement, and a powerful partnership with AI.

It offers a uniquely visual and engaging approach, taking readers through a journey that combines timeless principles with cutting-edge technology. With meticulously crafted visual charts and frameworks, the book transforms abstract ideas into accessible guides, allowing readers to "see" how life's intricate processes and choices fit into a larger, interconnected whole.

At the heart of this book is the SOAR framework—Situation, Objectives, Actions, Results—which, when combined with AI, becomes a dynamic force for life transformation. The synergy between SOAR and AI (or "S+AI") is revolutionary. SOAR provides a structured process for navigating life's challenges and goals, while AI serves as a constant companion—ready to offer guidance, motivation, and critical thinking on demand. Together, they form what the author aptly calls "I AM + AI," a partnership designed to keep readers adaptable, continuously prepared for new advancements in AI, and empowered to live a better life story.

Visual representations are one of the book's hallmarks, turning theoretical models into intuitive, practical tools. These charts don't just illustrate ideas; they serve as roadmaps for aligning actions with aspirations. The "Big Picture" chart, for instance, provides a comprehensive view of the journey from past experiences to present choices and future goals, helping readers see how each choice and experience fits into a bigger story. Each visual is crafted to make complex processes feel accessible and actionable.

This is more than self-improvement—it's a uniquely immersive way to engage with one's life story, where every choice adds to an evolving narrative that adapts to take advantage of new AI innovations.

The book's focus on "I AM" as an ever-present, adaptive persona is both profound and empowering. Here, "I AM" represents anyone and everyone—it embodies the reader's potential and their personal journey of growth. By centering self-improvement around "I AM," the book makes progress a deeply personal endeavor, encouraging readers to understand their past, embrace their NOW, and prepare for a future enhanced by AI.

With the guiding principles of "Job #1: Feel Good NOW" and "Job #2: Plan to Feel Better," this approach to well-being emphasizes living fully in the present while setting intentional plans that align with each reader's evolving goals and prepare them for whatever AI—and life—may bring.

Young adults, in particular, stand to gain immeasurably from this guide. The book recognizes the complexities of young adulthood and the myriad choices that define it, without prescribing a single path. Instead, it provides adaptable tools, offering the SOAR process as a steady framework in choice-making and life story improvement.

With AI as a tool for self-expansion, readers are invited to cultivate a long-term relationship with technology—one where AI serves as a mentor, planner, and supporter that grows with them. This empowering approach is particularly valuable for a generation ready to integrate technology seamlessly into their lives.

Beyond its structured approaches and visual guides, the book synthesizes insights from positive psychology, management theories, and personal development, creating a holistic framework for living well. By integrating well-established methods like Maslow's hierarchy of needs and Drucker's management principles with AI's ever-evolving capabilities, the book builds a bridge between personal growth and technological advancement. It demystifies complex theories and makes them actionable, relevant, and even enjoyable.

This is a book to return to repeatedly, each read-through revealing new layers and insights.

Ultimately, this book is more than a guide; it's a toolkit for thriving in a world that often feels overwhelming. Through its unique approach, readers are encouraged to embrace growth, make thoughtful choices, and live a life story that feels genuinely fulfilling. As you embark on this journey with "I AM + AI," prepare to see your world differently, to embrace new opportunities with renewed vigor, and, most importantly, to shape a life story that feels undeniably your own.

I AM+AI

INTRODUCTION

> ## *QUICK START*
>
> 1. AI (Machine) soon will dramatically change how people think, feel and act.
>
> 2. I AM (Person) can choose to adapt to keep up with AI and optimize the millions of opportunities created by AI…or not.
>
> 3. I AM + AI = Synergy to help I AM feel better NOW, make better choices and live a better life story.

Humanity is not merely at a crossroads of history creation, we are NOW at a spaghetti-like intersection of new and fast changing situations being created by AI that lead in all different directions, affecting virtually everything.

- AI (Artificial Intelligence): Computer simulation of human intelligence.

I AM is used as an example of a person.

- I AM: A fictional character acting as an example of I AM's perspectives on SOARing ideas and life story improvement.

People who choose to adapt to AI can get the synergy benefits of Big Picture understanding and SOAR improvement of anything, all enhanced with AI.

- SYNERGY: Two things working together that create better results than the sum of the individual contributions.

Synergy is often described as $1 + 1 = 3$.

It is a powerful concept known to multiply strengths, mitigate weaknesses, and create a dynamic environment where collective efforts lead to far-reaching and impactful results. It emphasizes the power of collaboration, making it a cornerstone of successful teams, partnerships, and projects.

It is important to note that synergy can be applied to virtually every concept in this book. Its use can give higher quality results, faster learning and skill development, greater creativity, increased efficiency, more motivation and greater confidence.

Give AI a try. Experiment. Play with it…it won't break or get embarrassed.

BOOK OVERVIEW

I AM + AI's intent is to help you make better choices and live a better life story. You can improve the life story you are creating every day by making better choices, starting today.

Your life story is the account of everything that happens in your life. It is the legacy you leave your family, friends and to the world. *I AM + AI* is intended to help you create a continuously improving life story, from NOW on.

To improve your life story:

1. Understand the Big Picture, a snapshot of how life story puzzle pieces seem to fit together.
2. Understand the Fundamental Flows continually moving with and through you.
3. Make better choices NOW to create better experiences, which can create better memories.
4. Accomplish Job #1 and Job #2 at every NOW.
5. Navigate an improving life story by SOARing.
6. Enhance all of the above by synergizing with AI.

I AM + AI shows you how, with visual presentations and clear descriptions, I AM's perception of important ways the world of improvement seems to work. It presents a "Big Picture" of how the puzzle pieces of your life fit together in the grand scheme of things. It shows you the Fundamental Flows that impact your life 24/7/365. Then, you can choose to navigate the flow toward accomplishing whatever you want in life!

It is especially useful to young people and others in critical choice-making periods of life to help make better choices. It is useful for everyone wanting to improve their choice-making abilities, live better life experiences and create better life stories…or to see their children and grandchildren do so.

Young adulthood is a period in life when many critical choices are frequently made. Sometimes, young adults have enough experience and knowledge to make good choices. However, many others may need help in navigating through the choice process and dizzying array of alternatives available to them.

Young adults in particular face many opportunities to make choices that may define their entire lives. All choices have consequences and some of the choices can be painful reminders for the rest of their lives.

AI assists you in creating and managing plans for any time span, from tomorrow on through your customized life story plan. You can develop a relationship with AI as a 24/7/365 mentor, teacher, conversationalist, manager, critical thinker, problem solver, motivator, or advisor to help you make better choices and develop better plans. AI can monitor your plans and give you on-going feedback whenever you desire.

AI encourages your growth by suggesting more and better questions about any topic. *I AM + AI* discusses more than 250 of life's most important topics, each of which is easy for you to expand your knowledge through AI.

I AM

I AM + AI stars I AM, a fictional character so named to reflect Rene Descartes 1637 statement that "I think, therefore I am". I AM acts as an example of I AM's perspectives on SOARing ideas and life story improvement. I AM is apolitical, nonpartisan, impartial, unbiased, non-discriminatory, unprejudiced, inclusive, not of any sex and is neutral in any other divisive orientation.

I AM is always at NOW intending to think better, feel better and act better from NOW on. Because NOW is so key, NOW is always capitalized to remind I AM of its importance.

I AM + AI life story improvement is based on the SOAR process.

- SOAR: Acronym of Situation, Objectives, Actions, Results.
- SOARing: Using the SOAR intentional improvement process to feel better and live a better life story.
- SOARing Process: The SOAR method to reach objectives and navigate life.

This is how it applies to I AM.

S = Situation	I AM living life.
O = Objectives	To feel good NOW, feel better tomorrow and live a better life story.
A = Actions	By enjoying NOW, using the SOARing life improvement process and using an AI mentor 24/7 to assist and enhance everything important.
R = Results	Feel good NOW, feel better tomorrow and live a better life story.

The SOAR framework can be used in every situation every day. It is scalable from a nanosecond up to a lifetime. It has wide application throughout the living life process; from writing a paragraph, to creating new ideas, to solving a problem, to generating an organization's plan, to pursuing an opportunity, to living a better life story, and every other process, each of which can be enhanced by the synergy afforded by AI.

I AM + AI is presented as unique visual frameworks, supported by text explanations.

A simple visual chart forms the basis of SOARing. It puts into practice the old adage that a picture is worth 1,000 words. A picture communicates more information and relationships much faster than words. A picture also results in higher retention and understanding than text only.

I AM + AI presents these hundreds of concepts within the SOARing framework. It puts into one place improvement concepts from psychology, positive psychology, business management, new age, science, religion, philosophy, self-help, and others. It eliminates the confusion of not knowing where a word or concept fits into the overall, grand scheme of things.

Tired of reading self-help books/articles/hints and then not much happens to improve your life? With *I AM + AI,* you can plug all the self-help ideas into the Big Picture to see where they fit and how they relate to each other.

The universe is complex, to state the obvious. In the spirit of KISS (Keep It Super Simple), the information is arranged like a pyramid, with more information as the pyramid base gets broader. The top represents the simplest, most fundamental points. These are in "Quick Start" sections. The next level down expands with ample main content. The base, which can be of any size, represents the more expansive information available through AI.

I AM + AI is the centerpiece for better understanding very complex topics, like a human being. The structural framework makes it easy to plug-in new information from favorite sources, gurus, authors, internet, course studies, etc.

It is easily personalized to help create your profile or help you understand others better by profiling them. It is complemented with examples, forms and inspiration to create Improvement Plans, individual profiles, workbooks, new topics, additional definitions and other analysis tools.

I AM + AI can be thought of as **"I AM's Life Story Improvement Manual"**.

I AM + AI is intended to help you live a better life story by making better choices using the SOARing improvement process...the common denominator of all improvement processes. (See Common Denominator chart in Appendix)

SOARing can help you make better choices by using the SOARing Process to:

1. Continuously improve your essence; Body/Mind/Soul/Spirit (BMSS), Guidance System and Toolbox.
2. Focus thoughts and feelings on the most important topics.
3. Improve your feelings by improving your thoughts.
4. SOAR on topics aligned with your Vision and Focal Points.

A SOARing Experience (SE) is the form I AM uses at every situation that I AM chooses to improve. The chain of successful SEs creates I AM's living a better life story from NOW on.

Use the Feelings Platform to keep score of your progress with your most important feedback mechanism...your feelings. I AM's overall intent is to live in positive energy as much of the time as possible. Your life story is measured by how you feel, not by what others think. You can easily monitor your feelings by using Chart F.

> *The secret to continuous improvement and living a better life story:*
> *Live in positive energy, make better choices,*
> *enjoy today and manage the creation of feel -better tomorrows,*
> *by SOARing and enhancement by AI.*

ABOUT THE AUTHOR

"I wish I had known all this when I was younger"

How many times have you thought or said that sentiment during your life story journey? I know that I have said it plenty of times and that it has become an inspiration for this book. I want to try to help others "know all this" at earlier ages. Perhaps someone in your family would benefit from such a learning experience?

With each of my major learning experiences, I felt this sentiment.

By age 31, I had my MBA and enough (four Fortune 500 companies) exposure to know how the big kids did things in advertising, brand management and new product management. I escaped into entrepreneurship to carve my place in the world of business. I started several companies from scratch and hoped for the best.

My experiences opened my eyes to the high value of KISS. One of my mentors drilled into me, "If you can't reduce it to one page, you haven't thought about it enough." Thus, one-pagers with ample 1-2-3 bullet points became standard practice.

I have noted that in the new world of AI, many queries are responded to with a one-pager. I suspect that AI learned a thing or two from my personal mentor of years ago. He became CEO of various major operations.

The world and things tend to evolve into complexity, so I adopted KISS, one-pagers and drawings of frameworks of how things interrelate to become my primary go-to practices. This was a natural fit because I am blessed with a good IQ, but am also blessed with a low ability to memorize things and have CRS (Can't Remember Stuff). So, I try to make things as simple as I can in an attempt to understand and remember them.

When KISSing, the process seeks to go up the pyramid of details to discover the root causes/key issues of the topic and then to address them.

As I grew and tried to improve, I discovered that there was a common thread of processes all around me. Processes like decision-making, problem solving, the Scientific Method, the practice of medicine, the simple process of travel and many others that all boil down to the SOARing process.

- **S**ituation: I AM's perception of the set of circumstances Here NOW.
- **O**bjectives: I AM's desired improvements to help I AM feel better, achievable by an intended time.
- **A**ctions: The process of I AM doing things or taking steps to achieve the Objectives.
- **R**esults: The consequences, effects, or outcomes from I AM's Actions.

With this discovery, I created and marketed the SOARing Achievement Manager manual and pocket planner/organizer. It was based on the SOAR framework, Management by Objectives and time management.

As things turned out, other of my ventures took off and I had the opportunity to put SOARing into daily practice creating and managing businesses with thousands of employees through the years.

The SOARing mindset was instrumental in creating and managing several multi-million dollar businesses. Eventually, the successes allowed me to semi-retire at 49 and retire at 55. Since then, I have had the pleasure of living the "Give Back" life phase and have been able to continue SOARing on many projects.

In my life journey, I have been reminded frequently of my father's early advice to "Do as I say, not as I do". Perhaps you have heard the same? What I have written here tends to be a bit idealistic and short of the painful experiences life throws our way. That is by intent. A positive model gives people a framework to aspire to and build from.

I have made my share of bad choices. More than a few have been significant life changers. Hopefully, my experiences and studies have helped me refine the framework of life improvement to the point of helping others make better choices and live better life stories.

I AM and I wish you a life of feel-good NOWs, choice enhancement by synergizing with AI as your companion, always being the best you can be and living the best life story you can!

Aloha!

SITUATION

I AM's perception of the set of circumstances Here NOW.

SITUATION

Our world is becoming more and more complex every day. As a result, people are having a tougher time keeping up with all the changes and are becoming more and more negatively stressed. That distress is manifesting in physical and psychological problems.

I AM + AI offers SOARing frameworks and AI directional guidance to help I AM and others better cope with massive change and make the most of all the opportunities these changes present.

In essence, the current situation is unfolding with many problems and some huge opportunities.

QUICK START

PROBLEMS

1. CHANGE: The explosion of AI and knowledge is rapidly altering the relationships among things, people, resources, technologies, self-confidences, etc.

2. COMPLEXITY: This new knowledge and changing relationships dramatically increase life's complexity.

3. NEGATIVE STRESS: The increase in complexity is increasing the negative stresses people feel.

4. NEGATIVE STRESS PROBLEMS: The negative stresses can manifest in various negative feelings, along with many possible physical and psychological problems.

OPPORTUNITIES

1. SOARing: Reveals the Big Picture secrets of how the world of improvement seems to work and how to apply these secrets to help I AM make better choices NOW and create a better life story.

2. AI: Shows how to use AI as a cutting-edge tool to assist I AM with continuing improvement and living a lifetime of an expanding life story.

PROBLEMS

1. KNOWLEDGE EXPLOSION = BIG CHANGES

The explosion of knowledge continually changes the relationships among things.

As human knowledge grows, especially due to rapid technological advances and greater access to information, shifts are seen in how things are interconnected. For example, technology impacts economics, which then influences social structures. This interconnectedness changes how we understand and interact with the world, requiring us to constantly update our knowledge base and adapt our skills.

As we learn more, especially with new technology and lots of information available, things in the world start to connect differently. For example, how we use our phones affects our jobs and our social lives. This makes the world a more complicated place.

2. INCREASING COMPLEXITY

These continual changes cause exponential increases in complexity.

With more information and interconnections, systems become more complex. This isn't just about having more knowledge, but also about the increasing difficulty of understanding how different parts of a system affect each other. For instance, the global economy is influenced by countless factors including technology, politics, social trends, and environmental changes, making it challenging for individuals to grasp and predict.

With everything connected, life gets trickier. It's harder to understand how changes in one area, like the economy, might affect other areas, like jobs or the environment. This means we have to think about a lot of things at once, which can be overwhelming.

3. INCREASING NEGATIVE STRESS

The increase in complexity increases negative stress for people.

As complexity increases, so does the difficulty in making decisions and predictions. People must consider a wider range of factors and potential outcomes, leading to decision fatigue and cognitive overload. This is particularly evident in areas like career choices, where the paths are no longer linear and the outcomes are uncertain. The effort to keep up and make informed decisions can be highly stressful.

When life is more complicated, it can be tough to make decisions because there's so much to think about. This can make people feel stressed because they're always trying to keep up and make the right choices.

There is an increasing feeling that the Peter Principle has matured in many leadership roles in government, big and small business, and organizations of all sizes. The Peter Principle suggests that many people rise through their organizational hierarchy to their level of incompetence. This increases stress to the individual as well as to their organization.

4. NEGATIVE STRESS PROBLEMS

Negative stress can manifest across different parts of people. These are all negative energy generating negative feelings.

1. Emotional Responses like: Anxiety. Restlessness. Lack of motivation or focus. Irritability or anger. Overwhelmed. Sadness or depression.

2. Cognitive Effects like: Memory problems. Poor judgment. Constant worrying. Negative thinking. Indecisiveness. Obsessive or compulsive behaviors. Suicidal thoughts.

3. Physical Symptoms like: Headaches and migraines. Muscle tension and pain. Fatigue. Digestive issues. Sleep disturbances. Changes in menstrual cycle for women. Increased heart rate and chest pain. Weakened immune system.

4. Behavioral Changes like: Eating changes. Angry outbursts. Drug or alcohol misuse. Social withdrawal. Decreased exercise. Procrastination. Nervous habits.

These issues reflect a complex web of challenges that interact across different domains of life, impacting overall well-being and development.

The negative stress resulting from navigating this complex and rapidly changing world manifests in various forms across different SOARing Life Domains.

1. CAREER: Job loss. Unemployment. New Job. Skills Lack. Workplace Discrimination. Work-Life Balance. Retirement. Schooling needs. Missed promotion.

2. ENVIRONMENT: Housing. Moving. New/old house. Possessions. Living conditions. Pollution exposure. Jail. Crime. Lawsuits. Maintenance. Costs. Urbanization. Neighbors.

3. FINANCE: Income. Expenses. Net worth. Economic Dependency. Poverty. Inflation. Savings. Debt. Taxes. Investments. Payments. Financial literacy. Homelessness.

4. HEALTH: Weight. Substance Abuse. Physical Inactivity. Deaths in family. Mental Health. Access to Healthcare. Illness. Injury. Poor lifestyle.

5. IMPROVEMENT: Overwhelm from Choices. Pressure to Succeed. Finding purpose. Self-esteem. Keeping up with change. Education and skill development. Procrastination.

1. LEISURE: Inadequate skill levels. Lack of time. Activities cost. Hand-held addiction. TV. Non-athletic. Uncomfortable outdoors. Limited interests. Can't travel. Teams.

2. RELATIONSHIPS: Marriage. Divorce. Separation. Infidelity. Pregnancy. Abuse. Holidays. Family. Friends. Neighbors. Memberships. Dating. Sex. Boss. Employees.

3. SPIRITUALITY: Beliefs. Anti---------ism. Values. Religions. Sects. Differences. Traditions. Search for meaning. Interfaith Challenges. Spiritual Well-being.

Negative stress can come from anywhere at any time. It tends to increase at certain times of life as certain situations unfold. It tends to happen at points in life where major changes are happening. When they happen, they can be flash events or long-smoldering problems over time.

Every problem can be addressed as a Topic in the SOARing Process or by a professional. In SOARing, I AM shows how to address problems and perhaps turn problems into opportunities.

OPPORTUNITIES

SOARing

I AM's natural state is living life in positive energy. That is, experiencing the positive emotions of feeling good NOW and planning to feel better in the future.

As such, I AM tries to find opportunities where others find problems. Having a positive mindset helps I AM find positive emotions, such as:

Advancement	Curiosity	Healed	Optimistic
Affection	Delight	Healthy	Passion
Alignment	Eagerness	Hopeful	Peace
Alive	Empathy	Improvement	Pleasure
Amusement	Empowered	Informed	Positive
Appreciated	Energized	Inspired	Progress
Awakened	Enthusiastic	Interested	Safe
Beauty	Excitement	Invigorated	Satisfaction
Better	Expansion	Joy	Self-Actualizing
Bliss	Flourishing	Kindness	Selfless
Calmness	Free	Love	SOARing
Carefree	Fulfillment	Motivated	Spiritual
Cheerful	Gratitude	New Person	Successful
Confident	Growth	Normal	Thriving
Contentment	Happy	Oneness	Up

Sometimes, the negative energy of stress takes I AM out of positive energy and into negative energy.

Anger	Grief	Overwhelmed	Self-Consciousness
Anxiety	Guilt	Pain	Selfish
Blame	Hatred	Panic	Shame
Boredom	Hostility	Pessimism	Sorrow
Depression	Impatience	Powerless	Stressed
Despair	Insecure	Pressure	Suffering
Difficulty	Irritated	Rage	Threatened
Disapproval	Jealousy	Regret	Troubled
Down	Misery	Resentment	Unhappy
Embarrassment	Negative	Sadness	Worry
Failure	Nervous	Self-Centered	Worthless

When in negative energy, it is I AM's responsibility to get back into positive energy as soon and safely as possible.

I AM looks at I AM's life as a journey. It is like a highway from here NOW to a desired destination. I AM measures the journey, not in miles, but in feelings. The more of the journey in positive feelings, the better the journey!

I AM's journey is mostly a smooth, enjoyable trip in positive energy with positive feelings. But periodically, I AM hits a pothole or bump in the road. This can be a stressful, negative energy event. I AM tries to avoid these challenges, but sometimes they are out of I AM's control and they just happen.

SOARing has helped I AM develop resilience. Resilience is I AM's ability to adjust to and bounce back from challenging life experiences. This adaptability and toughness helps I AM cope with the potholes and bumps in the road.

Bumps and potholes are an inevitable part of life. I AM knows they exist various places along the road. I AM also knows that beyond the bumps and potholes, there is much more open road ahead brimming with opportunities and positive emotions. I AM SOARs out of the bumps and potholes back into positive energy and enjoyment of the journey toward I AM's desired destination.

SOARing has helped I AM identify the desired destination. SOARing has helped I AM develop I AM's personal roadmap to get to the destination. SOARing has helped I AM prepare for the bumps and potholes. SOARing has helped I AM know how to get out of the bumps and potholes. SOARing has helped I AM keep things in perspective and to always keep an eye on the overall journey and desired destination.

Some of the ways SOARing helps I AM are to:

✓ Gain and maintain control of I AM's life.

✓ Feel good in the present.

✓ Try to feel even better in the future.

✓ Address the most important Topic in every Situation.

✓ Continuous improvement through SOARing.

✓ Make better-feeling choices at NOW.

✓ Live in NOW.

✓ Get out of negative energy by finding feel-better thoughts.

✓ Navigate both problems and opportunity.

✓ Understand how the Big Picture influences all choices.

✓ Identify I AM's Vision.

✓ Use I AM's Guidance System to SOAR toward that Vision.

✓ Use AI to advise and mentor I AM's life story journey.

✓ Make I AM's life better.

KEY ELEMENTS

- **BIG PICTURE:** I AM's perspective of how the world of improvement seems to work, all on one chart! The Big Picture provides I AM with a broader worldview and allows I AM to bring a bigger perspective to every NOW. This knowledge and understanding helps I AM make better choices and decisions.

- **LIFE STORY:** Every moment I AM lives creates an additional part of I AM's lifetime. Wherever I AM is NOW, I AM wants to make the life story better from NOW on. I AM's life story is like a piece of the Big Picture puzzle. The better I AM's life story, the better the entire puzzle.

- **NOW:** The present moment in time is the place where I AM lives. From NOW, I AM can look back at the past and look ahead to the future. But, I AM lives, makes choices, and creates a life story in the present.

  ○ JOB #1: At every NOW, I AM focuses on accomplishing Job #1. To feel good NOW!

  ○ JOB #2: At every NOW, I AM focuses on accomplishing Job #2. To plan to feel better in the future.

- **SATISFACTION:** I AM's life story is built of need/want satisfactions and dissatisfactions. The more satisfactions, the better I AM's life story. I AM satisfies needs to live and satisfies wants to grow and thrive.

- **GUIDANCE SYSTEM:** This represents much of what I AM has become to NOW. It is how I AM navigates the ups and downs of life. I AM has built in the past the Guidance System that arrives at NOW. Should it not be working to I AM's liking, I AM can choose to improve it at any NOW.

- VISION: I AM has chosen I AM's long-term visualization of the ideal I AM aspires to create. This is I AM's "Dream". The Vision is the big idea that everything else is focused toward.

- FOCAL POINTS: These are I AM's most important long-term centers of attention that guide the pursuit of I AM's vision. These act as a roadmap guiding I AM's life story journey.

  - BODY, MIND, SOUL, SPIRIT: I AM feels much better when these are aligned.

  - POSITIVE MINDSET: If I AM arrives at every NOW feeling positive energy, I AM will attract more positive energy and has a great chance to create an enjoyable NOW and better feeling futures. A positive mindset is one of I AM's most important attributes. Having a positive mindset makes I AM's life easier in many aspects.

  - WELL-BEING: I AM's major focus is on the five elements of well-being…per Martin E. P. Seligman in his ground-breaking positive psychology book "Flourish".

    1. Positive Emotions: Everything in *I AM + AI* orients toward I AM living as much time as possible in positive emotion/energy. The continuous focus is on how I AM feels at NOW. At every NOW, I AM has two jobs. Job #1 is to feel good NOW. Job #2 is to plan to feel better in the future.

    2. Engagement: When I AM is totally into and flowing with a task, I AM is engaged. At every NOW, I AM chooses to focus on something. I AM tries to focus on Topics that engage I AM.

    3. Meaning: SOARing is intended to give more meaning to I AM's NOW and for the life story journey. I AM tries to focus on only the most important Topics, those that give I AM the most meaning.

    4. Accomplishments: SOARing is all about accomplishing improvements. The S is the current Situation defined. The O is the improvement being sought. The A is the Action plan to accomplish the O. The R records the accomplishment of the O.

    5. Positive Relationships: Building and nurturing a group of family, friends and associates is key to I AM's improvement and the living of a better life story. The close network can serve as mentor, confidant, master mind, or advisor to I AM at any moment of need. I AM appreciates I AM's support group.

  - TOOLBOX: What I AM brings along to every NOW to assist with fixing any problem and pursuing any opportunity. I AM has about 50 tools in the Toolbox.

- **SIS (SOARING IMPROVEMENT SYSTEM):**

  - SOARing PROCESS: How I AM manages the intentional improvement of I AM's life story. I AM's core operating system. How I AM improves anything.

- ○ FEELINGS PLATFORM: The unique visual framework that helps I AM manage I AM's feelings at every NOW. Feelings are how I AM keeps score. Positive feelings are good and where I AM wants to be most of the time. Negative feelings are not so good, but I AM knows how to get back to positive feelings. When I AM knows I AM's feelings, I AM knows how successful I AM is being NOW in the pursuit of a better life story.

- ○ IMPROVEMENT PYRAMID: An inspiring visual to help I AM manage all the journey steps that create a better and better life story. I AM's life and viewpoint keeps getting more and more beautiful as I AM ascends the pyramid.

- **LIFE DOMAINS:** Keeps I AM focused on the most important areas of I AM's long-term interests and activities.

- **CHOICE CYCLE:** The most important 1-2-3 process I AM does at every NOW. The better the choices, the better I AM feels NOW and in the future.

- **CELEBRATION:** What happens when I AM feels good R's.

JOB #1 = To Feel Good NOW!

SOARing PROCESS *(CAUSE)*

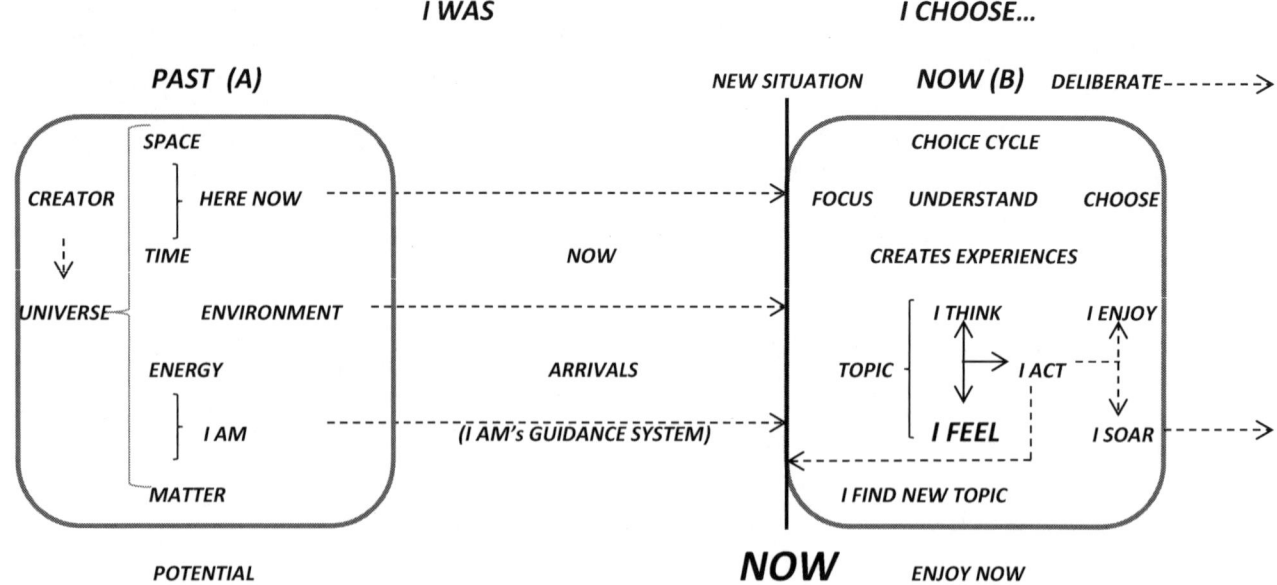

I WAS

I CHOOSE...

PAST (A)

NEW SITUATION | NOW (B) | DELIBERATE - - - - - - - ->

SPACE

CREATOR | HERE NOW

TIME

UNIVERSE | ENVIRONMENT

ENERGY

I AM

MATTER

CHOICE CYCLE

FOCUS UNDERSTAND CHOOSE

CREATES EXPERIENCES

I THINK | I ENJOY

TOPIC | I ACT

I FEEL | I SOAR

I FIND NEW TOPIC

NOW

ARRIVALS

(I AM's GUIDANCE SYSTEM)

POTENTIAL

NOW

ENJOY NOW

FEELINGS PLATFORM *(EFFECT)*

I FELT

I FEEL...

NOW (F)

PAST NOWs (E)

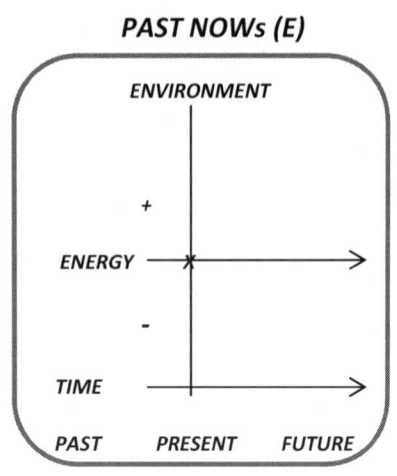

ENVIRONMENT

+

ENERGY

-

TIME

PAST PRESENT FUTURE

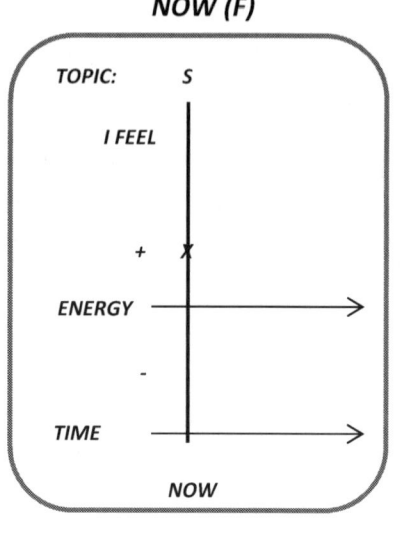

TOPIC: S

I FEEL

+

ENERGY

-

TIME

NOW

NOW, I AM HERE to ENJOY

PICTURE

JOB #2 = To Plan to Feel Better in the Future!

SOARing PROCESS *(CAUSE)*

I SOAR

FUTURE (C)

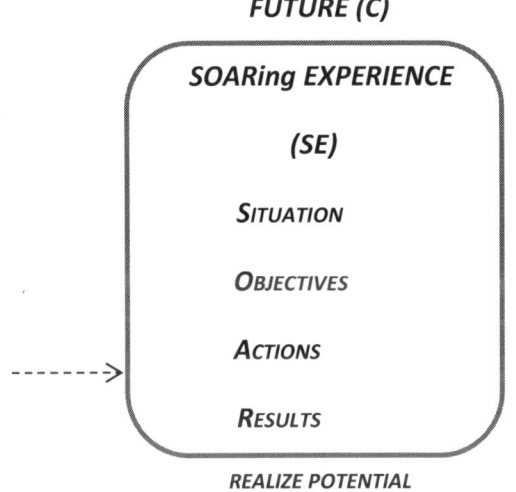

SOARing EXPERIENCE

(SE)

SITUATION

OBJECTIVES

ACTIONS

RESULTS

REALIZE POTENTIAL

LIFE STORY (D)

GUIDANCE

SYSTEM   VISION

FOCAL POINTS

SOARing

LIFE DOMAINS

MANAGED by SE's & AI

IMPROVEMENT PYRAMID

FEELINGS PLATFORM *(EFFECT)*

I FEEL BETTER

BETTER NOWs (G)

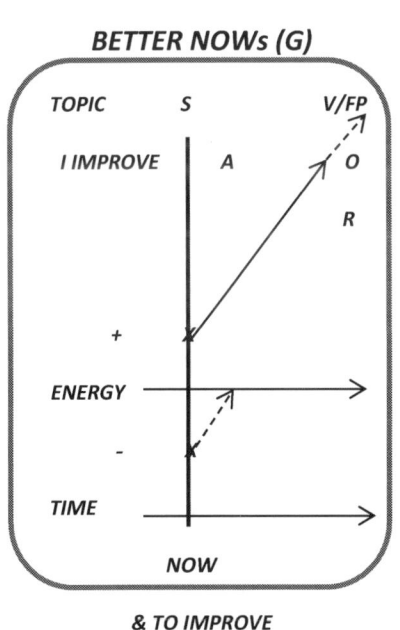

BETTER LIFE STORY (H)

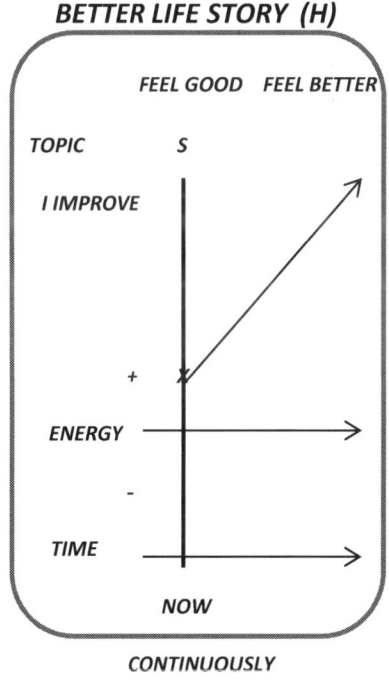

& TO IMPROVE   CONTINUOUSLY

17

BIG PICTURE ESSENCE

QUICK START

1. The Big Picture is the unique visual framework for all SOARing, giving I AM context and a big perspective for creating a bigger, better and continuously expanding life story.

2. It provides a foundation for helping I AM make better choices, the key to a better life story.

3. All SOARing starts with a focus on I AM at NOW, looking back at the past, enjoying NOW and looking ahead to a better future.

4. At each NOW, I AM has two jobs:

   - JOB #1 is to feel good NOW.

   - JOB #2 is to plan to feel better in the future.

5. I AM uses the SOARing Process to manage improvement, both NOW and in the future.

6. I AM manages the most important measure, I AM's feelings, with the Feelings Platform.

7. The Feelings Platform reflects I AM's feelings about things being done in the SOARing Process.

The Big Picture is a KISS perspective of the way I AM sees how the world of improvement seems to work.

Having this perspective, I AM can choose to expand on and improve on any of the wondrous details of life throughout I AM's lifetime. With the understanding of the Big Picture, I AM can enhance I AM's ability to make better choices. Good choices are the key to living a better life story.

The Big Picture gives I AM a broad context within which choices and actions can be evaluated for the best alternatives. The better I AM understands, the better alternatives become available for finding the best choices. The use of AI can further expand I AM's perspective and the generation of alternatives.

The Big Picture helps I AM prioritize Topics in I AM's life. From the millions of available alternatives at every NOW, I AM tries to address the most important Topics at each NOW.

The Big Picture shows I AM's perspective of the natural flow of time and the universal process of improvement. Time flows left to right, from the past, to NOW, to better NOWs and to a better life story. The process flows top to bottom, from the SOARing Process (causes) to the Feelings Platform (effects).

In essence, I AM lives life at NOW and tries to feel good. While at NOW, I AM makes choices to try to create a better feeling future.

Understanding these time and process flows, along with their relationships, can help I AM feel good.

NOW, feel better in the future and live a better life story.

The Big Picture represents much of how the world of improvement seems to work. The world is extraordinarily complex, but how it seems to work can be boiled down to the single Big Picture.

I AM

I AM navigates life by using the Big Picture both horizontally and vertically.

HORIZONTALLY

I AM lives life partially by time.

The flow of time happens left to right in the form of the:

- SOARing Process (Activities), shown in Charts A, B, C and D.
- Feelings Platform (Feelings), shown in Charts E, F, G and H.

I AM lives at NOW. From NOW, I AM can look back at the past, feel NOW and look ahead to the future.

SOARing PROCESS (I CHOOSE…)

- A. The past has helped I AM develop I AM's Guidance System.
- B. I AM arrives at NOW to focus on a Topic and choose what to do about it.
- C. The most important NOW Topics are acted upon by SOARing Experiences (SEs).
- D. I AM manages a lifetime of SEs toward I AM's Vision, guided by AI and Focal Points.

FEELINGS PLATFORM (I FEEL…)

- E. The development of I AM's feelings in history.
- F. How I AM feels NOW about the Topic…positive energy (+), negative energy (-).
- G. Improvement Plan to SOAR to try to achieve something that will make I AM feel better.
- H. The lifetime accumulation of improved Topics that help make I AM feel better.

VERTICALLY

I AM also lives partially by managing life.

I AM has chosen to have two jobs to try to accomplish at every NOW.

- JOB #1: To feel good NOW.
- JOB #2: To plan to feel better in the future.

These jobs are managed in pairs at each time period. For instance, at NOW, I AM does the activities in the SOARing Process and then views feelings feedback in the Feelings Platform.

If I AM accomplishes both jobs most of the time, I AM can create and live a better life story. I AM's job accomplishments are measured by how I AM feels, not by what others think.

JOB #1 (To Feel Good NOW)

- A. I AM's potential gets developed and is aimed at NOW, along with Here NOW and Environment.
- B. I AM's big perspective helps I AM look for and find the most important Topics and make better choices through the I Think-I Feel-I Act cycle to help I AM enjoy NOW.
- E. The feelings from learned and unlearned lessons of the past are available to I AM at NOW.
- F. I AM in positive energy, enjoying NOW.

JOB #2 (To Plan to Feel Better in the Future)

- C. I AM SOARing with a SOARing Experience for each priority Topic.
- D. I AM's continual managing of I AM's Life Domains, guided by AI and Focal Points toward I AM's Vision.
- G. I AM planning to achieve improved future NOWs by SOARing.
- H. I AM managing to achieve continuous improvement to live a better life story.

By navigating and understanding the flows of the Big Picture, I AM can make more informed, strategic and impactful choices at NOW. Better choices add up to living a better life story.

NAVIGATE the FLOW with INTENTION

JOB #1

QUICK START

I AM believes that this lifetime is intended to be lived in positive energy as much time as possible.

To live that belief, I AM tries to accomplish two jobs at every NOW.

- JOB #1: To feel good NOW.

- JOB #2: To plan to feel better in the future.

Job #1 is accomplished at NOW if I AM's feelings are in positive energy.

The Big Picture chart is split into two halves, dividing left and right sides. The left side represents Job #1 and the right side represents Job #2. Job #1 is influenced by the Past and is accomplished at NOW. Specifically, I AM completes the phrase "I Feel…" with current feelings.

The past can significantly influence I AM's NOW feelings. For instance, if I AM's recent experiences have been in positive energy, it is likely that I AM arrives at NOW feeling good.

The past produced all that I AM has become up to NOW. What I AM has become was influenced by the environment and I AM's interaction with that environment.

I AM's Guidance System has been developed by I AM over the past and is a big part of determining what I AM has become and what I AM can become from NOW on. The Guidance System starts with I AM's stated Vision…the long-term visualization of the ideal I AM aspires to create.

I AM also has created the guidelines I AM has chosen to follow in order to get I AM to I AM's Vision. These guidelines are I AM's Focal Points. If I AM is following I AM's Focal Points toward I AM's Vision, I AM probably arrives at most NOWs feeling good.

On the other hand, I AM may have had recently one or more negative feeling experiences. That negative energy may carry over to NOW. At every NOW, I AM has a choice to continue the past negative feelings or to change them by thinking feel-better thoughts.

One thing that can have a big influence on I AM's feelings arriving at NOW is I AM's mindset. A positive mindset creates many more positive energy NOWs!

SOARing PERSPECTIVE

The easiest way for I AM to know NOW feelings is to complete the phrase "I Feel…" If the response is a word of positive energy, I AM is enjoying NOW with good feelings. If the response is negative energy, I AM is not enjoying NOW.

I AM has accumulated a list of some of the most frequently used positive words that I AM answers when I AM is feeling good. I AM feels…

Advancement	Curiosity	Healed	Optimistic
Affection	Delight	Healthy	Passion
Alignment	Eagerness	Hopeful	Peace
Alive	Empathy	Improvement	Pleasure
Amusement	Empowered	Informed	Positive
Appreciated	Energized	Inspired	Progress
Awakened	Enthusiastic	Interested	Safe
Beauty	Excitement	Invigorated	Satisfaction
Better	Expansion	Joy	Self-Actualizing
Bliss	Flourishing	Kindness	Selfless
Calmness	Free	Love	SOARing
Carefree	Fulfillment	Motivated	Spiritual
Cheerful	Gratitude	New Person	Successful
Confident	Growth	Normal	Thriving
Contentment	Happy	Oneness	Up

On the other hand, if I AM uses any of these negative words, I AM needs to get back to thinking "feel-better" thoughts.

Anger	Grief	Overwhelmed	Self-Consciousness
Anxiety	Guilt	Pain	Selfish
Blame	Hatred	Panic	Shame
Boredom	Hostility	Pessimism	Sorrow
Depression	Impatience	Powerless	Stressed
Despair	Insecure	Pressure	Suffering
Difficulty	Irritated	Rage	Threatened
Disapproval	Jealousy	Regret	Troubled
Down	Misery	Resentment	Unhappy
Embarrassment	Negative	Sadness	Worry
Failure	Nervous	Self-Centered	Worthless

If I AM is in negative energy, I AM tries to think feel-better words. I AM can do this by changing I AM's thoughts about the Topic, or by redirecting thoughts to a better feeling Topic.

AI PERSPECTIVE

Feeling good is commonly associated with:

1. Physical Well-being: Often, feeling good starts with physical health and comfort. This might mean being free from pain, feeling energized, or experiencing physical relaxation.

2. Emotional Balance: Feeling good emotionally usually involves a sense of happiness, contentment, or joy. It can also mean the absence of negative emotions like anxiety, sadness, or anger, or it could be the successful management of these emotions.

3. Mental Health: Good mental health is a crucial component. This includes feeling mentally clear, focused, and at peace. It might also involve a sense of resilience or the ability to handle stress effectively.

4. Social Connection: Feeling connected to others, whether through friendships, family relationships, or broader community ties, can contribute significantly to feeling good. Social interactions that are positive, supportive, and meaningful are key.

5. Accomplishment and Purpose: Achieving objectives or making progress in personal or professional areas can lead to a sense of accomplishment, which often contributes to feeling good. Additionally, engaging in activities that are meaningful or purposeful can enhance this feeling.

6. Leisure and Enjoyment: Engaging in hobbies, interests, or simply taking time for relaxation and leisure activities can also be a significant aspect of feeling good. This includes anything that brings joy, relaxation, or entertainment.

7. Optimism and Positivity: A general sense of optimism or having a positive outlook on life can contribute to a feeling of well-being. This doesn't mean ignoring life's challenges, but rather having a hopeful attitude towards them.

8. Self-Esteem and Confidence: Feeling good about oneself, having self-confidence, and possessing a healthy level of self-esteem can greatly influence overall feelings of well-being.

9. Balance and Harmony: This refers to a sense of balance in life – between work and play, social time and solitude, activity and rest. Achieving a harmonious balance tailored to one's personal needs can lead to feeling good.

10. Spiritual or Existential Peace: For some, feeling good might also include a sense of spiritual fulfillment or a feeling of being at peace with existential questions.

Overall, feeling good is a multifaceted experience that encompasses physical, emotional, mental, and social well-being. It's also subjective, so what makes I AM feel good might be different for another person.

JOB #2

QUICK START

I AM believes that this lifetime is intended to be lived in positive energy as much time as possible.

To live that belief, I AM tries to accomplish two jobs at every NOW.

- SOARing JOB #1: To feel good NOW.
- SOARing JOB #2: To plan to feel better in the future.

1. Job #1 is accomplished at NOW if I AM's feelings are in positive energy.

2. Job #2 is planned at NOW. I AM creates an Improvement Plan to try to create better feeling NOWs in the future.

3. Job #2 is accomplished when I AM celebrates the Results of the Improvement Plan and experiences better feeling NOWs.

Continuously accomplishing both leads to I AM living a journey of a better life story.

The Big Picture chart is split into two halves, dividing left and right sides. The left side represents Job #1 and the right side represents Job #2.

Job #2 is about making a plan to SOAR towards a better Life Story. This is where I AM goes SOARing!

SOARing is the intentional improvement process I AM uses to feel better and live a better life story.

I AM can SOAR from any NOW, positive or negative. Frequently, positive is seen as an opportunity and negative is seen as a problem. Whether defined as an opportunity or as a problem, SOARing brings I AM positive energy.

- OPPORTUNITY: A Situation that makes it possible for I AM to do something I AM needs or wants to do, improve, or newly create.
- PROBLEM: A Situation I AM defines as unacceptable, unresolved, broken, or harmful that needs to be fixed or solved.

Positive energy pursues the opportunity. Positive energy solves the problem.

Life is full of problems and opportunities. Improve both by SOARing!

SOARing PERSPECTIVE

Job #2 is about SOARing to improve I AM's chances of having better NOWs in the future. There are no guarantees in life, but I AM has learned that by making plans NOW for I AM's future, I AM can dramatically increase the odds of having a better feeling future. By planning, I AM takes more control over life, rather than be buffeted about by others and surrendering control to life's inevitable ups and downs.

I AM plans improvements with SOARing.

At each NOW, I AM tries to improve the priority Topics. I AM goes through the Choice Cycle to determine what is most important and then I AM can SOAR to improve it.

Job #2 is unique in that I AM can be in either positive or negative energy at NOW to improve. This means that <u>at any NOW feeling</u>, I AM can seek to improve the future by SOARing. When in negative energy, I AM seeks to get back to positive energy as soon and safely as possible. When in positive energy, I AM uses the positive energy base to seek higher and higher improvements into the future.

AI PERSPECTIVE

The concept of "feeling better in the future" generally refers to the hope or expectation that one's emotional, physical, mental, or overall life situation will improve over time. This outlook is crucial for motivation, resilience, and mental health. Here's a more detailed breakdown of what it means:

1. Emotional Improvement: If you're going through a tough emotional time, feeling better in the future might mean overcoming sadness, stress, anxiety, or other negative emotions. It involves the hope or expectation that you will find happiness, contentment, or peace.

2. Physical Health Recovery: For those experiencing physical health issues, feeling better in the future could refer to healing from illness or injury, improving physical health, or gaining strength and vitality.

3. Mental Health Progress: If you're dealing with mental health challenges, feeling better might mean managing symptoms effectively, developing healthier coping mechanisms, or achieving a more balanced and positive mental state.

4. Personal or Professional Development: This could involve achieving objectives, improving personal or professional circumstances, or experiencing growth and success in various aspects of life.

5. Improved Relationships: For some, feeling better in the future might mean healing, strengthening, or developing personal relationships, finding new social connections, or resolving interpersonal conflicts.

6. Overcoming Adversity: It often involves the hope or expectation of overcoming current challenges or difficulties, whether they're personal, professional, financial, or otherwise.

7. Increased Happiness and Well-being: Generally, it encompasses an overall increase in happiness, satisfaction, or well-being in life.

8. Optimism and Hope: This outlook represents a fundamental optimism or hope for the future, believing that things can and will get better.

9. Personal Resilience: It also implies a sense of resilience and the ability to bounce back from setbacks, using current challenges as a stepping stone to a better future.

10. Planning and Action: Often, feeling better in the future is linked to the plans and actions taken in the present. This might involve setting objectives, making positive changes, or seeking support and resources.

In essence, the meaning of feeling better in the future is tied to a sense of progress and improvement. It's a forward-looking perspective that plays a crucial role in motivating people to navigate through current difficulties and work towards a more positive and fulfilling future

THE SOARING PROCESS

QUICK START

To manage I AM's life story improvement, I AM uses the SOARing Process.

- SOARing PROCESS: The SOAR method to reach objectives and navigate life.

On the Big Picture, the SOARing Process is the visual framework that helps I AM manage the intentional improvement of I AM's life story. It is represented in Charts A-D.

The focus is on SOAR.

S: SITUATION = This is I AM's understanding of what is going on NOW.

O: OBJECTIVES = This is I AM's setting of clear, and achievable Objectives.

A: ACTIONS: This is I AM taking the steps necessary to achieve the Objectives.

R: RESULTS: This is I AM measuring the outcomes of I AM's Actions.

The SOARing Process actions create Feelings Platform feelings. It shows what actions I AM takes to try to succeed at feeling good NOW (Job #1) and feeling better in the future (Job #2).

The SOARing Process shows how to manage I AM's life story improvement.

This visual framework helps I AM manage the three NOWs, plus manage the pursuit of I AM's better life story.

A thumbnail of each follows.

CHART A

- **PAST:** The time before NOW.

In Chart A, the key is the Guidance System I AM has developed and brings to every NOW. A positive Guidance System flows positive energy throughout I AM's life.

1. I AM's past has created all that I AM has become until NOW.

2. The past has also created the Here NOW and Environment that have become all that they have become until NOW.

3. I AM uses I AM's Guidance System to live life making focused choices.

   - GUIDANCE SYSTEM: I AM's Vision and Focal Points…the guides of I AM's life story journey.

- VISION: I AM's long-term visualization of the ideal I AM aspires to create.

  I AM's Vision: Everyone enjoying NOW & living a better life story.

- FOCAL POINTS: The most important long-term centers of attention guiding pursuits of I AM's Vision.

  1. Feel good NOW, satisfying needs and wants.
  2. Align body, mind, soul and spirit in positive energy.
  3. Employ SOARing Improvement System.
  4. Practice well-being daily.
  5. Improve I AM's Toolbox.
  6. SOAR NOW!

CHART B

- **NOW:** The present moment in I AM's clock time.

In Chart B, I AM wants to sidestep the millions of time-wasting alternatives available and focus only on what is most important NOW. I AM tries to look for and find Topics that are within the Focal Point guidelines and aimed at I AM's Vision.

1. At every NOW, I AM arrives to join Here NOW and Environment as NOW Arrivals.

2. These three NOW Arrivals create a new Situation at NOW.

3. I AM responds to the new Situation.

4. I AM goes through the Choice Cycle.

5. I AM chooses a Topic by focusing on the most important issue.

6. I AM thinks, feels and acts on each Topic (for nanosecond or longer time).

7. I AM's acts can be to enjoy NOW (Job #1), move on to a different Topic, or to enjoy NOW and to plan for SOARing improvement.

This process can be summarized as: Choices create experiences, which can create memories.

- Choices: Every action or decision I AM makes is a choice. These choices determine what I AM encounters or engages with.

- Experiences: The choices I AM makes lead to different experiences. For example, deciding to travel, take a new job, or meet someone will create an experience.

- Memories: Experiences are stored as memories. These are the mental impressions or recollections of the events and feelings that occurred during the experience.

This sequence reflects how I AM's choices influence what I AM experiences and how I AM remembers those experiences. Strive to make better choices and create a better life story.

CHART C

- **FUTURE:** The time after NOW.

In Chart C, I AM SOARs!

I AM has memorized and habituated the process and applies it to new Situations.

1. With I AM's Vision and Focal Points in mind, I AM creates a SOARing Experience (SE).
2. A SE is the SOAR format that produces and helps manage the Improvement Plan.
3. The Improvement Plan is the series of steps intended to be taken to reach Objectives,
4. I AM manages each SOARing Experience through time and process to a Result.
5. Better NOWs are created by successfully monitoring, measuring and managing a continuous stream of SOARing Experiences.
6. The SOARing Experience is, quite simply, the process to improve anything.
7. It is used each time I AM chooses to improve something.
8. I AM can have many SEs going at the same period of time and on many different Topics.
9. The many SEs are long-term managed by the Improvement Pyramid.

CHART D

- **BETTER LIFE STORY:** From NOW on, living more and more of life in positive energy seeking higher and higher emotional levels.

In Chart D, I AM uses the Improvement Pyramid as the overall management system of I AM's life. It focuses on I AM's most important life domains, filtered through I AM's Focal Point guidelines and toward I AM's Vision.

1. The Improvement Pyramid is I AM's primary life management system.
2. It helps I AM manage the many SOARing Experiences generated in I AM's Life Domains, improving I AM's Toolbox. fixing problems and pursuing opportunities,
3. Life Domains are the most important areas of interest and activity in I AM's Here NOW, such as; career, environment, finances, health, improvement, leisure, relationships and spirituality.
4. A better life story is easier to create and live if I AM maintains the thinking of feel-better thoughts throughout the SOARing Process.

OVERVIEW

The SOARing Process can be used in a single SE, or repeated in a cycle where the results from one SE become the starting point for the next. The R of one SE becomes the S of the next SE. This helps I AM keep growing and improving. It is a way to actively and intentionally navigate life, making sure that I AM is always moving forward in a meaningful way toward I AM's Vision.

THE FEELINGS PLATFORM

QUICK START

To measure I AM's life story improvement, I AM uses the Feelings Platform.

- FEELINGS PLATFORM: The scorecard I AM uses to understand how well I AM is doing with the SOARing Process.

- The Feelings Platform reflects I AM's feelings about things being done in the SOARing Process.

On the Big Picture, the Feelings Platform is the visual framework that helps I AM monitor and manage I AM's feelings. It is represented in Charts E-H.

Feelings are I AM's way of judging what I AM thinks about a Topic. They are a part of the Think-Feel-Act Triangle I AM uses for each Topic. I AM wants to invest as much time as possible in positive energy. I AM's feelings tell I AM if I AM is in positive or negative energy by how I AM feels.

Topics can be specific or general. I AM can have feelings about a single word or event or the Topic can be about I AM's general state feelings.

I AM's Job #1 is to feel good NOW. The Feelings Platform gives feedback if I AM is being successful doing Job #1 or not. I AM's Job #2 is to plan to feel better in the future. I AM is being in positive energy if I AM feels good about the plan.

The Feelings Platform visually reflects I AM's feelings at NOW. If I AM's X is in positive energy, I AM is being successful. If I AM's X is in negative energy, I AM needs to keep thinking feel-better thoughts to get back into positive energy.

Feelings are the critical measure of how I AM is enjoying life. They are how I AM keeps "Score" in the game of life. The score of the game is the single metric that summarizes how the game is going. Likewise, "I Feel…" is the single metric that summarizes how I AM's life is going at NOW.

The Feelings Platform helps I AM keep score at NOW and encourages thinking better thoughts of how to score more and better feelings in the future. How I AM can feel better (score more) in the future is planned by I AM at NOW.

The Feeling Platform's purpose is to help I AM monitor, measure and manage I AM's feelings. I AM has learned that when I AM's feelings get monitored and measured, they get better managed. With better management, I AM has a better opportunity to live a better life story.

In SOARing, I AM seeks to live a better life story from NOW through the last chapter. Progress is measured by how I AM feels at each NOW. The more of I AM's time in positive energy, the better the life story. Also, the higher the quality of positive energy, the better the life story.

The Feelings Platform monitors the level of I AM's energy at each NOW based on I AM's answer to "I FEEL…" The answer becomes the X location on the NOW Line. I AM wants to have the X in positive energy as much of the time as possible.

At every NOW, I AM has feelings and also has some question about what will happen next in I AM's life.

What happens next in I AM's life depends to some extent on the choices I AM makes at NOW. I AM has the opportunity to think and feel about what I AM wants and needs in future NOWs. Normally, I AM thinks about things that would make I AM feel better. I AM visualizes these things as positive energy opportunities. I AM SOARs to try to make them happen in I AM's future NOWs.

The Feelings Platform unfolds in four timeline phases, always seen from NOW. I AM looks back at how I AM became I AM, looks at I AM Here NOW and looks ahead at how I AM can improve for I AM's lifetime.

EASY SUMMARY

CHART E	PAST	I AM
CHART F	NOW	HERE NOW
CHART G	FUTURE	TO IMPROVE
CHART H	LIFE STORY	CONTINUOUSLY

CHART E

1. I AM is represented by an X somewhere on the vertical NOW Line.
2. Past NOW's created all that I AM has become until NOW.

CHART F

- **HERE NOW:**

1. At precisely NOW, I AM zeros in on a focus…the Topic. The Topic is the most important thing to I AM at NOW.
2. How I AM feels about the Topic causes the X to be located appropriately on the NOW Line.
3. X above the Energy Line reflects I AM's feelings of positive energy.

4. X below the Energy Line reflects I AM's feelings of negative energy.

5. I AM's X location is most important in SOARing because it summarizes I AM's starting position in living a better life story.

CHART G

- **To IMPROVE:**

1. I AM can choose to improve from the current situation on this Topic.

2. If the X is in negative energy, I AM wants to get back to positive energy as quickly and safely as possible.

3. If the X is in positive energy, I AM may want a longer-term plan to maintain or improve that Topic.

4. I AM then plans improvement using the SOARing Experience (SE) form.

5. From the X, the Improvement Line created by the SE extends up (to reflect the Actions taken over time) and into the future (to reflect the time necessary to get the intended Results).

CHART H

- **CONTINUOUSLY:**

1. I AM continuously SOARs to feel better through I AM's lifetime.

2. Daily attention to doing Job #1 and Job #2 successfully leads to a better life story.

3. Job #1 and Job #2 can be accomplished by managing the Improvement Pyramid.

The Feelings Platform visual framework can help you:

- Easily see where your feelings are at any time.
- Visualize where you are and where you want to be.
- Relate your feelings to next steps.
- See opportunities for mindset and perspective adjustment.
- Identify and name your current emotions.
- Recognize chances for recasting problems into opportunities.
- Make better choices to improve direction and next steps from NOW.
- More easily see relationships in your "mind's eye".
- Quickly eliminate Topics that don't fit with creating a better life story.
- Remember how to create a better life story.

OVERVIEW

The Feelings Platform is like an internal scorecard that helps I AM stay aligned with I AM's Vision and to navigate life effectively.

I AM continuously monitors feelings. Doing so helps I AM make better choices, improves actions and ensures that I AM's efforts in the SOARing Process are leading toward satisfaction and success.

PAST

PAST: THE TIME BEFORE NOW.

THE BIG PICTURE

JOB #1 = To Feel Good NOW!

SOARing PROCESS *(CAUSE)*

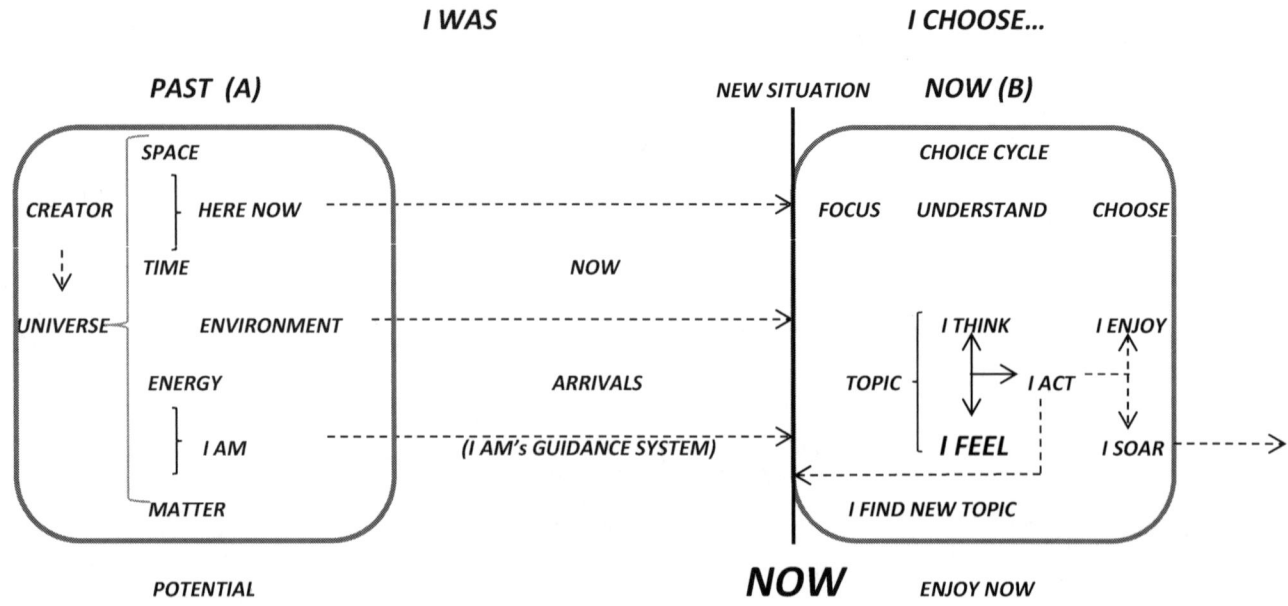

FEELINGS PLATFORM *(EFFECT)*

I FELT

I FEEL...

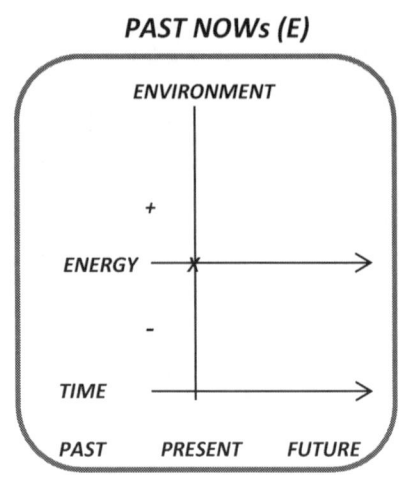

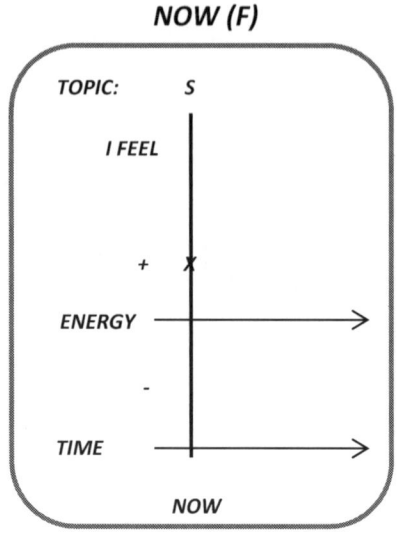

NOW, I AM HERE to ENJOY

SOARing PROCESS

PAST   Chart A

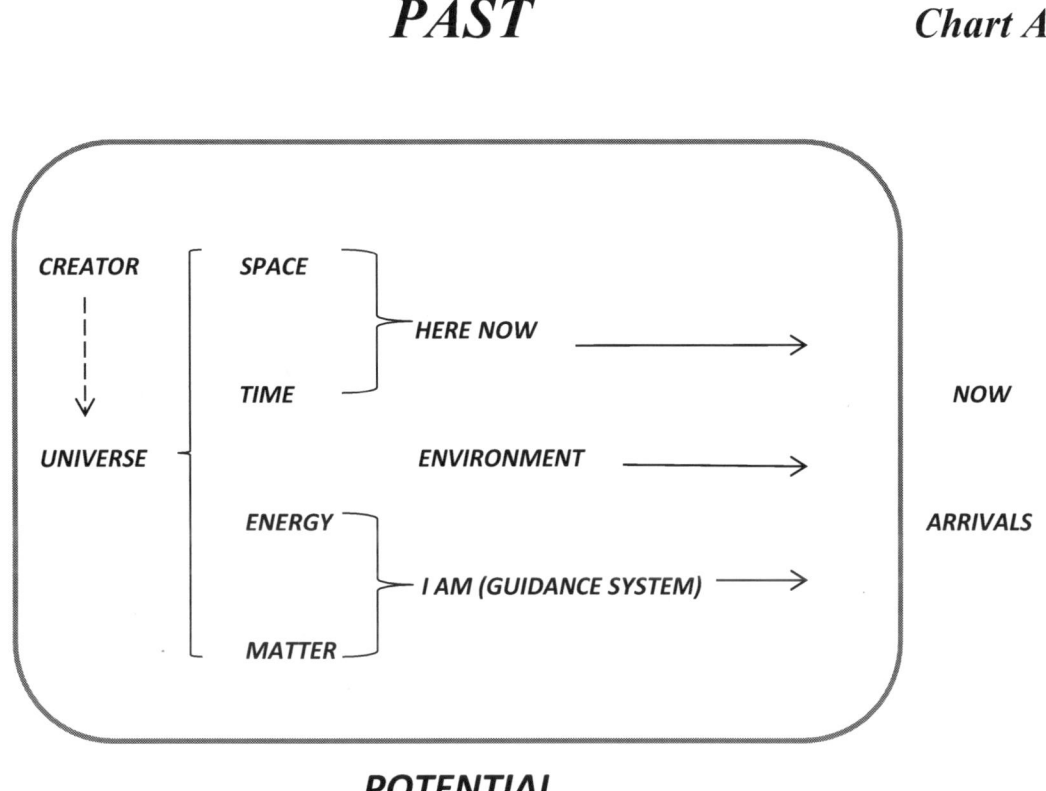

POTENTIAL

All of history happened in the past.

I AM looks back from NOW and perceives the past as Past NOWs.

- PAST: The time before NOW.
- PAST NOWs: NOWs that have happened in the past.
- NOW: The present moment in I AM's clock time.

Past NOWs were NOWs back in history, but become NOWs upon arrival at NOW. They are the yesterdays I AM looks back at today.

Past NOWs give I AM perspectives for NOW. They give context to every Situation. They influence how I AM addresses every who, what, when, where, why, and how. They have helped I AM to be all that I AM has become until NOW.

Past NOWs have provided I AM with:

- Mistakes from which I AM learned…or not.
- A general level of need satisfaction on Maslow's Hierarchy of Needs.

- Context for understanding change, the environment, power, economics, governments and all the other processes important to living life.
- Cultural identity with language, traditions, family, and sense of belonging.
- A basis for building I AM's Toolbox.
- Inspiration to create improvements, like leaving the world a better place for I AM's children and their children.
- A vast storehouse of collective knowledge, insights, how-to processes, moral and ethical guidelines, etc.
- Millions of success stories in all aspects of living, if only I AM is wise enough to recognize, understand and implement them in I AM's life.

The past can serve as a solid foundation for I AM to make better choices at every NOW.

This chart represents the basic universal components that I AM brings to every NOW in the form of NOW Arrivals.

In the beginning, believed to be about 27 billion of our years ago, the Creator created the universe.

- CREATOR: That which brought our universe into existence.
- UNIVERSE: All of space, time, energy and matter.
- SPACE: A continuous area which is available for use.
- TIME: I AM's clock time.
- ENERGY: The vibrational power flowing throughout the universe that is part of everything.
- MATTER: The material substance that constitutes the observable universe, and together with energy, forms the basis of all objective phenomena.

Space and time team to form Here NOW.

- HERE NOW: Space and time arranged as a specific place at a specific moment of clock time.

The time part of HERE NOW is I AM's clock time so it arrives with the passage of time in seconds, minutes, hours, days, weeks, months, years, etc. I AM does not control time, but can manage I AM's relationship with time.

The here part is controlled by I AM to some degree. I AM can choose to be at home, at work, on the golf course, in Dallas, in Paris, in an airplane, driving a car, etc.

Space, time, energy and matter team to form the Environment.

- ENVIRONMENT: Everything in the universe except Here NOW and I AM.

I AM has some limited control over I AM's environment. Generally, I AM has more control over things the closer they are to I AM. I AM has more control within the range of I AM's senses (hearing, seeing, tasting, touching, smelling and intuition), especially if I AM has access to the internet and other communication tools.

I AM

Energy and matter team to form I AM and other objective phenomena.

- I AM: A fictional character acting as an example of I AM's perspectives on SOARing ideas and life story improvement.

People have been studied and defined for many centuries. Many of these analyses have led to a great deal of understanding of all things human and invite deeper study beyond this narrative.

In creating I AM's life story up to NOW, I AM has developed a Guidance System to help guide I AM into the future. At NOW, I AM has an idea of what is most important to I AM. What is important to I AM takes the form of I AM's Guidance System. It aims I AM toward I AM's Vision and helps guide I AM to that Vision with Focal Points.

I AM's Guidance System has been described through the ages as; core self, character, inner self, self-concept, personal philosophy, moral compass, authentic self, psychological philosophy, inner voice, conscience and others. I AM prefers the general term Guidance System

- GUIDANCE SYSTEM: I AM's Vision and Focal Points…the guides of I AM's life story journey.

This Guidance System has been created by I AM from past history…all the environments, people, social interactions, experiences, education, successes, failures, trials, errors, etc. Every different person creates their own customized Guidance System.

I AM's Guidance System:

- VISION: I AM's long-term visualization of the ideal I AM aspires to create.

I AM's Vision is "Everyone enjoying NOW and living a better life story".

I AM's thinking, feeling and acting is oriented toward that Vision. The thinking, feeling and acting on the Focal Points are how I AM plans to get to the Vision. I AM is guided by I AM's Focal Points at every NOW. I AM's Guidance System can be a model for others or be totally customized by the individual.

In SOARing, the emphasis is on I AM improving from where I AM is NOW to where I AM wants to be in the future. That is done by making choices aimed at the Vision and within the parameters set by I AM's Focal Points.

- FOCAL POINTS: The most important long-term centers of attention guiding pursuits of I AM's Vision.

Briefly, I AM has chosen these as I AM's Focal Points. (Everyone is free to choose their own)

1. FEEL GOOD NOW, SATISFYING NEEDS AND WANTS
   - FEEL GOOD NOW: Job #1
   - SATISFYING NEEDS: Topics I AM must have, satisfied.
   - SATISFYING WANTS: Topics I AM would like to have, satisfied.

2. ALIGN BODY, MIND, SOUL & SPIRIT (BMSS) IN POSITIVE ENERGY

   o BODY: The physical structure part of I AM.

   o MIND: A nonphysical part of I AM that is responsible for thinking, reasoning, feeling, remembering, imagining, perceiving, ideating, sensing, etc.

   o SOUL: A nonphysical part of I AM that is everything that makes I AM alive instead of dead.

   o SPIRIT: A nonphysical part of I AM that is the spiritual connection between I AM and I AM's chosen god.

   o POSITIVE ENERGY: Good energy vibrations that I AM can align with and feel good.

3. EMPLOY SOARing IMPROVEMENT SYSTEM (SIS):

   o SOARing PROCESS: The SOAR method to reach objectives and navigate life.

   o FEELINGS PLATFORM: The scorecard I AM uses to understand how well I AM is doing with the SOARing Process.

   o IMPROVEMENT PYRAMID: The visual framework for helping I AM navigate I AM's life story.

4. PRACTICE WELL-BEING DAILY

   o WELL-BEING: Positive energy, engagement, meaning, accomplishments and positive relationships.

5. IMPROVE TOOLBOX

   o IMPROVE: Make better.

   o TOOLBOX: I AM's distinctive attributes.

6. SOAR NOW!

   o SOAR: Acronym for Situation, Objectives, Actions, Results.

   o SOARing EXPERIENCE (SE): The Situation, Objectives, Actions, Results format that produces and helps manage the Improvement Plan.

I AM intends daily life for I AM to be feeling good, satisfying needs and wants and planning for feeling even better tomorrow.

The Vision sets the desired destination. The Focal Points provide guidelines or a roadmap of the way to get to the desired destination. SOARing Experiences (SE) on Life Domains provide the focus to get to the desired destination.

   • LIFE DOMAINS: I AM's most important areas of long-term interest and activity.

Past NOWs have provided I AM with a life of many significant experiences. With each experience has come the opportunity to contrast between things I AM likes and things I AM does not like. The likes and dislikes start attracting into different groups. I AM prefers to invest I AM's resources (time, talent, treasure) into the likes and what is most important to I AM. Those are I AM's Life Domains.

Primary Life Domains: (Alphabetically, with examples)

1. *Career:* Employment. Work. Job. Vocation. Profession. Skills. Education.

2. *Environment:* Surroundings. Housing. Safety. Security. Freedom. Government. Media. Quality of Life. Community. Location.

3. *Finance:* Economics. Income. Net Worth. Wealth. Cash. Liquidity. Savings. Investments. Expenses. Risk.

4. *Health:* Physical. Mental. Emotional. Stress Management. Well-Being. Positive Mindset.

5. *Improvement:* SOARing. Self-Actualization. Personal Growth. Inspiration to others. Purpose. New Ideas. Strengths. Weaknesses. Mindfulness. Knowledge. Personal Management. Self-Esteem. Optimism.

6. *Leisure:* Fun. Arts. Sports. Passions. Hobbies. Collections. Creations. Volunteering. Advocacy. Play. Games.

7. *Relationships:* Family. Friends. Romance. Social. Significant Others. Co-workers. Teams. Memberships. Other Volunteers. Schoolmates. Clubs. Committees.

8. *Spirituality:* Religion. Giving. Beliefs. Alignment. Appreciation. Gratitude. Connection to something bigger. Oneness. Faith.

NOW ARRIVALS

The three key parts of the universe arrive at every NOW as a new Situation.

1. Here NOW arrives giving the Situation a place and time.

2. Environment arrives giving the Situation everything else in the universe except I AM.

3. I AM arrives giving the Situation human involvement.

For a detailed expansion of NOW Arrivals, see the NOW ARRIVALS Chart.

With these arrivals, the who, what, when, where, why and how components are in place for I AM to pursue:

- JOB #1: To feel good NOW.

- JOB #2: To plan to feel better in the future.

SUMMARY

Here NOW provides the place and time. The Environment provides all the surroundings and I AM provides the potential.

- POTENTIAL: I AM's energy capacity for what I AM can become in the future.

I AM arrives at NOW with a Vision and the Focal Points to help I AM pursue the Vision. I AM arrives with an innate sense that wherever I AM is NOW, I AM can improve. I AM knows I AM has not yet realized I AM's full potential.

I AM brings I AM's Guidance System to each NOW. I AM's Guidance System significantly influences how I AM looks at the Situation and what choices I AM makes.

I AM's Guidance System, in an evolving form, is with I AM for I AM's lifetime. It plays a big role in the creation and management of I AM's life story. A better Guidance System generally leads to a better life story.

FEELINGS PLATFORM

PAST NOWs

Chart E

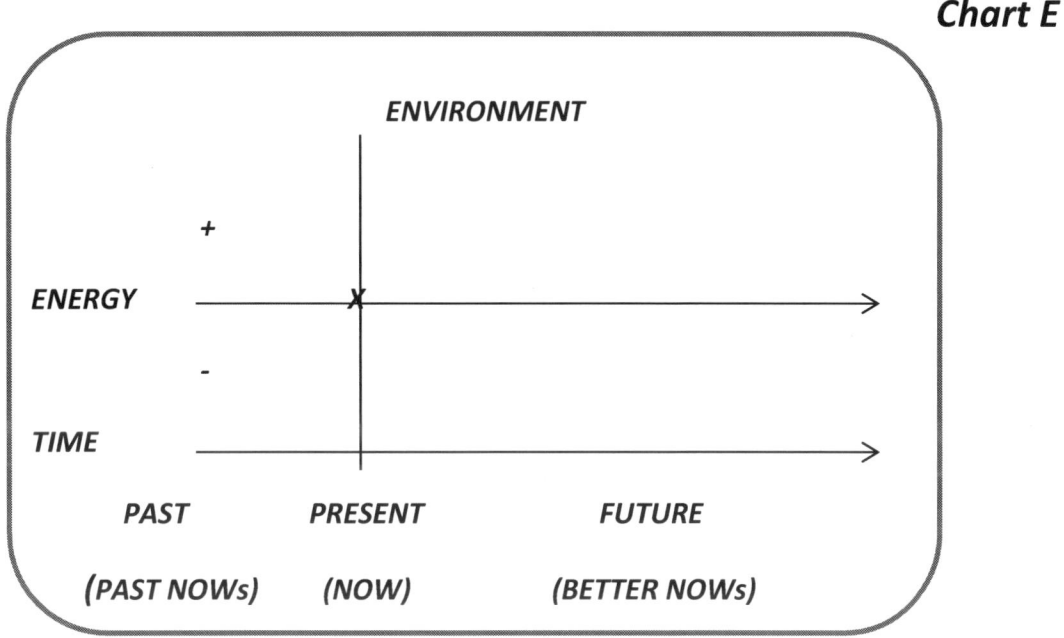

Chart E reflects I AM's feelings about things being done in Chart A.

I AM is the main character around whom each Feelings Platform centers. I AM shows how the Feelings Platform works, examples of what I AM thinks important and how I AM chooses to try to create and live a better life story from NOW into the future.

I AM (X) is always at NOW, so I AM's perspective can be back to the past (Past NOWs), to the present (NOW), or ahead to the future (Better NOWs) and a better life story.

The central focus of all platforms is I AM's location on the NOW Line. Everything else is related to X marks the spot…how I AM feels NOW. The X is always somewhere along the NOW Line. If I AM is feeling positive energy, I AM's X is on the NOW Line above the Energy Line. If I AM is feeling negative energy, I AM's X is on the NOW Line below the Energy Line.

The chart is a simple three lines and an X. From this simple beginning, I AM can expand and manage I AM's life of feeling good, feeling better and living a better life story from NOW on into the future.

The vertical line above NOW is the NOW Line.

- NOW LINE: The vertical line representing the present moment in time.

The NOW Line moves to the right along the Time Line with the passage of time.

Horizontally, there are two lines (arrows) representing the flows of energy and time.

The bottom horizontal line represents time.

- TIME: I AM's clock time.
- TIME LINE: The horizontal arrow representing the concept of time moving forward.
- PAST NOWs: NOWs that have happened in the past.
- NOW: The present moment in I AM's clock time.
- BETTER NOWs: I AM feeling better in future NOWs than I AM feels NOW.

The top horizontal line represents energy.

- ENERGY: The vibrational power flowing through the Universe that is part of everything.
- ENERGY LINE: The horizontal arrow separating positive energy from negative energy.
- POSITIVE ENERGY: (+) Good energy vibrations that I AM can align with and feel good.
- NEGATIVE ENERGY: (-) Bad energy vibrations that I AM can align with and feel bad.

The Feelings Platform represents all history coming together here NOW in the form of I AM and the environment. It reflects all that I AM and the environment have become until their arrival at NOW.

- PAST NOWs: NOWs that have happened in the past.
- NOW: The present moment in I AM's clock time.
- I AM: A fictional character acting as an example of I AM's perspectives on SOARing ideas and life story improvement.
- X: I AM.
- ENVIRONMENT: Everything in the universe except Here NOW and I AM.

The past is the development time of I AM being able to experience feelings at NOW. The past has influenced I AM in everything I AM brings to NOW…how I AM thinks, feels and acts.

ENVIRONMENT

I AM exists and lives within and as a part of a larger environment. This environment has had a large influence on all that I AM has become. I AM's development in the past has been aided by being surrounded by civilization's advancements and many positive energy intending entities, such as:

- Parents, family, heritage, ancestry, culture, society
- Social groups and systems
- Economic systems
- Governments
- Legal systems

- Education systems
- Information systems
- Communications systems
- Safety and security systems
- Health systems
- Sports organizations for all sports
- Freedom
- Capitalist system
- Research and scientific institutions
- Religious freedom
- Monetary systems
- Free-trade systems
- Transportation systems
- Entrepreneurial systems
- Corporate systems
- High technology
- Support groups for everything
- Special interest groups
- Etc.

All these groups share the common goal of people helping themselves and other people improve their lives.

I AM has been influenced by these and other groups since long before I AM was born. All the influences from the environment are summarized into I AM's Toolbox and I AM's Guidance System. These are intended to broadly represent all that I AM has become to NOW.

I AM's TOOLBOX

- TOOLBOX: I AM's distinctive attributes.
1. *ABILITIES:* I AM's having the capacity to do something.
2. *APTITUDES:* I AM's having the natural ability to do something.
3. *ATTITUDES:* I AM's positive or negative feeling or thinking about a situation, thing, person or group.
4. *AWARENESS:* I AM's field of knowledge or perception of a situation or facts.
5. *BEHAVIORS:* I AM's actions in response to external or internal stimuli.

6. *BELIEFS:* Things I AM accepts to be true repeated over and over again.

7. *CHARACTER:* I AM's distinctive mental and moral qualities.

8. *COMPETENCE:* I AM's ability to use knowledge, abilities and skills to successfully perform tasks.

9. *CONFIDENCE:* I AM's belief in I AM's abilities to succeed.

10. *EDUCATION:* I AM in the process of receiving and/or giving knowledge.

11. *EMOTIONS:* I AM's strong feelings.

12. *ETHICS:* The principles of morally right conduct by I AM.

13. *EXPERIENCES:* What I AM goes through or takes part in that helps I AM learn, grow, or feel something.

14. *FEELINGS:* I AM's emotional responses.

15. *FREE WILL:* I AM's capability to freely make choices, decisions and to take action.

16. *HABITS:* I AM's behaviors that are routine, repeated regularly and usually subconscious.

17. *INTELLIGENCE:* I AM's ability to solve complex problems or to make choices with results benefiting I AM.

18. *INTENTION:* I AM's plan to do specific things on purpose to reach objectives.

19. *INTUITION:* I AM's ability to know something without having to think about it.

20. *JUDGMENT:* I AM's ability to make a choice or form an opinion after careful thought.

21. *KNOWLEDGE:* All that I AM knows about a Topic or Topics.

22. *LESSONS:* Things I AM has learned.

23. *MEMORY:* I AM's ability to remember things from the past.

24. *MINDSET*: I AM's mental state of thoughts, attitudes and beliefs reflecting either positive or negative energy.

25. *MOODS:* I AM's temporary, general emotional state at a particular time.

26. *MORALS:* The ethical values or principles I AM uses to guide I AM's behavior.

27. *NEEDS:* Topics I AM must have.

28. *OPINIONS:* I AM's thoughts, beliefs or judgments about someone or something, based on facts or not.

29. *PASSIONS:* Strong interest or enthusiasm I AM has for something.

30. *PERCEPTIONS:* I AM being aware through the senses or the mind.

31. *PERSONAL RESOURCES:* Time, talent and treasure are the three personal resources that I AM can offer to any SOARing Experience.

32. *PERSONALITY:* I AM's characteristic sets of cognitions, emotional patterns and behaviors.

33. *PERSPECTIVES:* I AM's particular way of looking at situations and topics.

34. *PRINCIPLES:* The fundamental rules I AM lives by.

35. *RESISTANCE:* I AM's reluctance or refusal to accept or comply with something.

36. *SKILLS:* I AM's having the capacity to do something well.

37. *STRENGTHS:* I AM's physical and nonphysical positive qualities.

38. *TALENTS:* I AM's having the natural ability to do something well.

39. *TEMPERAMENT:* I AM's natural frame of mind.

40. *THOUGHTS:* Products of I AM's thinking, like ideas, perceptions and opinions.

41. *TRAITS:* I AM's distinguishing characteristics.

42. *VALUES:* The moral, social or aesthetic principles I AM uses as guidelines for what is good, desirable or important.

43. *WANTS:* Topics I AM would like to have.

44. *WEAKNESSES:* I AM's physical and nonphysical negative qualities.

45. *WISDOM:* I AM having knowledge, experience and good judgment.

I AM's Toolbox joins I AM's Guidance System at every NOW to represent all that I AM is NOW.

I AM's GUIDANCE SYSTEM

- GUIDANCE SYSTEM: I AM's Vision and Focal Points…the guides to I AM's life story journey.

I AM's Vision is to help everyone enjoy NOW and to live a better life story. I AM is guided towards the Vision by I AM's Focal Points.

- ○ Feel good NOW, satisfying needs and wants.
- ○ Align BMSS (Body, Mind, Soul, Spirit) in positive energy.
- ○ Employ SOARing Improvement System.
- ○ Practice well-being daily.
- ○ Improve I AM's Toolbox.
- ○ SOAR NOW!

I AM's Toolbox and Guidance System have been long in development to the point they are NOW. They are a major influence on AM's choices. Continual improvement of both can help I AM make better and better choices toward a better life story. AI can be of great assistance to I AM, especially in helping I AM to improve I AM's Toolbox attributes.

The I AM Feelings Platform is focused on Past NOWs. This is known territory. I AM has invested all of this lifetime in the past. It houses all the memories, knowledge, habits, skills, successes, failures and everything else I AM has experienced. The past has created all that I AM has become until NOW.

I AM + AI has a primary goal of helping I AM feel better at every NOW, no matter where I AM has been. That goal is achievable by I AM when I AM continually thinks feel-better thoughts.

NOW

NOW: THE PRESENT MOMENT

IN I AM's CLOCK TIME.

THE BIG PICTURE

JOB #1 = To Feel Good NOW!

SOARing PROCESS *(CAUSE)*

SOARing PROCESS *(CAUSE)*

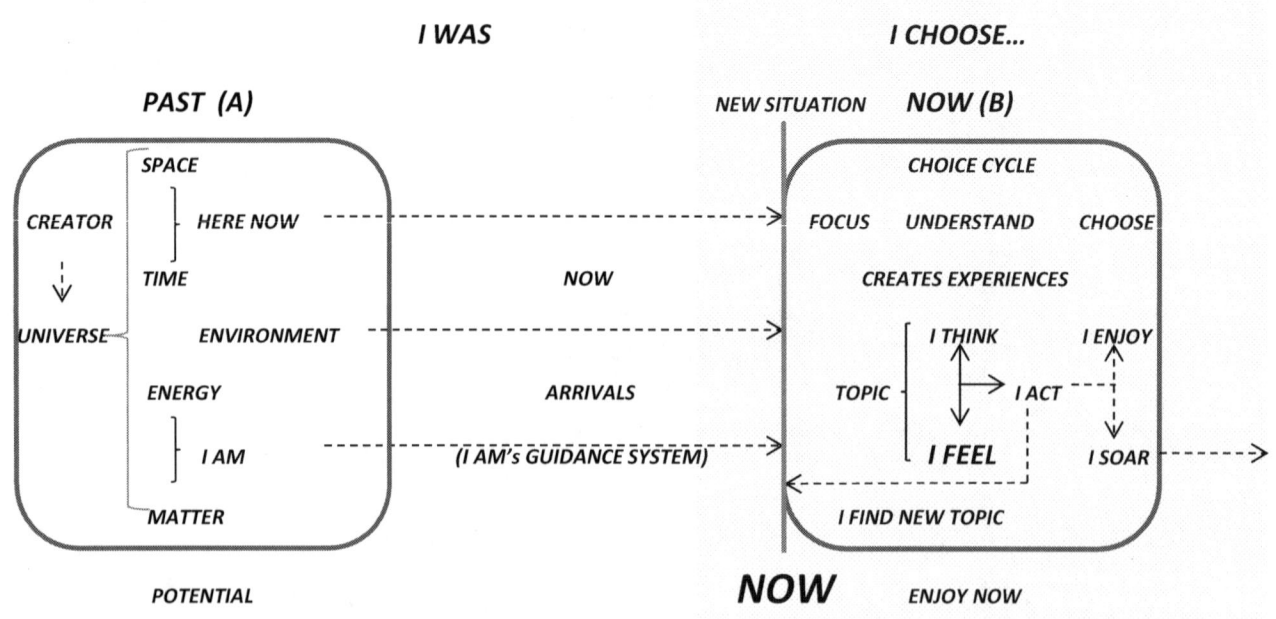

SOARing PLATFORM *(EFFECT)*

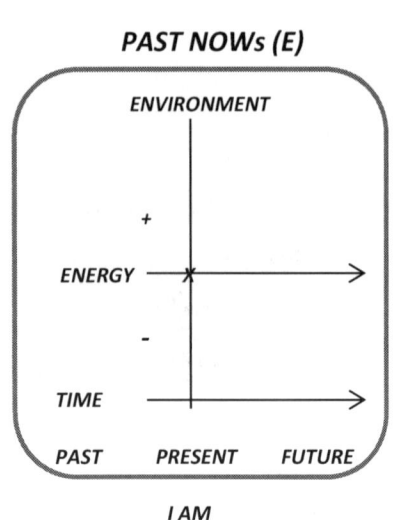

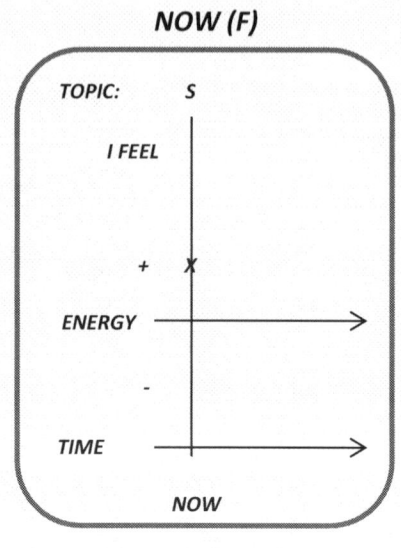

SOARing PROCESS

NOW

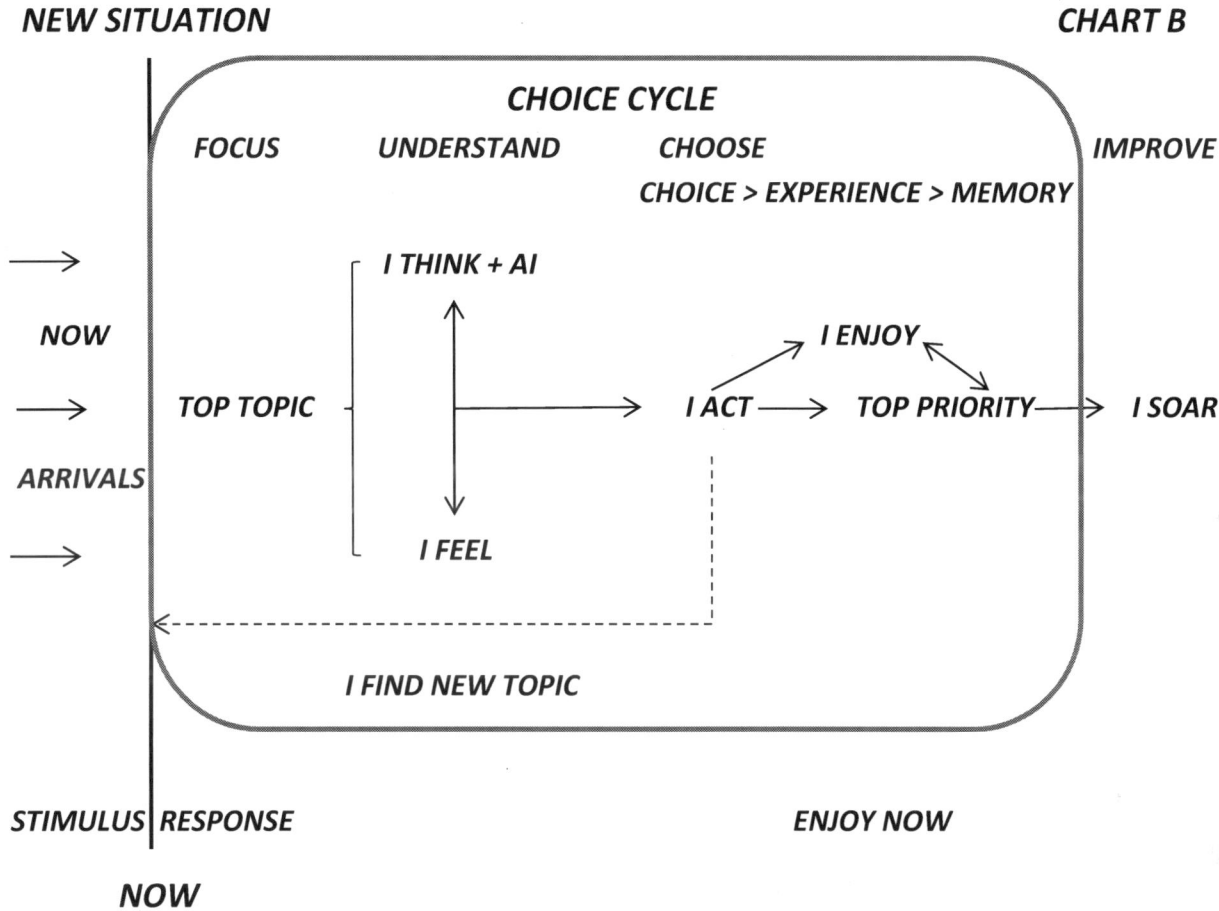

NEW SITUATION   **CHART B**

CHOICE CYCLE

FOCUS   UNDERSTAND   CHOOSE   IMPROVE

CHOICE > EXPERIENCE > MEMORY

NOW

I THINK + AI

I ENJOY

TOP TOPIC   I ACT → TOP PRIORITY → I SOAR

ARRIVALS

I FEEL

I FIND NEW TOPIC

STIMULUS | RESPONSE   ENJOY NOW

NOW

The function of the Choice Cycle is to help I AM choose what to do NOW and what to do next.

- CHOICE CYCLE: I AM's I Think, I Feel, I Act process of making choices at NOW.

I AM intends to use the Choice Cycle to focus on Topics that help I AM accomplish Job #1 (Enjoy NOW) and Job #2 (Live better NOWs in the future).

This SOARing Process chart represents, in a very simplified way, the process I AM goes through to make choices at every NOW. It conceptualizes what happens at the NOWs in I AM's life story journey.

It is I AM's overall intent to enjoy the living process. Enjoying the process is easier when I AM focuses on Topics aligned with I AM's Guidance System.

QUICK START

1. I AM, Environment and Here NOW arrive at NOW as New Arrivals.

2. They create a new Situation at NOW as a stimulus for I AM.

3. I AM responds through the Choice Cycle.

4. The Choice Cycle has two parts.

   - Topic Choice.
   - The Think-Feel-Act Cycle.

5. I AM makes choices on each part.

   - Chooses the Topic.
   - Chooses an action to take on the Topic.
     - Enjoy.
     - Enjoy and SOAR.
     - Find another Topic.

6. Each choice creates an experience, which can create a memory.

7. This process can happen instantly or more deliberately over a span of time.

I AM's life is centered around NOW. It is where I AM lives , breathes and makes choices.

SOARing charts reflect this with the NOW Line prominent and pretty much the center of attention on all charts.

NOW is a most interesting place that needs further exploration.

1. NOW

In SOARing, NOW is defined as the present moment in I AM's clock time.

Clock time serves well to identify a precise point in time. From a practical standpoint, I AM perceives NOW as a moment in time. That moment can be thought of as a bit longer than an absolute pinpoint in time. It is like the amount of time it takes I AM to go through the Choice Cycle process. The moment could be a nanosecond or longer.

Because NOW is a moment in the flow of time, NOW simply happens as time moves forward. I AM has no control over time. It happens. I AM can only work with time. I AM assumes that time will keep unfolding into the future and chooses to go with the flow.

When NOW happens, things change.

- CHANGE: Something different.

Change itself is one of the few constants in the universe. Change is always there at NOW because time advances and NOW is always moving along the Time Line sweeping I AM along with it.

NOW is the change between a minute ago and a minute in the future, between yesterday and tomorrow. It is the transition between old and new, memories and dreams, past and future. It is I AM's closing of the last chapter lived and the beginning of the next chapter to be lived in I AM's living a better life story.

Every NOW is the leading edge of I AM's thoughts, feelings and actions. It offers I AM the opportunity to change I AM's life, to get a fresh start, to get a chance to create a better future. It offers I AM the opportunity to forget past negative energies and to focus on present and future positive energies.

Most of all, change offers I AM the opportunity to Enjoy NOW! Enjoy NOW means that I AM is in positive energy, above the Energy Line. Being in positive energy enjoying life is the key to living a better life story. Living a better life story is living life in positive energy as much time as possible.

When NOW happens, the change creates a new Situation.

- SITUATION: I AM's perception of the set of circumstances Here NOW.

The set of circumstances around I AM is ever changing because of the complex mix of place, time, surroundings and the whims of I AM. Everything is changing all the time. Ancient Greek Heraclitus chronicles this in the famous quip that one can never step in the same river twice. I AM changes, the river changes and the Situation changes every moment.

The Situation is the who, what, when, where, why and how of the circumstances as perceived by I AM. At every NOW, I AM is faced with a new Situation. Each Situation can be perceived as either an opportunity (+) or as a problem (-).

The Situation is the S in SOARing and is the foundation for all things SOARing.

The Situation stimulates responses from I AM.

- STIMULUS: A Situation that causes I AM's responses.

The stimulus of the continuously evolving Situation in I AM's life compels I AM to make choices.

2. TOPIC CHOICE

The making of choices at NOW is the most important thing I AM does at NOW! Every choice changes the course of history.

I AM's first response to a new Situation is to do something.

- RESPONSE: I AM's reaction to a stimulus.

Information about the Situation begins with that received through I AM's senses. I AM has five primary senses that provide information from the Environment and I AM's relationship with the Environment. They are: hearing, taste, touch, smell and vision. I AM also relies on what some call the 6th Sense…intuition.

- INTUITION: I AM's ability to know something without having to think about it.

Using these senses, I AM gathers focus information by using the Focus Funnel.

- FOCUS FUNNEL: A conceptual funnel that screens a mass of information down to only the most interesting information for I AM's further consideration.

The Focus Funnel is designed to screen out all the uninteresting information and leave only items that are of interest to I AM. These can become I AM's current focus.

The Focus Funnel is a four-stage filtering process of information. It filters huge amounts of information through a process that screens out all the clutter and leaves only the most interesting information for I AM. This process can happen almost instantaneously or can be long and considered.

STAGE 1: AWARENESS: I AM's field of knowledge or perceptions of situations or facts.

- All the information in the universe is buzzing around outside the Focus Funnel.

- Some of that information enters I AM's awareness, mostly by I AM's primary senses of sight, taste, smell, touch or hearing…plus intuition.

- Most of what enters I AM's awareness is fleeting and soon out of consciousness. Other incoming information can be interesting and potentially could become knowledge and go into lifetime memory (e.g. product brands, people names, locations, history, language, relationships, facts, etc.)

STAGE 2; ALTERNATIVES: Any group of two or more things from which I AM can choose.

- With consciousness come millions of alternative directions.

- I AM can go anywhere, think any thought, feel any emotion, do nothing, do anything I AM needs to do or wants to do.

- To improve, I AM must reduce the chaos of clutter by giving something I AM's attention.

STAGE 3: ATTENTION: I AM's taking notice of someone or something.

- I AM can choose to access some of that awareness by giving it attention. Or, attention can be forced entry, like TV commercials, road signs, another driver, a relative, another person, etc. Both can go through the filter and get I AM's attention. Attention is precious because it requires at least a little bit of I AM's time and talent resources.

STAGE 4: FOCUS: I AM's center of attention at NOW.

- Once someone or something important or interesting gets I AM's attention, I AM can choose to focus on that information, or not.

- If I AM chooses not to focus on this information, I AM can move on to other more important or interesting information.

- If I AM chooses to focus on the information, it becomes the Top Topic.

RESULT: TOPIC: I AM's focus of attention.

The Topic is the subject of the Choice Cycle and of the SOARing Process. It is the top priority of I AM at NOW because it focuses I AM's thoughts, feelings and actions.

Good Topic selection is key to living a great life story. What I AM thinks about, feels and acts upon creates I AM's life story.

Anything imaginable can be a Topic. Every word in every language, every person on Earth, every star in the universe, and everything else can be a Topic. I AM likes to be aware of a broad spectrum of things, ideas, and feelings. However, I AM can truly focus on only one thing at a time.

With everything in the universe available as Topics, I AM tries to follow the rule to focus on what is most important at NOW. That thing becomes the Topic for further thinking, feeling and acting.

I AM tries at every NOW to stay aligned within the guidelines of I AM's Guidance System (Vision, Focal Points) and I AM's Life Domains (Career, Environment, Finance, Health, Improvement, Leisure, Relationships and Spirituality). Most of I AM's Topics are in these important areas of I AM's living a better life story.

3. THINK-FEEL-ACT CYCLE

After a Topic is identified, I AM seeks to understand the Topic in this Situation.

The I Think, I Feel, I Act Cycle is the source of I AM's understanding of the Topic.

- I THINK, I FEEL, I ACT: A concept showing the interconnection of thinking, feeling and acting.

This cycle relates each element with each of the others. I Think is related to both I Feel and I Act. I Feel is related to both I Think and I Act. I Act is related to both I Feel and I Think.

This means that the Topic can enter the triangle at any point and flow through each of the others. Most Topics enter at I Think or I Feel. I Act usually happens after I Think and I Feel.

- I THINK: Thoughts I AM is thinking, like ideas, perceptions, opinions, etc.
- I FEEL: Emotions and feelings I AM is experiencing.
- I ACT: I AM taking action and doing things or taking steps toward an objective.

I AM's mind is responsible for, among other things, I AM's thinking, feeling, choosing and acting at every NOW to try to best cope with the ever changing Situation and new Topics.

The coping process can be virtually instantaneous (like confronting a poisonous snake ready to strike) or it can be extended over a period of time (like creating a long-term plan). Either way, the choices I AM makes at NOW can affect the remainder of I AM's life.

Understanding the who, what, when, where, why and how of the Situation and Topic is critical to I AM making better choices. I AM tries to know as much about the Topic as possible in the time allowed by the Situation. With knowledge comes confidence and the ability to make better choices.

The key to understanding is the creation of meaning. I AM understands the meaning of the Topic.

Meaning comes from the interaction between I Think and I Feel in the I Think, I Feel, I Act Cycle.

The process with I AM can begin with either I Think or I Feel. I AM believes it unwise to begin with I Act without first thinking and/or feeling. Immediate brash action can lead to poor outcomes.

The process usually begins with I Think. Such as, "I Think this is a good idea". Then I Feel gives positive or negative energy to the thought. Such as, "I feel it is a good idea". When both I Think and I Feel are positive energy, it is easy for I Act to get busy expanding the idea by SOARing.

Similarly, the process can begin with I Feel. Such as, "I'm really scared! I feel fear!". I AM acknowledges the negative emotion and then thinks of alternatives to eliminate the fear. I AM acts on the best alternative.

Or, I AM can begin with a positive feeling, such as "I love this person". I AM acknowledges the positive emotion and thinks of positive actions to expand the feeling of love.

I AM can go back and forth between I Think and I Feel trying to get energy alignment of the two. This is shown as the Interaction Line (the arrow representing the interaction between I Think and I Feel). This interaction between I Think and I Feel can be lightning fast or slow and deliberate.

- When both I Think and I Feel are positive energy (++), I AM usually chooses to expand this feeling and act by moving on to SOARing on this Topic.
  - I AM feels this is a good idea and wants to expand it by SOARing.
- When both I Think and I Feel are negative energy (--), I AM usually chooses to act by leaving this Topic and considering another important Topic.
  - I AM feels this is a bad idea and wants to address a different Topic.
- When I Think and I Feel are conflicting energies (+- or -+), I AM usually acts by moving on to another Topic or recasting this Topic. Conflicting energies are confusion…i.e. negative energy.
  - I AM feels uneasy because there is no alignment of energies.
  - Sometimes adjusting the definition of the Topic can resolve the stumbling blocks between I Think and I Feel.

When I AM answers the phrase "I Feel… ", that creates the location of the X on the NOW Line on the SOARing Platform (Chart F).

The X is always somewhere on the NOW Line to reflect I AM's feeling about the Topic NOW. If the feeling is positive energy, the X is placed above the Energy Line. If the feeling is negative energy, the X is placed below the Energy Line.

To more precisely locate the X, I AM can use a scale. The scale can be placed left of the NOW Line. The default scale is a + in positive energy and a − in negative energy. For a bit more detail, I AM can use the common school grading scale of A, B, C, D and F. A and B are positive energy. D and F are negative energy. For even greater detail, I AM can use the 10 (highest) down to 1 (lowest). The most precise scale I AM can use is the Abraham-Hicks Emotional Guidance Scale. (See Chart F-3)

4. CHOICES

I AM's response to the ever-changing Situation comes in the form of the choices I AM makes. Every new NOW offers I AM a chaos of thousands of choice alternatives. Choice alternatives surround I AM at every moment, but the choices I AM makes in choosing a Topic and the Think-Feel-Act choices are key.

At NOW, I AM has a world of alternatives available. I AM can think about anything, feel anything, do anything. The universe can be considered as nothing but opportunity for I AM. The universe is open for I AM to create anything. The alternatives are endless and can be a chaos that becomes overwhelming for I AM. To make the best of the Situation and not be overwhelmed, I AM needs to be able to make good choices.

Making good choices is one of the most important things I AM can do, every moment of every day.

- CHOICE: The act of selecting something after considering multiple alternatives. .

The quality of the choice is heavily influenced by the quality and quantity of the identified alternatives from which I AM chooses. I AM's choice can come only from the list I AM has developed of multiple alternatives, because I AM has set that as the parameters of consideration.

Therefore, I AM wants to create the best possible list of alternatives

This is one of the most important places where I AM + AI synergy really helps!

I AM and AI synergize together to meld I AM's best ideas with AI's best ideas. The result can be a synergized list of alternatives better than each separately could have produced. Synergy takes things I AM can do, every moment of every day to a higher level.

From the synergized list of alternatives, I AM can go through the process of making a choice.

The choices I AM makes at every NOW accumulate to form I AM's life story. Every choice changes that life story in some manner. Sometimes, a choice makes a major change in I AM's life forever and sometimes it makes big changes in the lives of others forever. Every choice changes the course of history. Every choice has consequences. Every choice is important.

I AM chooses to make I AM feel good NOW (Job #1) and feel better in the future (Job #2). I AM relies on I AM's Guidance System (Vision and Focal Points) to guide those choices in SOARing the right direction.

The initial, very important choice in the Choice Cycle is the choice of Topic. The next important choice is what I AM chooses to do with the Topic. The Topic becomes the subject and focus. The intention is to find the best feeling alternative. The action is what to do about the Topic. (Sound like a familiar process?)

This process creates direction for I AM.

- DIRECTION: The orientation I AM faces or moves.

Direction is very important to I AM because it aims I AM at a destination.

If I AM is aimed in the wrong direction, I AM will arrive at the wrong destination. Going to the wrong destination can waste huge amounts of I AM's time, talent and treasure. It is possible for the wrong direction to last a lifetime. That does not create a great life story. If I AM desires to live a better life story, I AM needs to aim in a positive direction with every choice.

Going a positive direction is easier when I AM is guided by a positive Guidance System.

At every NOW on every Topic, I AM has three choice options to pursue.

1. Enjoy NOW: This is I AM's Job #1, so it is important to do as much as possible.
2. Enjoy NOW and SOAR: This is doing Job #1 and planning Job #2, living a better life story.
3. Find a better feeling Topic: This is when the Topic isn't right for the Situation

When guided by a positive Guidance System, these choices become easier. If the Topic aligns with the Guidance System, I AM enjoys NOW. Then, I AM can choose to plan to maintain or improve the enjoyment of that Topic into the future. If the Topic does not align with the Guidance System, then I AM changes focus to another Topic that feels better.

Every Topic goes through the Choice Cycle of I Think, I Feel and I Act. Most Topics are rejected and I AM moves on to more important Topics. Those "Top Priority" Topics advance to the SOARing Experience.

- PRIORITY: Something I AM regards as more important than anything else at this time.

Maintaining priorities is one of I AM's important NOW tasks. For I AM, it is as easy as putting Topics in order of importance:

1. Most important. Do first. "Top Priority"
2. Second most important. Do this after number 1 is done as far as it must be done at this moment.
3. Third most important. Do this after number 2 is done as far as it must be done at this moment.

In the Choice Cycle, when I AM chooses to "Enjoy NOW and SOAR", I AM proceeds to improve the Topic by creating a SOARing Experience. (Chart C).

5. CHOICES > EXPERIENCES > MEMORIES

I AM's choices create experiences. The experiences can become memories.

EXPERIENCES

- EXPERIENCES: What I AM goes through or takes part in that helps I AM learn, grow, or feel something.

If I AM's choices are good, the experiences usually are perceived as positive energy. There can be a continuous chain of positive feeling experiences. Many of those experiences are commonplace and keep reinforcing I AM's positive mindset.

Experiences accumulate into I AM's life experiences.

- LIFE EXPERIENCES: The cumulative events, interactions, and situations I AM encounters over time. .

Characteristics:

- These are not just significant events, but everyday moments and lessons that contribute to personal growth and understanding of the world.

- Continuous and ongoing.

- Can range from mundane (like daily routines) to significant (like career choices).

- Both positive and negative experiences contribute to I AM's overall development.

Examples: Moving to a new city, forming relationships, daily work, travel experiences, or learning new skills.

Some of I AM's experiences are rare, euphoric moments of personal fulfillment or spiritual awakening. These experiences are Peak Experiences.

- PEAK EXPERIENCES: A profound, often transformative, moment that stands out as exceptionally meaningful, fulfilling, or joyful.

Characteristics:

- It is often associated with moments of heightened emotion, deep connection, or self-actualization.

- Short-lived but intensely memorable.

- Often described as "spiritual" or "euphoric" moments of personal transcendence.

- Linked to feelings of unity, purpose, or extreme satisfaction.

- Associated with the psychologist Abraham Maslow, who linked these moments to self-actualization.

Examples: I AM achieving a long-term personal goal, falling in love, the birth of a child, or an awe-inspiring moment in nature.

Part of I AM's life also gets remembered as Life Events.

- LIFE EVENTS: A significant occurrence or change in I AM's life that often has a lasting impact.

Characteristics:

- Life events are typically major milestones or transitions that can alter I AM's circumstances, perspective, or direction in life.

- Usually a one-time or infrequent occurrence.

- ○ Can be positive (marriage, graduation) or negative (loss of a loved one, divorce).
- ○ Often marks a transition from one phase of life to another.

Examples: I AM graduating from college, getting married, starting a new job, losing a loved one, or experiencing a major health crisis.

MEMORIES

When I AM makes a choice that leads to an experience, the associated memory is created or not created based on several factors related to how the brain processes and stores information. Here's a breakdown of how memory creation occurs:

1. Attention and Focus:

Role: For a memory to be created, the brain must pay attention to the experience. If I AM is deeply focused or emotionally engaged, the experience is more likely to be encoded into memory.

Impact: If I AM makes a choice that leads to a highly engaging or novel experience (like traveling somewhere new), I AM is more likely to remember it. Conversely, if I AM is distracted or the experience is routine (like driving the same route every day), the memory may not be as strong or may not form at all.

2. Emotional Significance:

Role: Experiences tied to strong emotions—whether positive or negative—are more likely to be stored as lasting memories. This is because emotions activate the amygdala, a part of the brain involved in emotional processing, which helps consolidate memories.

Impact: If I AM's choice leads to an emotionally significant experience (e.g., meeting someone important to I AM), the associated memory will likely be vivid. However, emotionally neutral or mundane experiences (e.g., grocery shopping) may not result in long-term memories.

3. Novelty and Uniqueness:

Role: The brain is wired to remember new, unexpected, or unusual experiences more easily than routine ones. When something is novel, it activates more areas of the brain, helping encode the experience into memory.

Impact: A choice that leads to a novel experience, like trying a new activity, is more likely to result in a strong memory. Repeated or familiar experiences may not leave a significant memory unless something new or different happens.

4. Repetition and Rehearsal:

Role: Repeating or consciously reflecting on an experience strengthens memory. This is often called memory consolidation, which is the process where short-term memories are transformed into long-term memories.

Impact: If I AM reflects on the experience after it occurs, talks about it, or thinks about it repeatedly, I AM is more likely to solidify it as a memory. A choice leading to a one-time, fleeting experience may result in a weak or no memory unless revisited mentally or through discussion.

5. Contextual Factors:

Role: The context in which the experience happens—such as I AM's environment, sensory stimuli (sights, sounds, smells), or people involved—helps shape whether the memory will be encoded.

Impact: If the experience occurs in a distinctive context or with strong sensory inputs (like hearing a specific song or smelling a unique scent), the brain may link the memory to those sensory cues. Choices that lead to experiences in less distinct or unremarkable contexts may result in weaker memories.

6. Sleep and Memory Consolidation:

Role: Memory consolidation happens during sleep. When I AM sleeps, I AM's brain organizes and stores information, determining which memories to retain and which to forget.

Impact: If the experience was particularly important or emotionally significant, I AM's brain is more likely to consolidate that memory during sleep. Lack of sleep or poor-quality sleep can hinder this process and weaken memory retention.

7. Stress and Cognitive Overload:

Role: High levels of stress or cognitive overload can either enhance or impair memory formation. Moderate stress may enhance memory encoding, while overwhelming stress or distractions can interfere with the process.

Impact: If I AM's choice results in a stressful situation, depending on the level of stress, the memory might be heightened or disrupted. In cases of cognitive overload, the brain may not be able to encode the experience properly, leading to gaps or no memory at all.

Strong memory creation is likely when I AM's choice leads to an experience that is novel, emotionally significant, highly focused, and repeatedly reflected upon.

Weak or no memory creation can happen when the experience is mundane, lacks emotional or sensory impact, occurs during distraction, or is not reinforced through reflection or sleep.

In essence, while I AM's choices automatically lead to experiences, whether or not those experiences become lasting memories depends on how the brain processes the event, the emotional or cognitive context, and whether the experience is consolidated after it occurs.

FEELINGS PLATFORM

NOW

Chart F

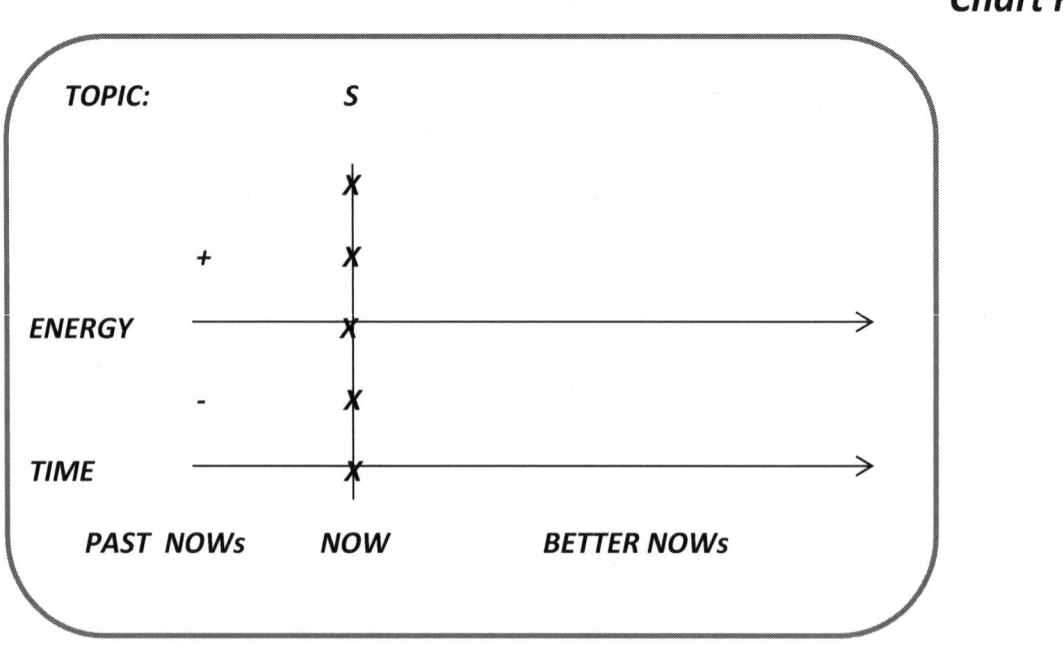

NOW, I AM HERE to ENJOY

Chart F reflects I AM's feelings about things being done in Chart B.

I AM is always living life in the Here NOW.

- HERE NOW: Space and time arranged as a specific place at a specific moment of clock time.

Here NOW is where I AM lives, works, plays and manages I AM's life story. For simplicity, NOW or Enjoy NOW is used with the assumption that I AM is always Here.

NOW is at the center of the overall framework and is visualized as the vertical line above NOW.

I AM (X) is always somewhere along the vertical NOW Line. Exact location is determined by how I AM feels about I AM's specific focus of attention (Topic).

How I AM responds to "I FEEL…" places the X into positive energy, negative energy or neutrality. If I AM's energy is positive, the X goes above the Energy Line. If I AM's energy is negative, the X goes below the Energy Line. Neutrality is the feeling I AM has when I AM does not have positive or negative energy about the Topic. In that case, X is placed at the intersection of the NOW Line and the Energy Line.

As shown on Chart F, I AM's X can be placed anywhere along the NOW Line. It is always on the NOW Line, but the location changes up or down with I AM's feelings about a Topic going up or down. The X can move very rapidly up and down with I AM's feelings, just like in the real life the chart reflects.

62

I AM tries to keep the X in positive energy as much time as possible.

EXPANDING CHART F

The NOW Feelings Platform represents I AM's arrival at NOW. I AM is Here NOW. I AM is in this place at this moment in I AM's clock time. I AM lives in the Here NOW.
I AM arrives at NOW with I AM's Guidance System leading the way into a new Situation.

- SITUATION (S): I AM's perception of the set of circumstances Here NOW.

The new Situation presents a new stimulus for I AM's response. Every new Situation requires choices… either conscious or unconscious. Essentially, I AM responds by using the six senses to become aware of, pay attention to and focus on a Topic.

- TOPIC: I AM's focus of attention.

The Topic is identified at the top of the chart.

I AM considers the Topic through the I Think, I Feel, I Act Cycle. The "I Feel…" answer places I AM's X at some point on the NOW Line. If I AM feels positive energy about the Topic, the X goes on the NOW Line above the Energy Line. If I AM feels negative energy about the Topic, the X goes on the NOW Line below the Energy Line.

The location of the X can be identified more precisely with the use of a scale on the NOW Line.

- I FEEL SCALE: Quantification of I AM's "I Feel…" on the NOW Line.

Adding a scale to the chart expands its usefulness because a scale adds valuable information for I AM. It's like being in school and getting a positive or negative grade on a test. Only limited information is gained. Much more actionable information is gained when A, B, C, D, F is added. Then I AM knows more precisely where I AM stands, has a direction to aim and can decide specific improvement targets for next time.

Several expansion choices are available to apply to the chart.

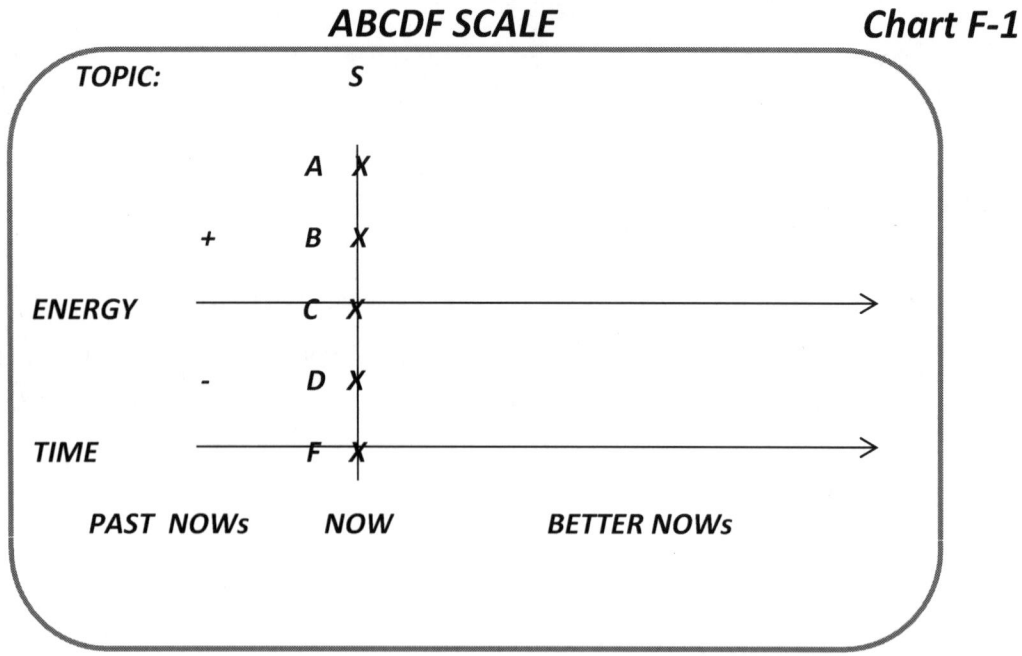

ABCDF SCALE   **Chart F-1**

1. ABCDF: As shown on the above chart. A is highest positive energy and F is the lowest negative energy.

When I AM responds to "I Feel…" the X can go to a spot on the NOW Line that approximates the strength of the feeling. The stronger the feeling, the higher it goes in positive energy and the lower it goes in negative energy.

This is a very simple scale, easily recognizable from classic grading scales.

This scale offers the added advantage of being able to put plusses and minuses on each letter. This gives I AM even more information to address. For example:

- A+
- A
- A-
- B+
- B
- B-
- C+
- C
- C-
- D+
- D
- D-
- F

54321 SCALE **Chart F-2**

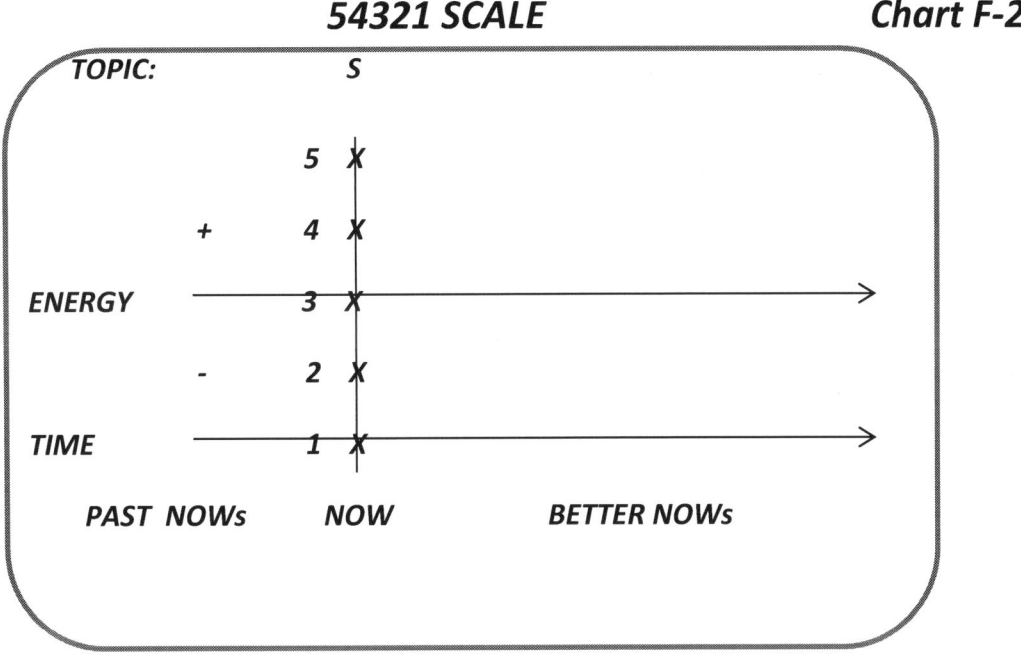

2. 54321: As shown on the above chart.

The same concept as the ABCDF Scale, except with numbers.

5 is highest positive energy and 1 is the lowest negative energy.

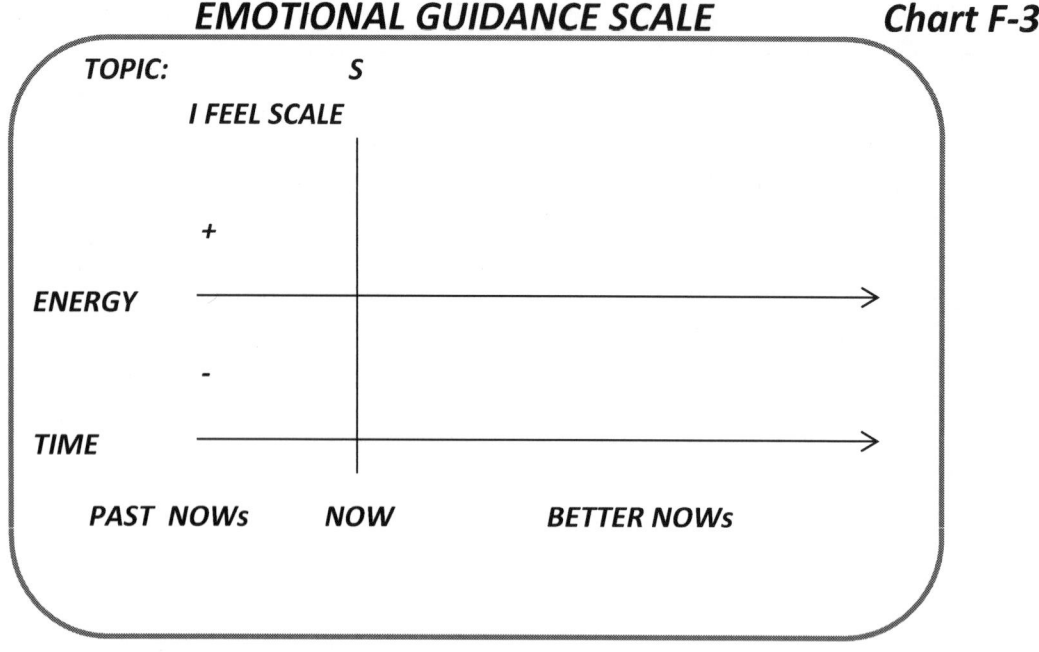

EMOTIONAL GUIDANCE SCALE   ***Chart F-3***

3. Abraham Hicks Emotional Guidance Scale: (See detail below)

A superb, copyrighted scale of emotions from the highest positive energy (love, joy, freedom, etc.) to the lowest negative energy (depression, grief, fear, etc.).

This is the best scale to use for more precisely ranking feelings. It provides a relative strength from highest emotions on down to lowest emotions.

I AM thinks in terms of levels when establishing Objectives. Within this scale, I AM can zero in on the relative level of current feelings. I AM seeks to climb up the levels instead of trying to jump from the bottom to the top in one big leap. Life generally doesn't work that way.

I AM's JOB #1 is to feel better NOW. On this scale, that is being in 1-7. I AM intends for these feelings to be the everyday I AM. I AM expects to dip down into 8 or lower only briefly and not very often.

When I AM does dip into negative energy (8-22), I AM's Objective is to return to positive energy (7) as soon as safely possible. The longer I AM is in negative energy, the more time it can take to get back into positive energy.

I AM's Job #2 is to plan to feel better in the future. That SOARing can be accomplished from any place on the NOW Line. I AM prefers to best accomplish this by SOARing from levels 7, 6, 5, 4, 3, 2, or 1 because I AM is coming from a place of positive energy, like a positive mindset.

ABRAHAM-HICKS EMOTIONAL GUIDANCE SCALE

I FEEL...

JOY, KNOWLEDGE, EMPOWERMENT, LOVE, FREEDOM, APPRECIATION	**1**	
PASSION	**2**	
ENTHUSIASM, EAGERNESS, HAPPINESS	**3**	
POSITIVE EXPECTATION, BELIEF +	**4**	
OPTIMISM	**5**	
HOPEFULNESS	**6**	
CONTENTMENT	**7**	X
BOREDOM	**8**	
PESSIMISM	**9**	
FRUSTRATION, IMPATIENCE, IRRITATION	**10**	
OVERWHELMED	**11**	
DISAPPOINTMENT	**12**	
DOUBT	**13**	
WORRY	**14**	
BLAME --	**15**	
DISCOURAGEMENT	**16**	
ANGER	**17**	
REVENGE	**18**	
HATRED, RAGE	**19**	
JEALOUSY	**20**	
INSECURITY, GUILT, UNWORTHINESS	**21**	
FEAR, GRIEF, DEPRESSION, DESPAIR, POWERLESSNESS	**22**	

NOW

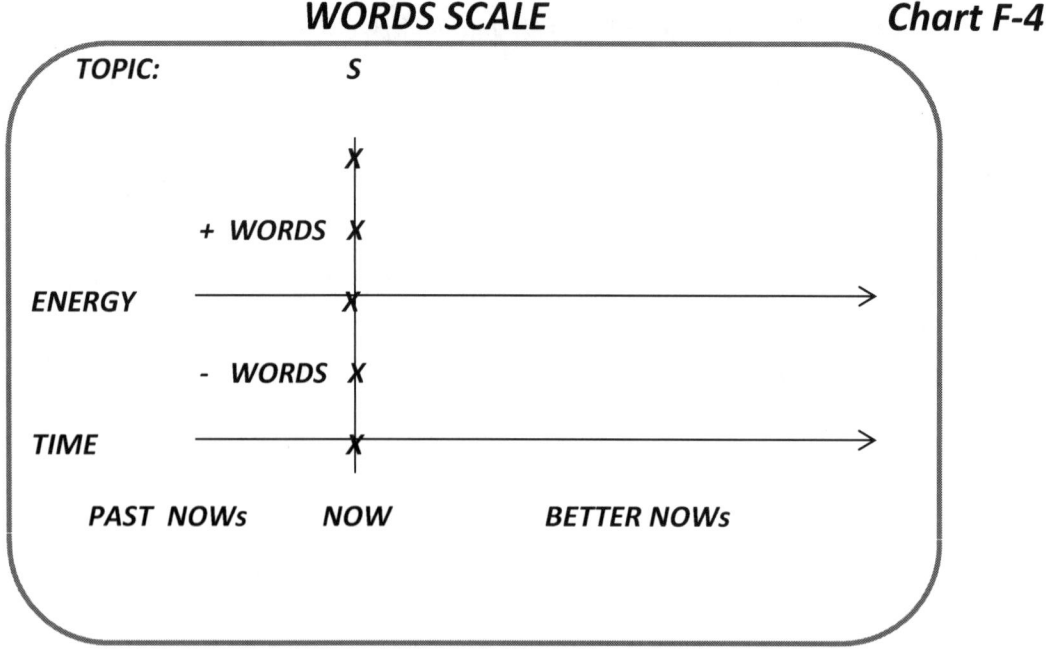

WORDS SCALE   *Chart F-4*

4. Words: A list of positive energy words and negative energy words from which to choose the most appropriate for the current feeling.

This is another great scale for getting precise in trying to identify feelings. I AM selects specific words from the Words List to describe precisely I AM's feeling about the Topic.

I FEEL...POSITIVE ENERGY

Advancement	Curiosity	Healed	Optimistic
Affection	Delight	Healthy	Passion
Alignment	Eagerness	Hopeful	Peace
Alive	Empathy	Improvement	Pleasure
Amusement	Empowered	Informed	Positive
Appreciated	Energized	Inspired	Progress
Awakened	Enthusiastic	Interested	Safe
Beauty	Excitement	Invigorated	Satisfaction
Better	Expansion	Joy	Self-Actualizing
Bliss	Flourishing	Kindness	Selfless
Calmness	Free	Love	SOARing
Carefree	Fulfillment	Motivated	Spiritual
Cheerful	Gratitude	New Person	Successful
Confident	Growth	Normal	Thriving
Contentment	Happy	Oneness	Up

POSITIVE (+)

ENERGY

NEGATIVE (–)

I FEEL...NEGATIVE ENERGY

Anger	Grief	Overwhelmed	Self-Consciousness
Anxiety	Guilt	Pain	Selfish
Blame	Hatred	Panic	Shame
Boredom	Hostility	Pessimism	Sorrow
Depression	Impatience	Powerless	Stressed
Despair	Insecure	Pressure	Suffering
Difficulty	Irritated	Rage	Threatened
Disapproval	Jealousy	Regret	Troubled
Down	Misery	Resentment	Unhappy
Embarrassment	Negative	Sadness	Worry
Failure	Nervous	Self-Centered	Worthless

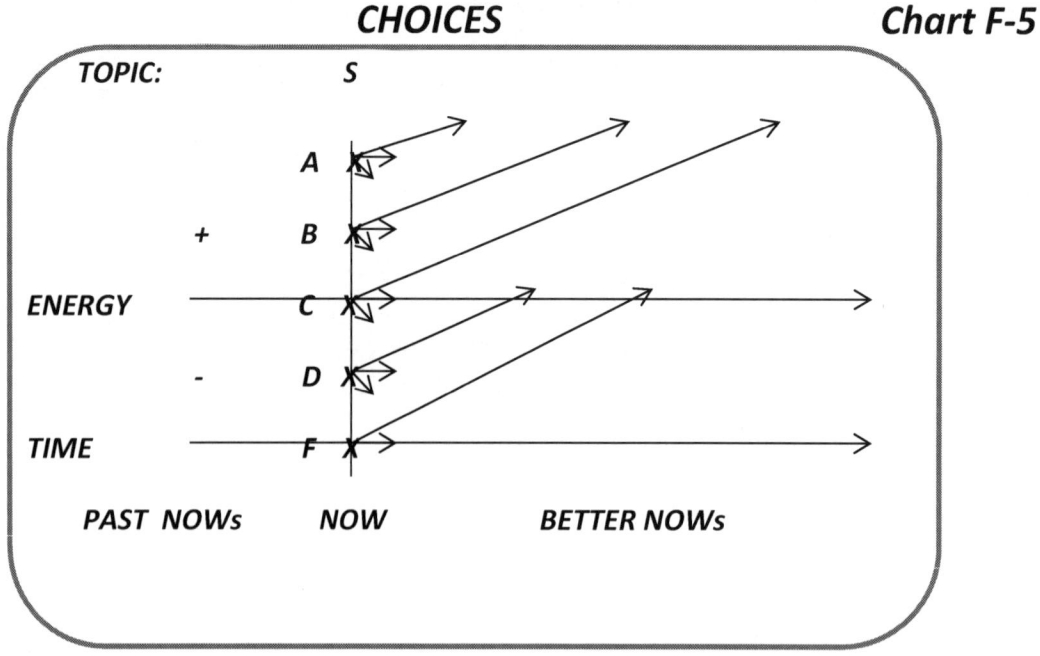

At every NOW, I AM must make choices about what to do next. Good choices elevate I AM into living a better life story.

- CHOICE: The act of selecting something after considering multiple alternatives.

At NOW, I AM can make choices aimed in three different directions.

1. IMPROVE: Make better.

I AM's choice to improve launches the Improvement Line (Arrow) up to the right.

If X is in positive energy, I AM's Objective is to stay in positive energy as long as possible and at higher and higher levels of positive energy.

If I AM's X is in negative energy, I AM's Objective is to return to positive energy as soon and safely as possible. I AM can accomplish this by focusing on feel-better thoughts, either on this Topic or by changing Topics.

Improvement is the choice I AM tries to make on all Topics that are important NOW and are within the guiding parameters of I AM's Vision and Focal Points. These are choices I AM must make to try to live a better life story.

2. STATUS QUO: The current situation at NOW.

Frequently, these choices are the easiest to make because I AM does not have to make any changes. I AM just keeps doing the same things as in Past NOWs.

This can be a good direction on Topics where I AM sees no opportunity or need for improvement and no problem is apparent that needs fixing. This is great when I AM is flowing with well-being, is aligned with I AM's Guidance System and is near the top of the scale. ENJOY!

However, I AM practices caution because the Situation is always changing and most Topics change over time. Things can be fantastic NOW, but the next moment can change dramatically. Topics and their associated feelings can also experience entropy and drift lower and lower over time and even start becoming a problem.

3. DECLINE: Get worse.

I AM tries to avoid these Topics. Why waste time and effort when I AM could be pursuing something important and aligned with I AM's Vision and Focal Points?

Because of I AM's positive Vision and Focal Points, I AM tries to enter every NOW with a positive energy mindset and attract Topics that fit with I AM's Vision and Focal Points. I AM looks for positive energy and generally finds positive energy.

I AM likes to SOAR on opportunities to improve. I AM also likes to fix problems and move on to pursue opportunities.

SOAR with Feel-Better Thoughts.

FUTURE

FUTURE: THE TIME AFTER NOW.

PICTURE

JOB #2 = To Plan to Feel Better in the Future!

SOARing PROCESS *(CAUSE)*

SOARing PROCESS *(CAUSE)*

I SOAR

FUTURE (C)

SOARing EXPERIENCE

(SE)

SITUATION

OBJECTIVES

ACTIONS

RESULTS

REALIZE POTENTIAL

LIFE STORY (D)

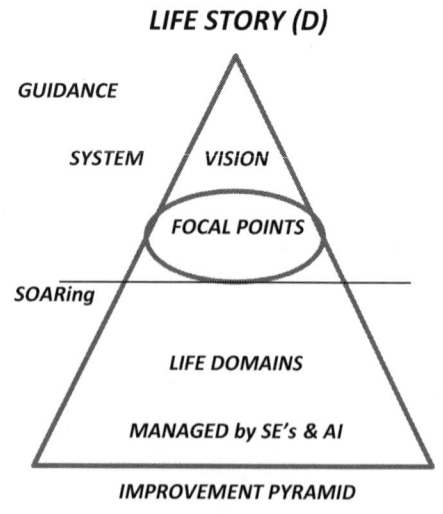

GUIDANCE

SYSTEM   VISION

FOCAL POINTS

SOARing

LIFE DOMAINS

MANAGED by SE's & AI

IMPROVEMENT PYRAMID

FEELINGS PLATFORM *(EFFECT)*

I FEEL BETTER

BETTER NOWs (G)

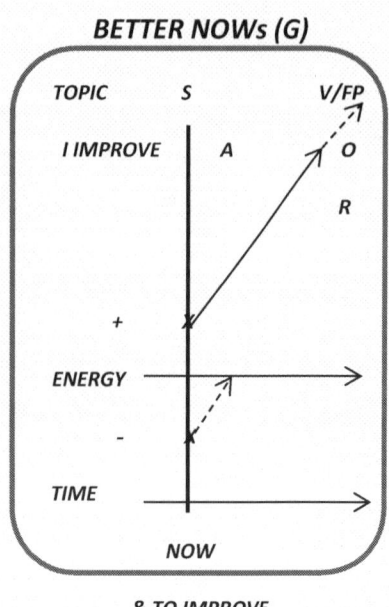

TOPIC   S   V/FP

I IMPROVE   A   O

                         R

+

ENERGY

-

TIME

NOW

& TO IMPROVE

BETTER LIFE STORY (H)

FEEL GOOD   FEEL BETTER

TOPIC   S

I IMPROVE

+

ENERGY

-

TIME

NOW

CONTINUOUSLY

SOARing PROCESS

FUTURE

CHART C

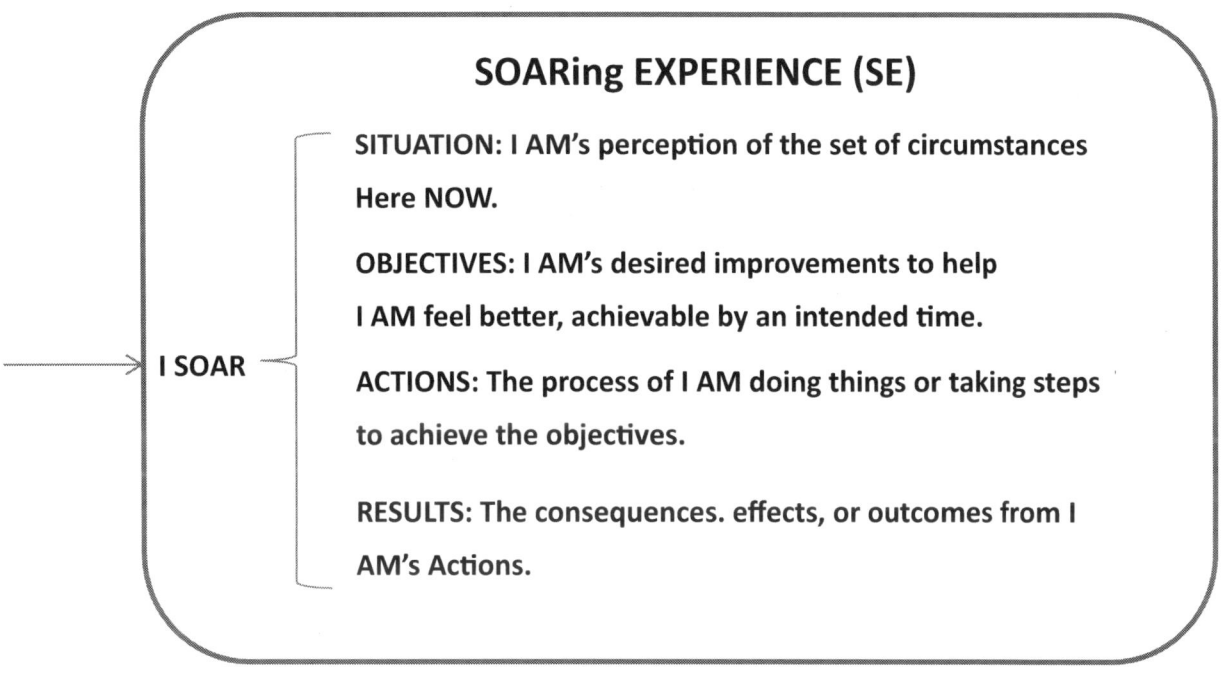

SOARing EXPERIENCE (SE)

I SOAR

SITUATION: I AM's perception of the set of circumstances Here NOW.

OBJECTIVES: I AM's desired improvements to help I AM feel better, achievable by an intended time.

ACTIONS: The process of I AM doing things or taking steps to achieve the objectives.

RESULTS: The consequences. effects, or outcomes from I AM's Actions.

REALIZE POTENTIAL

SOARing Experiences are the every moment, every day tool I AM uses to plan and manage I AM's life. SOARing Experiences are the workhorses of SOARing.

- SOARing EXPERIENCE: The Situation, Objectives, Actions and Results format that produces and helps manage the Improvement Plan.

(Please see the SE Form and sample SE in the Appendix)

Every Situation at every NOW has the opportunity for I AM to consciously or unconsciously create a SOARing Experience. I AM uses the process so frequently that it has become the automatic, habitual, go-to process in every Situation calling for improvement.

Every Situation can be viewed as an opportunity or as a problem. When I AM chooses to view the Situation as an opportunity, I AM uses the SE to plan and manage the pursuit of the opportunity. When I AM chooses to view the Situation as a problem, I AM uses the SE to plan and manage the fixing or solving of the problem. In either case, I AM can choose to feel better throughout the SE process and with the Results.

Some Situations call for immediate resolution, like when a bear suddenly appears on I AM's hiking trail. When the SE process is used regularly, the process can be almost instantaneous, hopefully with good Results.

Other times, the Situation can be very complex and require deliberate contemplation and extended time to create the SE, like preparing an annual plan and budget for the boss. Again, the SE provides the same process but it is extended over a longer timeline and is more complex.

Whatever the Situation, the core SE process is the same. All SEs have these five elements.

1. TOPIC: I AM's focus of attention.
2. SITUATION: I AM's perception of the set of circumstances Here NOW.
3. OBJECTIVES: I AM's desired improvements to help I AM feel better, achievable by an intended time.
4. ACTIONS: The process of I AM doing things or taking steps to achieve the Objectives.
5. RESULTS: The consequences, effects or outcomes from I AM's Actions.

In Actions, the SE produces an Improvement Plan for I AM to manage into the future.

I AM is always mindful to specify the Objectives before any Actions. I AM has observed that many actions in the world are seemingly taken without objectives. That is, people have a Situation, take Action and get all-over-the-place Results because they had no Objectives. This can bring unfortunate results to all.

The SE is used by I AM to pursue Job #2.

In I AM's quest to create and live a better life story, I AM has two jobs.

- JOB #1: To feel good NOW. (Enjoy NOW)
- JOB #2: To plan to feel better in the future. (SOAR)

Job #2 is accomplished by planning and making improvements at NOW that make I AM's life feel better in the future.

- IMPROVEMENT: The process of changing something for the better.

The word improvement has many similar words that give it more meaning. Such as: Positive change. Add value. Upgrade. More qualities. New. Better. Advancement. Strengthening. Increasing. Enhancement. Growth. Becoming. Add benefits. Self-actualize.

Improvement is a choice I AM makes. When I AM makes the choice to improve, the choice also means that I AM has chosen to expand. When I AM improves, I AM expands as a person and can expand everything in I AM's surroundings.

When I AM chooses to expand, I AM chooses intentional improvement.

- INTENTIONAL IMPROVEMENT: I AM's plan to do positive things on purpose to make I AM feel better.

Most improvements are inspired by I AM's desire to pursue an opportunity or to fix a problem.

- OPPORTUNITY: A Situation that makes it possible for I AM to do something I AM needs or wants to do, improve, or newly create.
- PROBLEM: A Situation I AM defines as unacceptable, unresolved, broken, or harmful that needs to be fixed or solved.

Both are appropriately addressed by SEs.

Opportunities are normally perceived as positive energy. Therefore, I AM uses the SE starting from positive energy with an Objective to improve to higher, longer positive energy. As I AM successfully pursues the opportunity, confidence grows, motivation is re-enforced and I AM feels better and better.

Problems are normally perceived as negative energy. Therefore, I AM uses the SE starting from negative energy with an Objective to get back to positive energy. That is, to fix the problem and get I AM back to normal positive energy.

At any NOW, I AM can choose to improve something. To improve anything, I AM creates a SOARing Experience (SE). The entire SE process can be completed very quickly in I AM's mind or can be longer and formalized on paper, cell, computer, etc. The steps remain the same in either.

1. CHOOSE TOPIC

Each SE is on a specific Topic. The Topic is the focus of the SE.

The Topic is I AM's most important choice at NOW. That is because it can set in motion a series of events that can consume significant resources of I AM and others,

- PERSONAL RESOURCES: Time, talent and treasure are the three personal resources I AM can offer to any SOARing Experience.

With the selection of a Topic for the SE, I AM starts to invest resources into the project. I AM tries to make sure the Topics selected are the most important and are potentially worth the resource investment.

Topics can be anything important in the NOW Situation. Such as, it could be facing a bear on a hiking trail, planning a vacation, or preparing a proposal for the boss or anything else. It is for whatever the priority is at this point in time.

Ideally, all Topics should be aimed at I AM's Vision, with the SE guided by I AM's Focal Points. And yes, facing a bear on the trail is probably top priority for I AM at that moment. I AM seeks to satisfy an urgent need for physiological health, safety and self-preservation. Sometimes, I AM might feel the same urgency in preparing a proposal for the boss.

The point is to create the SE for improvement of whatever Topic is most important.

2. UNDERSTAND the SITUATION

On each Situation, I AM tries to at least address the who, what, when, where, why and how. It is a simple, tried-and-true method of accumulating the key facts.

Another good method is to practice Situational Awareness.

- SITUATIONAL AWARENESS: I AM's awareness and understanding of the Here NOW situation with consideration for what could evolve in the future.

This method adds the element of anticipation of what might happen in the future if the current Situation continues to play out. This method works well in determining Objectives that I AM might adopt in order to improve the Situation.

3. CREATE SMART OBJECTIVES

Objectives set the direction for the entire SE. They point at the destination of I AM's journey. They describe the destination and the time desired to get to the destination.

Without Objectives, I AM is like an aimless boat in the open ocean of alternatives, capable of drifting anywhere. The Objectives give I AM a target destination for anywhere I AM desires to reach. They give I AM's Actions purpose.

I AM tries to make Objectives that are SMART.

- Specific: Exactly what I AM wants to achieve.
- Measureable: Numbers for quantification of progress along and at the end of the SE.
- Achievable: Possible to accomplish what by when.
- Relevant: Aligned with Vision and Focal Points.
- Time Specific: The time/date when the Objectives are to be reached.

I AM uses the word "To" at the beginning of every Objective statement in order to separate it from other statements and to indicate intended action. Like, "To create Objectives that are SMART".

4. PLAN ACTIONS

After I AM understands the Situation and has created Objectives, I AM plans the Action steps necessary to achieve the Objectives. These Action steps become the Improvement Plan.

- IMPROVEMENT PLAN: The planned series of steps intended to be taken to achieve the Objectives.

The Improvement Plan can be as simple as Steps 1-2-3 or as complex as the thousands of steps necessary to send a person to the moon and back.

For a simple example, I AM is in San Francisco (Situation). I AM wants to get to Dallas for a 7 p.m. dinner meeting tomorrow (Objective). I AM looks at what steps are necessary (Actions) to get to Dallas and back. Very briefly, the steps might be:

1. Determine necessary time to arrive by in Dallas. By 5 p.m. tomorrow evening.
   And, determine timing for return to San Francisco for the day after tomorrow.

2. Choose mode of travel to get to Dallas by tomorrow evening and return to San Francisco from available alternatives:
   - Rail
   - Air Only alternative capable of meeting Objective time.
   - Bus
   - Car
   - Walk

3. Check airline flights and book reservations. Time. Availability. Cost. Etc. Book flights.

4. Check rental car and book reservations. Time. Availability. Cost. Etc. Book car rental.

5. Check hotel and book reservations. Time. Availability. Cost. Etc. Book hotel.

6. Enjoy all the NOWs of making the journey happen.

Hopefully, I AM's journey will have been a wildly successful dinner meeting and trip. I AM celebrates (End Results)!!!

5. CELEBRATE RESULTS

- RESULTS: The consequences, effects, or outcomes from I AM's Actions.

Results happen throughout the duration of the SE. From start to finish, Results happen.

Every SE has a timeline of how long it is intended to take to go from the Situation to the Results. Sometimes the timeline is almost instant, but other timelines can be quite long. The longer the timeline, the more midpoints the plan has.

- TIMELINE: The length of time planned for managing an Improvement Plan from start through Results.

- MIDPOINTS: Intermediate points in time in the Improvement Plan where I AM reviews progress towards the Objectives.

Midpoints are very important to I AM because they give I AM a good idea as to whether or not I AM is on course to meet I AM's Objectives.

I AM monitors, measures and manages at each midpoint, or even more frequently.

- MONITOR: I AM to systematically check on progress towards I AM's Objectives.

- MEASURE: I AM to systematically evaluate quality and quantity measurements of progress towards I AM's Objectives.
- MANAGE: I AM to supervise, direct and control progress towards I AM's Objectives.

When I AM monitors and measures, I AM can better manage the journey. Each midpoint represents a new point in time. That means a new NOW and a new Situation. The Situation may have changed enough to make it prudent for I AM to adjust the Improvement Plan accordingly. Sometimes, only minor changes need to be made. Other times, the new Situation demands I AM reevaluate the Objectives and Actions. That may require a new SE.

Once the Improvement Plan is created and started, it must be constantly managed. (Chart D)

SUMMARY

As I AM has gotten familiar with SOARing, I AM notices that SOARing is the natural core of every process. It is simply the way processes work. Many other names have been given to the process as civilization has progressed and become more complex, but they all boil down to basic SOARing. The Common Denominator chart shows some of the specialized applications.

- COMMON DENOMINATOR: A quality shared by all members of a group.

The point is that SOARing is the basic, natural flow of the improvement process. Humans simply must seek to improve their lives and that of those around them. SOAR is the inherent process humans use to improve their lives.

SOARing merely simplifies it so I AM can use it at every Situation. It is a reminder for I AM to pay attention to each of the four steps, in order.

Before learning about SOARing, I AM tended to:

- Respond immediately with Actions, paying no attention to the Situation or Objectives.
- Forget that there must be Objectives for every improvement.
- Not give enough attention to understanding the Situation.
- Blaze past Results without celebrating.
- Not know or forget Job #1.
- Be oblivious to Job #2.
- Learn nothing new because of doing things the same old way as always.
- Pay no attention to the life story being written by I AM every day of living, no matter how good or how bad it might be.

With SEs, I AM is confidently paying attention to enjoy NOW and the planning for a better future. I AM realizes that only I AM is responsible for creating I AM's future through choices.

I AM creates SEs all day, every day. Some are complex and well considered over time. Others are almost instantaneous because I AM now has SOAR imbedded in I AM's Guidance System and Choice Cycle. I AM finds Topics that align with I AM's Guidance System. Those Topics get the SE treatment and I AM can thrive in improvement.

I AM normally has many SEs active each day. Each is addressed by priority and dealt with in an appropriately timely manner. Some can be accomplished almost instantly and the Results celebrated…or not. Other SEs require more time to play out. That means that I AM may have many SEs active the same day.

With many active SEs, I AM enlists the aid of the Improvement Pyramid (Chart D) to help manage multiple SEs.

- IMPROVEMENT PYRAMID: The visual framework for helping I AM navigate I AM's life story.

The SEs form the base of the pyramid. They all are aimed at I AM's Vision, being guided along the life journey by I AM's Focal Points.

FEELINGS PLATFORM

BETTER NOWs

PART 1   *CHART G*

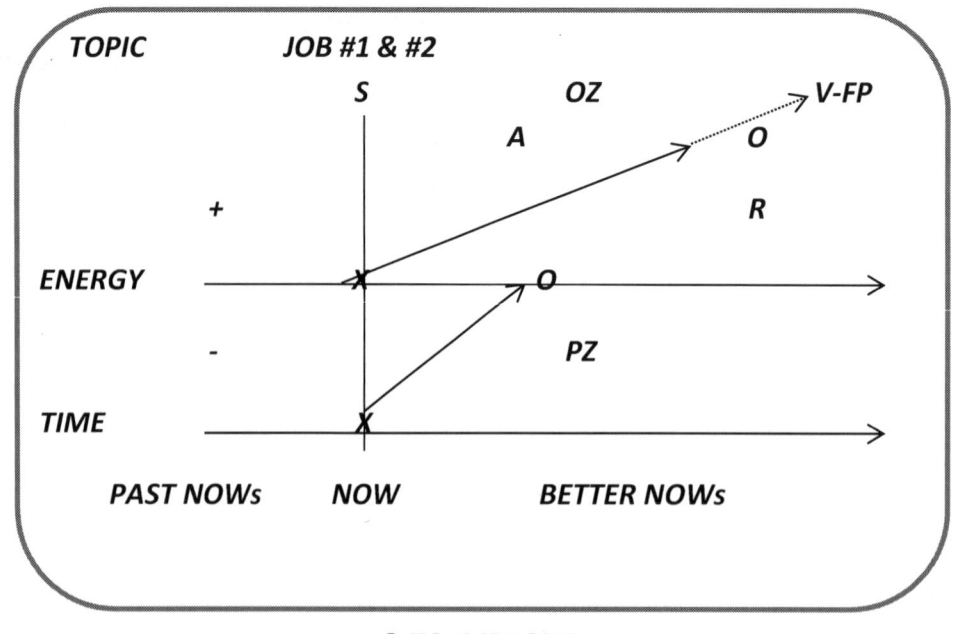

& TO IMPROVE

Chart G reflects I AM's feelings about things being done in Chart C.

Chart G is I AM's feelings picture of SOARing. It is SOARing's "Total Picture" chart.

This chart brings together all the basic elements of SOARing in one picture. It is a good reminder to I AM of all the SOARing parts working together to achieve Job #1 and Job #2 at every NOW.

The chart has two parts.

1. The part at NOW that gives I AM feedback on I AM's feelings on Job #1.

2. The part at NOW I AM uses to visualize Job #2 plans and feelings.

Note that both Job #1 and Job #2 happen at NOW. Job #1 reflects the feelings I AM has NOW. Job #2 reflects the feelings I AM has NOW about I AM's visualization of I AM's intended future.

I AM forgets things. So, I AM has created a Quick Start and a ready reference of all the definitions for the elements in this chart. The chart shows the relationships among all the various parts.

JOB #1

QUICK START

1. Chart G has a Topic…JOB #1. To feel good NOW.

2. The chart is focused on I AM's life NOW, represented on the NOW Line by I AM's X.

3. Every NOW is within the context of the left-to-right flows of energy and time.

4. Energy is divided into positive energy (+) and negative energy (-).

5. Time is divided into three parts.

   ○ Past NOWs (Past), into which I AM can look back.

   ○ NOW (Present), which is where I AM is.

   ○ Better NOWs (Future), into which I AM positively visualizes.

6. Every NOW has a situation (S) associated with it.

7. Every NOW presents an opportunity for I AM to accomplish Job #1.

8. The universe is prepared to help I AM accomplish Job #1, but I AM must choose to do so.

- TOPIC: I AM's focus of attention.
- JOB #1: To feel good NOW.
- X: I AM.
- X LOCATION: X placement on the NOW Line reflecting I AM's feelings.
- NOW: The present moment in I AM's clock time.
- NOW LINE: The vertical arrow representing the present moment in time.
- ENERGY: The vibrational power flowing throughout the universe that is part of everything.
- ENERGY LINE: The horizontal arrow separating positive energy from negative energy.
- POSITIVE ENERGY: (+) Good energy vibrations that I AM can align with and feel good.
- NEGATIVE ENERGY: (-) Bad energy vibrations that I AM can align with and feel bad.
- TIME: I AM's clock time.
- TIME LINE: The horizontal arrow representing the concept of time moving forward.
- PAST NOWs: NOWs that have happened in the past.
- BETTER NOWs: I AM feeling better in future NOWs than I AM feels NOW.
- S: Situation: I AM's perception of the set of circumstances Here NOW.

JOB #2

QUICK START

1. Chart G has a second Topic…JOB #2. To plan to feel better in the future. (To SOAR).

2. At NOW, I AM has three choices on a Topic.

   A. Enjoy NOW.

   B. Enjoy NOW & SOAR.

   C. Change Topics.

3. I AM chooses B on priority Topics.

4. I AM creates a SOARing Experience (S, O, A, R) to improve the Topic.

5. The Improvement Line is upwardly aimed at I AM's Vision, being guided by I AM's Focal Points.

6. If I AM's X starts in neutral or positive energy, I AM's intent is to SOAR higher in the Opportunity Zone.

7. If I AM's X starts in negative energy, I AM's intent is to SOAR back to positive energy.

- JOB #2: To plan to feel better in the future.

- O: OBJECTIVES: I AM's desired improvements to help I AM feel better, achievable by an intended time.

- A: ACTIONS: The process of I AM doing things or taking steps to achieve the Objectives.

- R: RESULTS: The consequences, effects, or outcomes from I AM's actions.

- V: VISION: I AM's long-term visualization of the ideal I AM aspires to create.

- FP: The most important long-term centers of attention guiding the pursuits of I AM's Vision.

- OZ: Opportunity Zone: The Feelings Platform upper right quadrant representing I AM's greatest chances for improvement.

- PZ: Problem Zone: The Feelings Platform lower right quadrant representing I AM's opportunity to return to the Opportunity Zone.

- IMPROVEMENT LINE: The solid arrow connecting the X to the O, representing I AM's Improvement Plan.

CHART G FLOW

1. The area right of the NOW Line, above the Energy Line, is the Opportunity Zone (OZ). The area right of the NOW Line, below the Energy Line, is the Problem Zone (PZ). Both of these represent areas where I AM can improve. I AM can choose to either pursue an opportunity from positive energy or to solve or fix a problem from negative energy.

2. I AM's X is always placed somewhere on the NOW Line, based on I AM's current feelings about the Topic. It reflects I AM's response to "I Feel…"

3. **S** (Situation) is I AM's perception of the current set of circumstances.

   The S is located above the NOW Line because every NOW is a new Situation. Every Situation has facts and feels. Facts represent the who, what, when, where, why and how of those circumstances. Feels represent I AM's feelings and emotions about those facts or perceptions about the Situation.

4. **O** (Objectives) are I AM's desired improvements to help I AM feel better, achievable by an intended time.

   The O is placed to the upper right of X because Objectives represent I AM's desire for improvement into the future. O is placed at a location appropriate for the length of the timeline and the height of the aspiration. The Objectives represent something I AM intends to achieve by a specific time through SOARing. Objectives are what by when. Objectives should be SMART (Specific, Measurable, Achievable, Relevant, Time-based) and in alignment with I AM's Vision and Focal Points.

5. Some Situations are identified by I AM as opportunities, which usually are felt as positive energy. When I AM's X is in positive energy, all intended Objectives, Actions and Results are intended to happen in positive energy. They are in OZ.

6. Sometimes I AM runs into Situations I AM identifies as problems, which usually are negative energy. When I AM's X is in negative energy, it is in PZ. The Objectives and intended Results are to solve or fix the problem and get back as soon and safely as possible into OZ positive energy.

7. The line between X and O is the Improvement Line. It represents I AM's Improvement Plan. It goes up to the right from X. X can be in positive or negative energy. I AM can improve from any NOW.

8. **A** (Actions) are the process of I AM doing things or taking steps to achieve the Objectives.

   The A is placed left of the O. It represents all of the Improvement Plan steps necessary to achieve the Objectives. It represents the who, what, when, where, why, and how of making happen the Improvement Plan.

9. **R** (Results) are the consequences, effects, or outcomes from I AM's Actions.

   The R is placed below the O. It reflects all I AM's facts and feels progress toward the Objective.

Interim Results are monitored at midpoints along the Improvement Line. If the steps being taken are working as planned, I AM stays on the Improvement Plan. If things are not going as planned, I AM adjusts or a revised SE may be in order.

10. Celebrate achievement of the Objectives!

MANAGING the SOARing EXPERIENCE

PART 2   **CHART G-1**

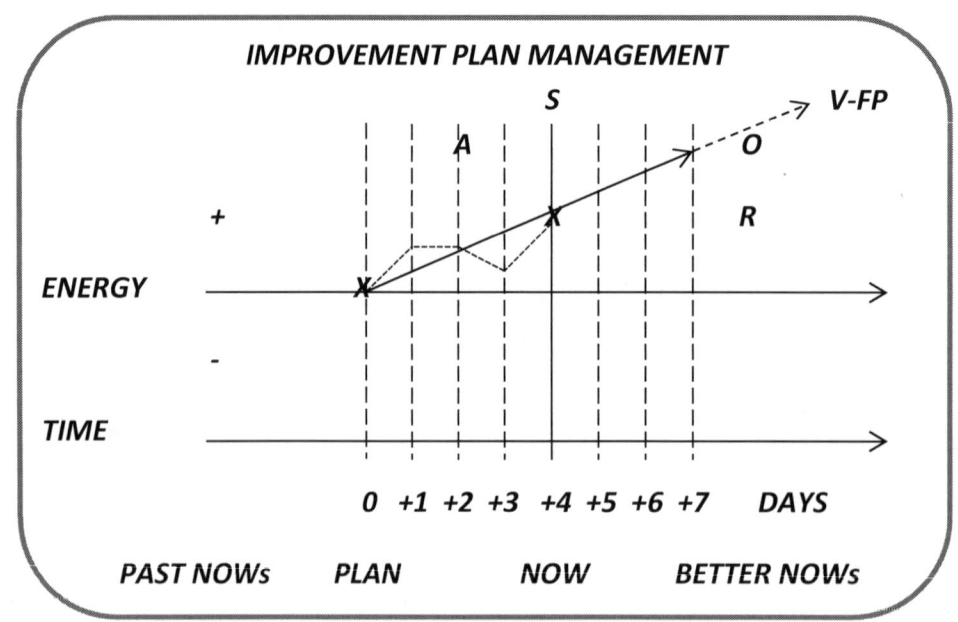

The SE creates the Improvement Plan that gets managed over a selected period of time. During the time between NOW and the Result, the plan must be monitored, measured and managed by I AM.

This example shows the basic Feelings Platform, plus various components working together in the described process. It shows I AM's perspective from NOW (Day 4,) looking back at progress, looking at the current Situation and looking ahead to accomplishing the Objective.

Conceptually, the process is as easy as 1-2-3.

1. The Improvement Plan starts with X at NOW…Day 0

2. I AM chooses the Objective (O) location…Day 7, Feeling Better

3. I AM monitors, measures and manages the Improvement Plan (solid arrow) from X to O and marks progress at midpoints.

This process can be applied to any time span from nanoseconds to a lifetime. Usual choices are nanoseconds, seconds, minutes, hours, days, weeks, months, years, and lifetime. This example uses days. The shorter time spans are for quick choices and fast actions. There can be hundreds of these a day. That is why I AM has memorized and habituated this SE process. The longer time spans are normally written and can be in great detail.

The days between the start of the Improvement Plan and the Objectives are Midpoints. Midpoints, as dashed vertical lines, are intermediate points in time in the Improvement Plan where I AM reviews progress toward the Objectives. These are Days +1, +2, +3, +4, +5, +6, and, if necessary, on further until Results (R) are decided. Or, the process could be shorter if the R is reached earlier.

In greater detail, the 1-2-3s are:

1. X at NOW…Day 0.

The Improvement Plan beginning (X) can be anywhere along the NOW line. Its location depends on I AM's feeling at that point in time about the Topic.

- The X reflects I AM's feelings.
- I AM's feelings reflect I AM's thoughts.
- I AM's thoughts reflect the Topic.
- The Topic is the most important focus in the Situation.
- When the Situation changes, the Topic, thoughts, feelings and X might change.

2. Place the O (Objective).

I AM tries to choose Topics that are aligned with I AM's Vision (V) and Focal Points (FP). Such Topics inspire I AM to improve on them because they are most important to I AM's living a better life story. In these cases, I AM is generally excited to try to improve on the opportunity and so the X location could be well into positive energy…up the NOW Line..

On the other hand, the Topic may reek of a big problem. Problems normally produce negative feelings. Negative feelings put the X below the Energy Line into negative energy. When the X starts in negative energy, I AM tries to get back to positive energy as safely and quickly as possible by thinking feel-better thoughts.

A great thing about the Improvement Plan is that it can start with any feelings and improve from there! The secret of climbing up the Improvement Line is I AM continually seeking to think feel-better thoughts.

On the chart, the Objective specifies what is to be accomplished by when. The "what" determines the improvement height above the level of the X. The "when" places the O at the amount of time planned for the achievement of the O. In the example, the O is set at Day +7 for achievement and significantly above the level of the X for improvement.

When the O is established, everything else falls into place. The Objective is what leads everything. I AM manages everything by the Objectives.

3. I AM monitors, measures and manages the Improvement Plan to the Objective.

The Improvement Line (solid arrow) connects the X on Day 0 and O on Day +7. From that, the A (Actions) automatically is placed above the arrow. The A represents all the action steps intended to be taken to achieve the Objective. Likewise, the R (Results) automatically is placed below the O, representing the results being achieved daily at the Midpoints.

With each day, progress is monitored, measured and posted to the Progress Line.

- PROGRESS LINE: The dashed line connecting the X and O, reflecting I AM's progress on I AM's Improvement Plan.

Progress is continually monitored, measured and managed throughout the Actions.

1. MONITOR: I AM to systematically check on progress towards I AM's Objectives.

2. MEASURE: I AM to systematically evaluate quality and quantity measurements of progress towards I AM's Objectives.

3. MANAGE: I AM to supervise, direct and control progress towards I AM's Objectives.

I AM monitors and measures each day and then manages progress or the lack thereof. I AM quits managing the SE when the Results are determined. At that point, I AM can switch efforts to another Topic or create another SE on the same Topic, using the Results of the completed SE as the Situation for the new SE.

Every SE is another word, sentence, paragraph or chapter in I AM's life story. I AM tries to feel better with each SE and continue creating a better life story SE by SE.

LIFE STORY

LIFE STORY: THE ACCOUNT OF EVERYTHING THAT HAPPENS IN I AM's LIFE.

PICTURE

JOB #2 = To Plan to Feel Better in the Future!

SOARing PROCESS *(CAUSE)*

I SOAR

FUTURE (C)

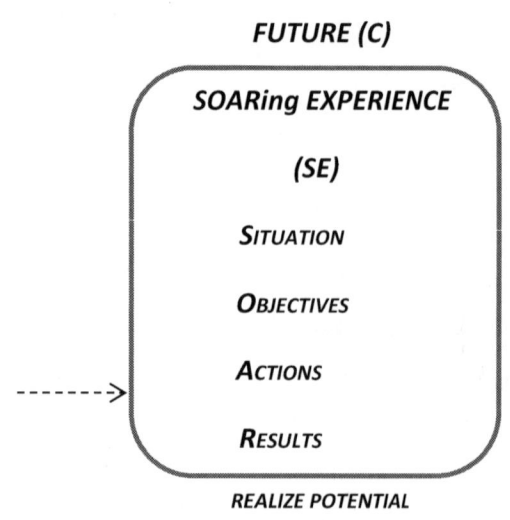

SOARing EXPERIENCE

(SE)

SITUATION

OBJECTIVES

ACTIONS

RESULTS

REALIZE POTENTIAL

LIFE STORY (D)

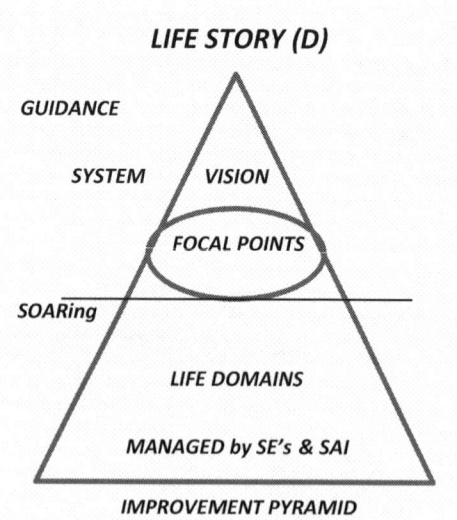

GUIDANCE

SYSTEM · VISION

FOCAL POINTS

SOARing

LIFE DOMAINS

MANAGED by SE's & SAI

IMPROVEMENT PYRAMID

FEELINGS PLATFORM *(EFFECT)*

I FEEL BETTER

BETTER NOWs (G)

TOPIC   S   V/FP

I IMPROVE   A   O

R

+

ENERGY

-

TIME

NOW

& TO IMPROVE

BETTER LIFE STORY (H)

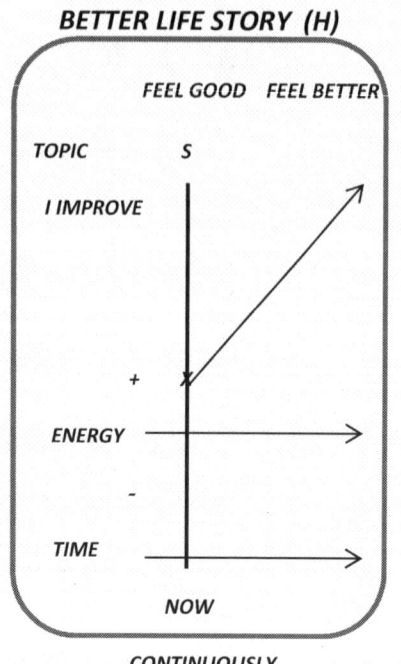

FEEL GOOD   FEEL BETTER

TOPIC   S

I IMPROVE

+

ENERGY

-

TIME

NOW

CONTINUOUSLY

SOARing PROCESS

LIFE STORY

Chart D

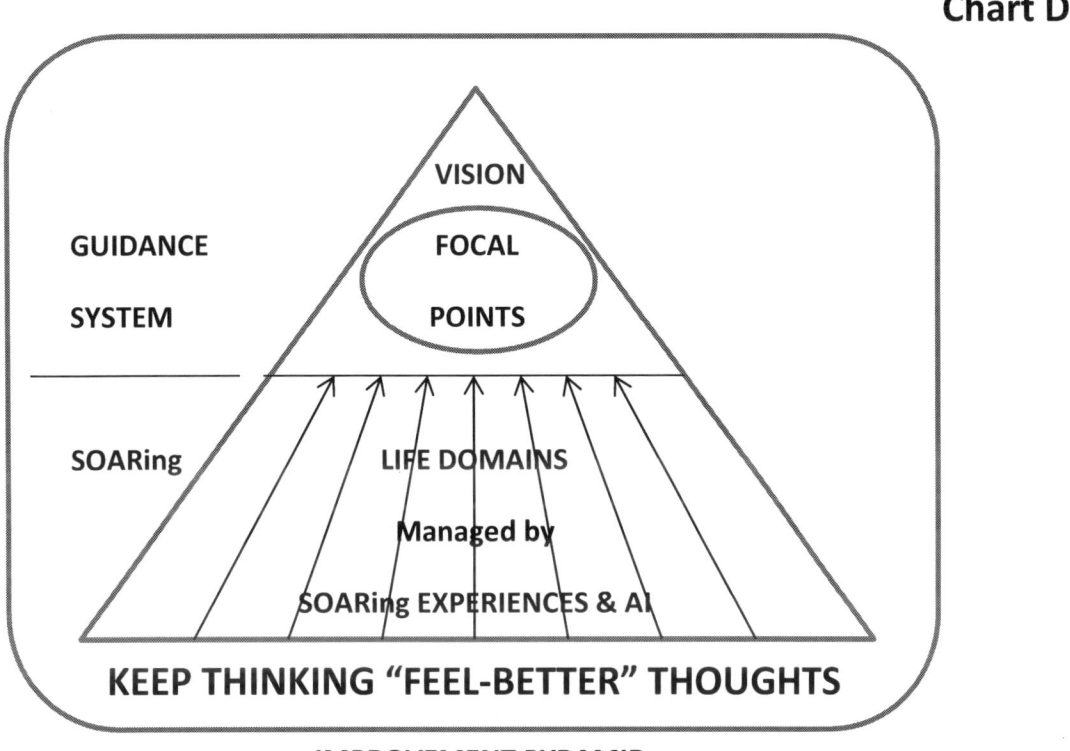

VISION

GUIDANCE
SYSTEM

FOCAL

POINTS

SOARing

LIFE DOMAINS

Managed by

SOARing EXPERIENCES & AI

KEEP THINKING "FEEL-BETTER" THOUGHTS

IMPROVEMENT PYRAMID

The Improvement Pyramid is an overview of how I AM manages I AM's life story improvement journey. It is the management tool for Job #2.

- IMPROVEMENT: The process of changing something for the better.
- IMPROVEMENT PYRAMID: The visual framework for helping I AM navigate I AM's life story.
- MANAGEMENT: I AM's being in charge of and responsible for I AM's life

Essentially, the process is 1-2-3, from the bottom of the pyramid up.

1. I AM creates a SOARing Experience (SE) on the most important Topic at NOW.
2. Frequently, the Topic is from I AM's Life Domains.
3. The SE is guided by I AM's Focal Points, aimed at I AM's Vision.

This process is repeated over and over again throughout I AM's life story improvement journey.

1. SOARing EXPERIENCE (SE)

SOARing Experiences are created as the result of I AM going through the Topic selection and Choice Cycle process at NOW.

- SOARing EXPERIENCE (SE): The Situation, Objectives, Actions, Results format that produces and helps manage the Improvement Plan.

- IMPROVEMENT PLAN: The planned series of steps intended to be taken to achieve the Objectives.

The Improvement Plan is created in Actions.

1. Climbing the Improvement Pyramid begins with I AM creating a SOARing Experience (SE)

2. Each SOARing Experience is on a separate Topic.

3. The SOARing Experience is the Situation, Objectives, Actions, Results of a Topic.

4. Situation: I AM's perception of the set of circumstances Here NOW. The Situation was created upon the NOW Ar- rivals' arrival at NOW.

5. Objectives: The desired improvements to help I AM feel better, achievable by an intended time.

6. Actions: The process of I AM doing things or taking steps to achieve the Objectives. This process creates the Improvement Plan.

7. The Improvement Plan is what guides I AM's Actions through time from the Situation to the Results

8. I AM implements the Improvement Plan, making it happen along the timeline of planned steps.

9. I AM monitors, measures and manages progress at appropriate midpoints to make sure the Improvement Plan is achieving the desired Results. Necessary adjustments are made along the timeline of the Improvement Plan.

10. Results: The consequences, effects, or outcomes of I AM's Actions. Results are monitored periodically during the Improvement Plan steps as well as at the end of the process.

11. The Results of one SOARing Experience can be used as the Situation of another link in a chain of SOARing Experiences on the same Topic.

12. Each SE can be any time length from a nanosecond to a lifetime.

13. As the SE is the day-to-day workhorse of SOARing, I AM tends to have a number of SE's actively being managed at almost the same time.

14. Management of multiple SOARing Experiences is accomplished by the Improvement Pyramid.

2. LIFE DOMAINS

Life Domains are the source of many. if not most, of I AM's SEs.

- LIFE DOMAINS: I AM's most important areas of long-term interest and activity.

Life Domains are a major focus of I AM's life management. They are the areas of life most important to I AM at each NOW. For I AM, the categories below are pretty stable through time, although the balance can change frequently. Everyone has their own set of Life Domains and different balances among them.

- BALANCE: The condition in which different elements are in appropriate proportions.

For I AM, maintaining balance among the domains is primarily a matter of priorities. Within the overall scheme of things, what is most important NOW becomes the priority. I AM remains flexible because the Situation is always changing and change can quickly modify priorities. I AM adapts to the new Situation and refocuses on the best balance.

Maintaining balance is an ongoing process, from second to second to the extent of a lifetime. I AM tries to step back from time to time and evaluate balance from the long-term perspective of creating a better life story. Then I AM makes adjustments as necessary.

The key for I AM is to stay focused on what is most important NOW.

Primary Life Domains: (Alphabetically, with examples)

1. *Career:* Employment. Work. Job. Vocation. Profession. Skills. Education.
2. *Environment:* Surroundings. Housing. Safety. Security. Freedom. Government. Media. Quality of Life. Community. Location.
3. *Finance:* Economics. Income. Net Worth. Wealth. Cash. Liquidity. Savings. Investments. Expenses. Risk.
4. *Health:* Physical. Mental. Emotional. Stress Management. Well-Being. Positive Mindset.
5. *Improvement:* SOARing. Self-Actualization. Personal Growth. Inspiration to others. Purpose. New Ideas. Strengths. Weaknesses. Mindfulness. Knowledge. Personal Management. Self-Esteem. Optimism.
6. *Leisure:* Fun. Arts. Sports. Passions. Hobbies. Collections. Creations. Volunteering. Advocacy. Play. Games.
7. *Relationships:* Family. Friends. Romance. Social. Significant Others. Co-workers. Teams. Memberships. Other Volunteers. Schoolmates. Clubs. Committees.
8. *Spirituality:* Religion. Giving. Beliefs. Alignment. Faith. Oneness. Appreciation. Gratitude. Connection.

I AM's balance can significantly affect I AM's success at Job #1 and Job #2. It is important for I AM to maintain appropriate balance by considering I AM's needs and that of others, especially family and health.

3. GUIDANCE SYSTEM

The top half of the Improvement Pyramid is the Guidance System.

- GUIDANCE SYSTEM: I AM's Vision and Focal Points…the guides of I AM's life story journey.

This Guidance System has been created by I AM with the aid of all that I AM has become…all the experiences, education, successes, failures, trials, errors, etc. Every person creates their own customized Guidance System.

I AM's Guidance System:

- VISION: I AM's long-term visualization of the ideal I AM aspires to create.

I AM's Vision is "Everyone enjoying NOW and living a better life story".

Much of I AM's thinking, feeling and acting is oriented toward that Vision. The thinking, feeling and acting on the Focal Points is how I AM plans to get to the Vision. I AM is guided by I AM's Focal Points at every NOW. I AM's Guidance System can be a model for others or be totally different to suit the individual.

In SOARing, the emphasis is on I AM improving from where I AM is NOW to where I AM wants to be at some point in the future. That is done by making choices aimed at the Vision and within the parameters set by I AM's Focal Points.

- FOCAL POINTS: The most important long-term centers of attention guiding pursuits of I AM's Vision

Briefly, I AM has chosen these as I AM's Focal Points. (Everyone chooses their own)

1. FEEL GOOD NOW, SATISFYING NEEDS AND WANTS

   - FEEL GOOD NOW: Job #1
   - SATISFYING NEEDS: Topics I AM must have, satisfied.
   - SATISFYING WANTS: Topics I AM would like to have, satisfied.

2. ALIGN BODY, MIND, SOUL & SPIRIT (BMSS) IN POSITIVE ENERGY

   - BODY: The physical structure part of I AM.
   - MIND: A nonphysical part of I AM that is responsible for thinking, reasoning, feeling, remembering, imagining, perceiving, ideating, sensing, etc.
   - SOUL: A nonphysical part of I AM that is everything that makes I AM alive instead of dead.
   - SPIRIT: A nonphysical part of I AM that is the spiritual connection between I AM and I AM's chosen god.
   - POSITIVE ENERGY: Good Energy vibrations that I AM can align with to feel good.

3. EMPLOY SOARing IMPROVEMENT SYSTEM (SIS):

- ○ SOARing PROCESS: The SOAR method to reach objectives and navigate life.
- ○ FEELINGS PLATFORM: The scorecard I AM uses to understand how well I AM is doing with the SOARing Process.
- ○ IMPROVEMENT PYRAMID: The visual framework for helping I AM navigate I AM's life story.

4. PRACTICE WELL-BEING DAILY

- ○ WELL-BEING: Positive energy, engagement, meaning, accomplishments and positive relationships.

5. IMPROVE TOOLBOX

- ○ IMPROVE: Make better.

- ○ TOOLBOX: I AM's distinctive attributes.

6. SOAR NOW!

- ○ SOAR: Acronym for Situation, Objectives, Actions, Results.

I AM's daily life is intended for I AM to be feeling good (Job #1), satisfying needs and wants and planning for feeling even better tomorrow (Job #2).

SUMMARY

I AM's Guidance System is critical to I AM's enjoying NOW and having better NOW's in the future. I AM continuously seeks to improve I AM's Guidance System.

I AM's Guidance System provides the roadmap for I AM to follow. It shows I AM the direction to go and the way to get there. If I AM strays off into the ditch, it shows I AM the way to get back into alignment with the roadmap and on course toward I AM's Vision.

**I AM SOARs with SOARing Experiences, guided by I AM's
Focal Points toward I AM's Vision.**

FEELINGS PLATFORM

BETTER LIFE STORY

Chart H

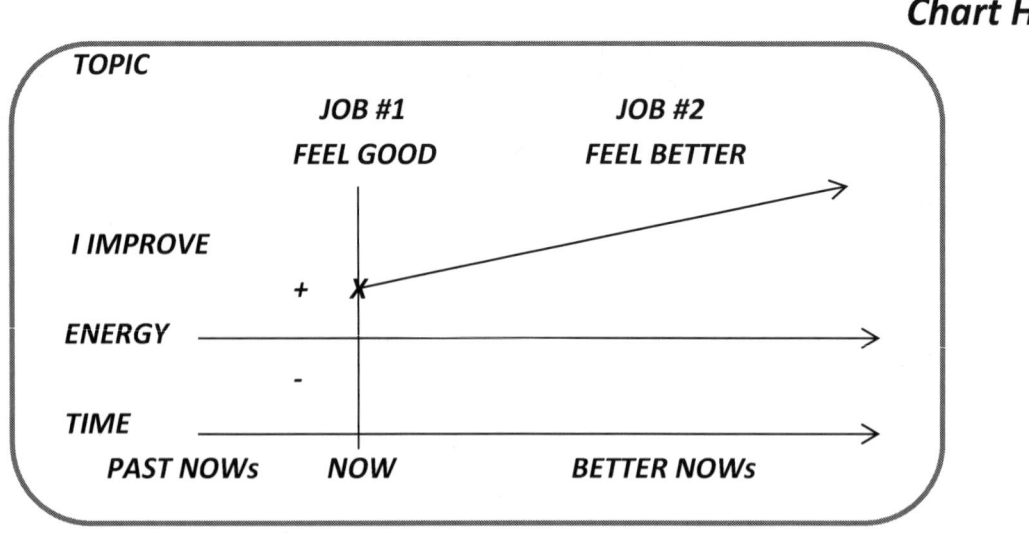

CONTINUOUSLY

Chart H reflects I AM's feelings about things being done in Chart D.

This chart is similar to Chart G but is for a lifetime of creating a superb life story.

I AM's core intention is to live a better life story.

- LIFE STORY: The account of everything that happens in I AM's life.
- BETTER LIFE STORY: From NOW on, living more and more of life in positive energy seeking higher and higher emotional levels.

To keep living a better and better life story, I AM embraces continuous improvement.

- CONTINUOUS IMPROVEMENT: I AM's journey of focusing on SOARing to improve I AM and I AM's surroundings.

Chart H represents I AM living a better and better life story.

1. I AM is in positive energy NOW.
2. S = Feeling good, enjoying NOW. (Job #1)
3. O = To feel better over the long-term future. (Job #2)
4. A = Continually improving by SOARing.
5. R = Feeling better and better from NOW on.

The chart shows the Improvement Line pointing up and right from the X.

- IMPROVEMENT LINE: The solid arrow connecting the X to the O, representing I AM's Improvement Plan.
- IMPROVEMENT PLAN: The planned series of steps intended to be taken to achieve the Objectives.

The Improvement Line can begin anywhere on the NOW Line. When I AM dips into negative energy, the X is below the Energy Line and the Improvement Line goes from the X up and right into positive energy. To make this happen, I AM uses the Choice Cycle to find and focus on feel-better thoughts. These can be finding more positives in the Topic, recasting the Topic or changing to a different Topic.

An important aspect of I AM's continuous improvement is using the Choice Cycle to make good choices of Topics. Topic choice is key because it:

1. Identifies what is most important to I AM at NOW.
2. Establishes the direction of I AM's future NOWs.
3. Creates a pattern of positive thoughts where the thoughts attract more and more like thoughts. (i.e. Law of Attraction).

I AM tries to focus Topic choices on both I AM's improvement and on helping the improvement of other things...people, products, education, environment, innovations, ideas, etc.

I AM improves I AM by SOARing with Topic choices in:

- Growing the Body, Mind, Soul, Spirit partnership.
- Enhancing I AM's Toolbox.
- Having and maintaining a positive mindset.
- Climbing Maslow's pyramid.
- Living in well-being daily.
  - In positive energy as much time as possible.
  - Being engaged in meaningful activities.
  - Nurturing relationships with others.
  - Enjoying achievements NOW while SOARing toward I AM's Vision.
- Adding WOW to passions.

I AM improves other things by SOARing with Topic choices such as:

- Give what I AM is capable of giving to others.
  - Time: Volunteer. Participate. Join. Serve. Befriend. Champion cause.
  - Talent: Teach. Mentor. Write book. How-to podcast. Leadership.
  - Treasure: Money. Goods. Endow. Donate. Support small businesses.

- I AM grows more, learns more and gains more dedication by teaching a Topic.
  - Embrace SOARing for living a better life story and share the passion.
  - Pick the best strengths from the Toolbox and share with others.
  - Change the world for the better with positive energy.

AI PERSPECTIVE

Other good ways to improve continuously are:

- Define Your Values and Objectives: Start by understanding what is truly important to you. What values do you want to live by? What goals do you aspire to achieve? This clarity will guide your choices and actions.

- Pursue Your Passions: Engage in activities and pursuits that you are passionate about. This not only brings joy but also helps you create a story that is uniquely yours.

- Embrace Learning and Growth: View life as a journey of continuous learning. Embrace new experiences, learn from your mistakes, and always seek to grow personally and professionally.

- Build Meaningful Relationships: The relationships you build along the way are a crucial part of your life story. Invest in deep and meaningful connections with family, friends, and new acquaintances.

- Overcome Challenges: Every great story involves overcoming obstacles. View challenges as opportunities to show your resilience and character.

- Leave a Positive Impact: Consider how you can contribute to the world around you. This could be through your work, volunteering, or simple acts of kindness. Making a difference adds profound meaning to your life story.

- Stay True to Yourself: In a world full of expectations and pressures, staying true to who you are is vital. Make choices that align with your inner self and values.

- Record and Reflect: Keep a journal or record of your experiences, thoughts, and feelings. Reflecting on your journey helps you appreciate your growth and learn from your experiences.

- Stay Open to Change: Life can be unpredictable. Stay open to new directions and paths that life may present to you.

- Enjoy the Journey: Lastly, remember to enjoy the journey. Find joy in the small moments, and don't get so focused on the destination that you forget to appreciate the journey.

A great life story is not just about achievements or milestones; it's about how I AM lives each day, the relationships nurtured, the challenges overcome, and the impacts made. I AM's life story is uniquely I AM's, so it is written.

Every life story leaves a legacy. I AM is trying to leave a legacy of self-actualization. That is, I AM living life being all that I AM can be.

- LEGACY: The long-lasting impact of a person's life.

Legacy is often thought of in terms of material wealth or achievements left behind, but it's much broader than that. It encompasses the impact you have on others, the memories you create, the changes you inspire in your community or circle, and the values and lessons you pass on. Here's how your life story contributes to your legacy.

1. Personal Impact: The way you live your life, the choices you make, and how you treat others all leave an imprint on those around you. Your kindness, resilience, and wisdom can inspire and positively influence others.

2. Shared Memories: The experiences you share with family, friends, and even acquaintances become part of their memories. The stories of your adventures, struggles, and triumphs can be retold and cherished for generations.

3. Values and Beliefs: The values you uphold and the beliefs you advocate for are often mirrored or adopted by those you interact with, especially younger generations. This can be a powerful part of your legacy.

4. Contributions and Achievements: Your contributions to your community, workplace, or field of interest, as well as personal achievements, are a part of your legacy. They reflect your passions, skills, and the impact you've made.

5. Inspirational Journey: Overcoming challenges and pursuing your passions can be incredibly inspiring to others. Your journey can motivate people to pursue their own goals and face their challenges with courage.

6. Emotional Legacy: The emotional support, love, and care you provide create an emotional legacy. This is often the most cherished aspect of a person's legacy.

Your life story, in its entirety, contributes to your legacy. It's not just about what you leave behind in a tangible sense, but also about the intangible - the way you've touched lives, influenced thoughts, and sparked changes. Each person's legacy is unique, shaped by their individual journey, actions, and interactions.

S+AI to create your legacy!

FUNDAMENTAL FLOWS

QUICK START

- FUNDAMENTAL FLOWS: The basic foundational flows from which other things develop.

  - NATURAL FLOWS: The fundamental processes in nature that operate independently of human intervention.

  - I AM FLOWS: The dynamic process unique to individuals, shaping thought, experiences, navigational choices, feelings and actions.

  - SOARing FLOWS: The systematic activities directed towards the achievement of specific objectives.

FUNDAMENTAL FLOWS

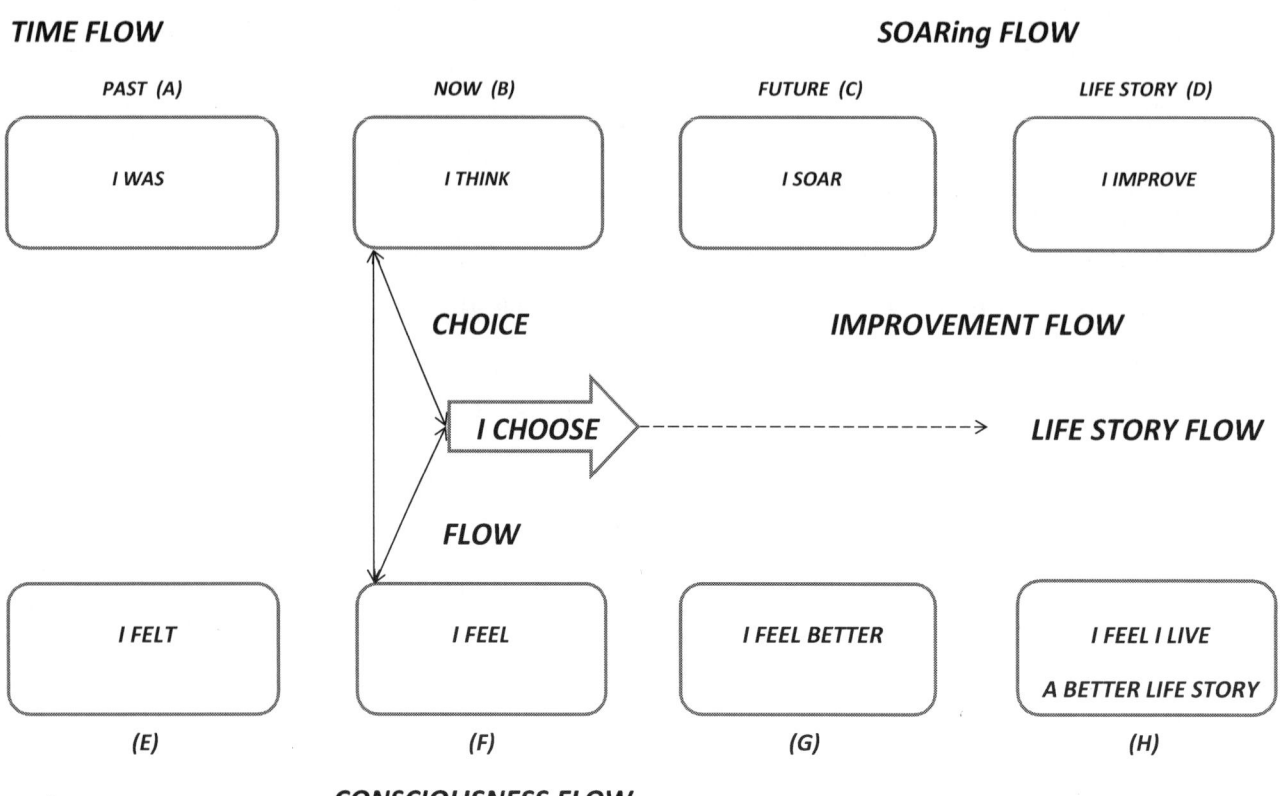

SPACE FLOW - ENERGY FLOW - MATTER FLOW

TIME FLOW   **SOARing FLOW**

PAST (A)	NOW (B)	FUTURE (C)	LIFE STORY (D)
I WAS	I THINK	I SOAR	I IMPROVE

CHOICE   **IMPROVEMENT FLOW**

I CHOOSE --------------------> **LIFE STORY FLOW**

FLOW

I FELT	I FEEL	I FEEL BETTER	I FEEL I LIVE A BETTER LIFE STORY
(E)	(F)	(G)	(H)

CONSCIOUSNESS FLOW

FUNDAMENTAL FLOWS

ESSENCE

QUICK START

1. Fundamental Flows represent the movement of I AM and the Big Picture through time.

2. The Big Picture is like a snapshot of I AM at NOW. It shows one point in time.

3. Fundamental Flows is like a movie of I AM at NOW as a single frame in the continuous movement of I AM's life story through time.

The Fundamental Flow chart represents I AM's perspective of some important ways the universe seems to flow. This flow is the movement I AM sees all around every moment of every day. I AM lives life as part of these movement flows.

- FUNDAMENTAL: The basic foundational principles upon which something is based.
- FLOW: The way things move and change over time, always interacting and affecting each other.
- FUNDAMENTAL FLOWS: The basic foundational flows from which other things develop.

The universe has a number of flows. I AM has identified key flows that are critically important for I AM to navigate every moment of every day.

1. NATURAL FLOWS

   - Space
   - Time
   - Energy
   - Matter

2. I AM FLOWS

   - Consciousness
   - Choice

3. SOARing FLOWS

   - SOARing
   - Improvement
   - Life Story

The Fundamental Flows provide the basic framework for all movements of I AM, I AM's environment, what I AM thinks, feels and acts, and everything else.

The Fundamental Flows form the foundational framework of the Big Picture. The Big Picture represents how I AM navigates the Fundamental Flows at each NOW.

CHART

The Fundamental Flows (FF) chart is in the same format as the Big Picture (BP), but shows a different perspective of how the universe seems to work according to I AM.

The biggest difference between the two is:

1. The Big Picture is like a snapshot of I AM at a specific point in time…NOW.

2. The Fundamental Flows is like a movie about I AM navigating on a river of NOWs.

The Fundamental Flows chart boxes (A-H) represent the corresponding boxes of Big Picture (A-H).

The top row (A-D) represents I AM's perspectives from NOW.

- o A = Looking back at the past where I AM was before NOW.
- o B = Looking inward at what I AM is thinking NOW.
- o C = Looking ahead to making tomorrow better than today by SOARing.
- o D = Looking at continuous improvement from NOW to the end of I AM's life story.

The bottom row (E-H) reflects I AM's feelings at each time frame.

- o E = Looking back at the past to what I AM felt. This could be a fraction of a second ago, an hour ago, a year ago or any other memory experience time.
- o F = Looking at how I AM feels NOW. If I AM feels positive energy/emotion, I AM is accomplishing Job #1.
- o G = Looking ahead with the desire to feel better in the future. This could be one second from NOW, or one hour, or tomorrow or any other time in the future. If I AM's plan to feel better in the future makes I AM feel good NOW, I AM is accomplishing Job #2.
- o H = Looking at how I AM feels about I AM's life story. I AM can monitor, measure and manage this feeling every day, every week, every month or at least every year.

The chart features the three types of flows that most apply to I AM at every NOW.

1. Natural Flows. These are flows given to I AM free of charge by the universe to use as the framework for I AM to choose to do about anything I AM wants to do.

- o Space Flow. This flow allows I AM to explore and expand any part of the universe. The world, as they say, is an oyster. I AM can expand in any space desired.

- Time Flow. This flow gives a constant timeline to I AM's life so I AM can do all the expanding, exploring and improving I AM cares to do. I AM is wise if I AM manages time with the importance it deserves.

- Energy Flow. Managing energy flow is the key to I AM's success. I AM tries to stay in positive energy as much time as safely possible. A positive energy mindset prepares I AM for addressing Job #1 and Job #2 at each NOW.

- Matter Flow. This flow gives I AM the opportunity to be anywhere in the universe at any time. I AM can choose to work from home, sit on the beach, save the environment, hang out, hike in the forest or do anything else I AM wants wherever I AM wants to do it.

2. I AM Flows. These are flows that I AM controls to help I AM deal with every new NOW Situation.

- Consciousness Flow. This flow allows I AM to enter into participating with all the actions and interactions of the universe.

- Choice Flow. This flow allows I AM to become all that I AM can be. Choices create the future. Bad choices create bad futures. Good choices open the world for I AM to create all that I AM can be.

3. SOARing Flows. These are flows involved with I AM's improvement from NOW.

- SOARing Flow. This flow allows I AM to try to improve anything. At each NOW, I AM has the opportunity to SOAR with SOARing Experiences (SEs) on the moment's most important Topic.

- Improvement Flow. This flow allows I AM to monitor, measure and manage the SEs over a period of time. The Improvement Pyramid guides this process.

- Life Story Flow. This flow encourages I AM to periodically review the whole of I AM's life story, with emphasis on what improvements have been accomplished since the last review.

The Fundamental Flows and the Big Picture work together:

- To help I AM focus on NOW

- To navigate life into the future.

NATURAL FLOWS

QUICK START

- NATURAL FLOWS: The fundamental processes in nature that operate independently of human intervention.

  - SPACE FLOW: The dynamic and continuous movement of space.

  - TIME FLOW: I AM's perception and experience of time passing.

  - ENERGY FLOW: The dynamic movement and utilization of energy.

  - MATTER FLOW: The movement and transformation of matter through different states and locations.

FUNDAMENTAL FLOWS

SPACE FLOW   **ENERGY FLOW**   **MATTER FLOW**

TIME FLOW

SOARing FLOW

PAST (A)	NOW (B)	FUTURE (C)	LIFE STORY (D)
I WAS	I THINK	I SOAR	I IMPROVE

CHOICE

IMPROVEMENT FLOW

I CHOOSE - - - - - - - - - - - - - - → LIFE STORY FLOW

FLOW

I FELT	I FEEL	I FEEL BETTER	I FEEL I LIVE A BETTER LIFE STORY
(E)	(F)	(G)	(H)

CONSCIOUSNESS FLOW

SPACE FLOW

QUICK START

- SPACE: A continuous area that is available for use.

Space is the full dimension of the universe. It is the length, width and depth of the area in which I AM exists and SOARs.

- SPACE FLOW: The dynamic and continuous movement of space.

Space Flow emphasizes the fluidity and the constant evolution of space as it responds to time, energy, matter, and human activities.

Space Flow is a concept that challenges the traditional notion of space as a static, unchanging entity. Instead, it views space as an active participant in the interactions and processes that define our world.

Space Flow can be observed in how architectural designs shape and are shaped by human movement, light, and environmental conditions. For instance, the way a building's layout channels the flow of people through corridors, staircases, and communal areas demonstrates how space is not just a backdrop but a dynamic component that guides and influences behavior.

Space Flow can also apply to urban environments where the flow of traffic, the arrangement of public spaces, and the distribution of resources like energy and water illustrate how cities are living systems with spaces that adapt and evolve over time.

In the digital realm, Space Flow can be seen in the organization of virtual spaces, where information flows through networks, creating dynamic interactions in social media platforms, websites, and online communities.

EXAMPLES

Urban Development: Space flows as cities expand, with new buildings, roads, and infrastructure transforming landscapes over time.

Migration and Settlement: Human populations move across space, settling in new areas and creating cultural and demographic shifts.

Transportation Networks: The flow of vehicles, goods, and people through roads, railways, and airways illustrates the dynamic use of space over time.

Ecosystem Dynamics: Space flows as plant and animal species migrate, expand their habitats, or face changes due to environmental factors.

Architectural Design: Space is shaped and transformed through the design and construction of buildings, altering how people interact with their environment.

Territorial Boundaries: Over time, space flows as national borders change due to wars, treaties, and diplomatic negotiations.

Expansion of the Universe: Space itself flows as the universe expands, with galaxies moving farther apart over billions of years.

Agricultural Land Use: Space flows as land is cleared, cultivated, and harvested, changing the landscape with each season.

Exploration of Outer Space: Space flows as human-made satellites, probes, and spacecraft move through the solar system and beyond, exploring new frontiers.

Urban Sprawl: The spread of urban areas into surrounding rural regions demonstrates the flow of space as development encroaches on natural landscapes.

Digital Space Expansion: The growth of the internet and virtual environments reflects the flow of digital space, connecting people across the globe.

Spatial Organization in Art: Artists use space to guide the viewer's eye, creating depth, perspective, and balance in visual compositions.

Public Spaces: Parks, plazas, and squares are dynamic spaces where people gather, interact, and experience communal life.

Trade Routes: Historically, space flows as trade routes connect distant regions, facilitating the exchange of goods, culture, and ideas.

Personal Space: The concept of personal space flows as individuals navigate social interactions, respecting or violating invisible boundaries.

Geographical Exploration: Space flows as explorers chart new territories, mapping previously unknown regions and expanding human knowledge.

Landscaping and Garden Design: Space is creatively shaped and transformed in gardens and landscapes, reflecting aesthetic and functional considerations.

Cultural Space: The flow of cultural practices, traditions, and languages through different regions illustrates how space influences identity and heritage.

Military Strategy: Space flows as armies maneuver across terrains, occupying strategic positions, and altering the control of regions.

Virtual Reality: In virtual reality environments, space flows as users navigate digital worlds, experiencing immersive spatial interactions.

These examples illustrate how space is dynamic and flows through various aspects of life, from physical environments to digital realms, influencing how people live, interact, and understand their surroundings.

FUNDAMENTAL FLOWS

SPACE FLOW - ENERGY FLOW - MATTER FLOW

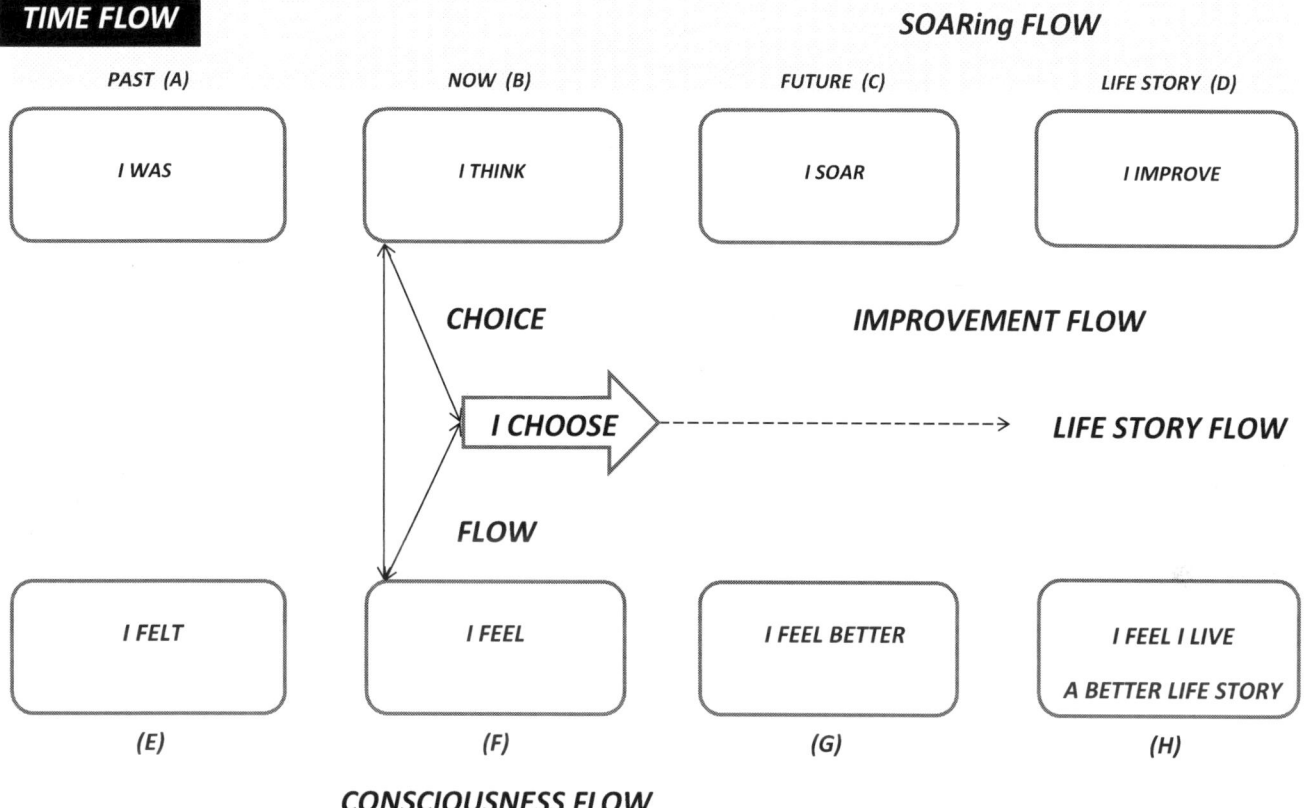

TIME FLOW

SOARing FLOW

PAST (A) — I WAS

NOW (B) — I THINK

FUTURE (C) — I SOAR

LIFE STORY (D) — I IMPROVE

CHOICE

IMPROVEMENT FLOW

I CHOOSE

LIFE STORY FLOW

FLOW

I FELT (E)

I FEEL (F)

I FEEL BETTER (G)

I FEEL I LIVE A BETTER LIFE STORY (H)

CONSCIOUSNESS FLOW

TIME FLOW

QUICK START

- TIME: I AM's clock time.

Time is a fundamental part of the world that helps I AM know when events occur. It acts as a universal measure, ordering moments from the past, through NOW and into the future. I AM uses it to track everything that happens.

- TIME FLOW: I AM's perception and experience of time passing.

I AM's perception can vary based on I AM's activities, focus and emotions. While time itself is the ticking of the clock, Time Flow is how I AM experiences these moments. I AM thinks of time as the framework, like a calendar, and Time Flow as I AM's personal journey through that calendar.

On the Fundamental Flows chart, Time Flow is shown in the upper left. It represents, from left to right, the flow of time from past, to NOW, to future, to a life story of I AM's lifetime.

Time is a very important flow in the modern world. Everything is scheduled. I AM runs I AM's life by what time it is. I AM runs late and gets frazzled. I AM arrives on time at an appointment and then has to wait. I AM wants it NOW!

NOW has become the center of I AM's life. I AM lives, breathes, exists, thinks, feels, acts and asks for more at NOW. From NOW, I AM can look back at the past, look ahead to the future and visualize a life story I AM dreams about living "someday".

NOW is the center of I AM's life and is so important that it is capitalized throughout the book.

EXAMPLES

Aging Process: Time flows through the natural progression of life stages, from infancy to old age, affecting physical and mental development.

Historical Events: The passage of time shapes the sequence of historical events, influencing cultural, social, and political changes.

Project Deadlines: In work and school, time flows as projects progress from initiation to completion, often marked by deadlines.

Seasonal Changes: The flow of time is evident in the cyclical changes of the seasons, affecting the environment and human activities.

Learning and Skill Development: Over time, learning new skills or gaining knowledge involves a gradual process of practice, mistakes, and mastery.

Technological Evolution: Time drives the progression of technology, from early inventions to advanced modern devices and systems.

Cultural Evolution: Over centuries, cultures evolve as traditions, languages, and customs adapt to changing times.

Generational Shifts: Time flows through the succession of generations, each bringing new perspectives, values, and innovations.

Economic Cycles: Time influences economic patterns, with economies experiencing periods of growth, recession, and recovery.

Construction Projects: Time flows as buildings and infrastructure are designed, constructed, and eventually aged or replaced.

Natural Disasters and Recovery: The aftermath of natural disasters unfolds over time, from immediate impact to long-term recovery and rebuilding.

Plant Growth: The flow of time is evident in the stages of plant growth, from seed germination to full maturity and eventual decay.

Phases of the Moon: Time flows as the moon cycles through its phases, influencing tides, cultural rituals, and timekeeping.

Literary and Artistic Movements: Over time, art and literature evolve through different movements, each characterized by unique styles and themes.

Social Change: Time drives social movements and reforms, with changes in laws, norms, and public attitudes occurring over years or decades.

Human Life Cycles: Time flows through the stages of human life, from birth, childhood, and adulthood to death, shaping personal narratives.

Environmental Changes: The flow of time is seen in long-term environmental changes, such as climate change, erosion, and deforestation.

Scientific Discoveries: Time allows for the accumulation of knowledge through research, experimentation, and the gradual acceptance of new scientific ideas.

These examples demonstrate how time flows through various aspects of life, nature, and human society, influencing growth, change, and continuity.

FUNDAMENTAL FLOWS

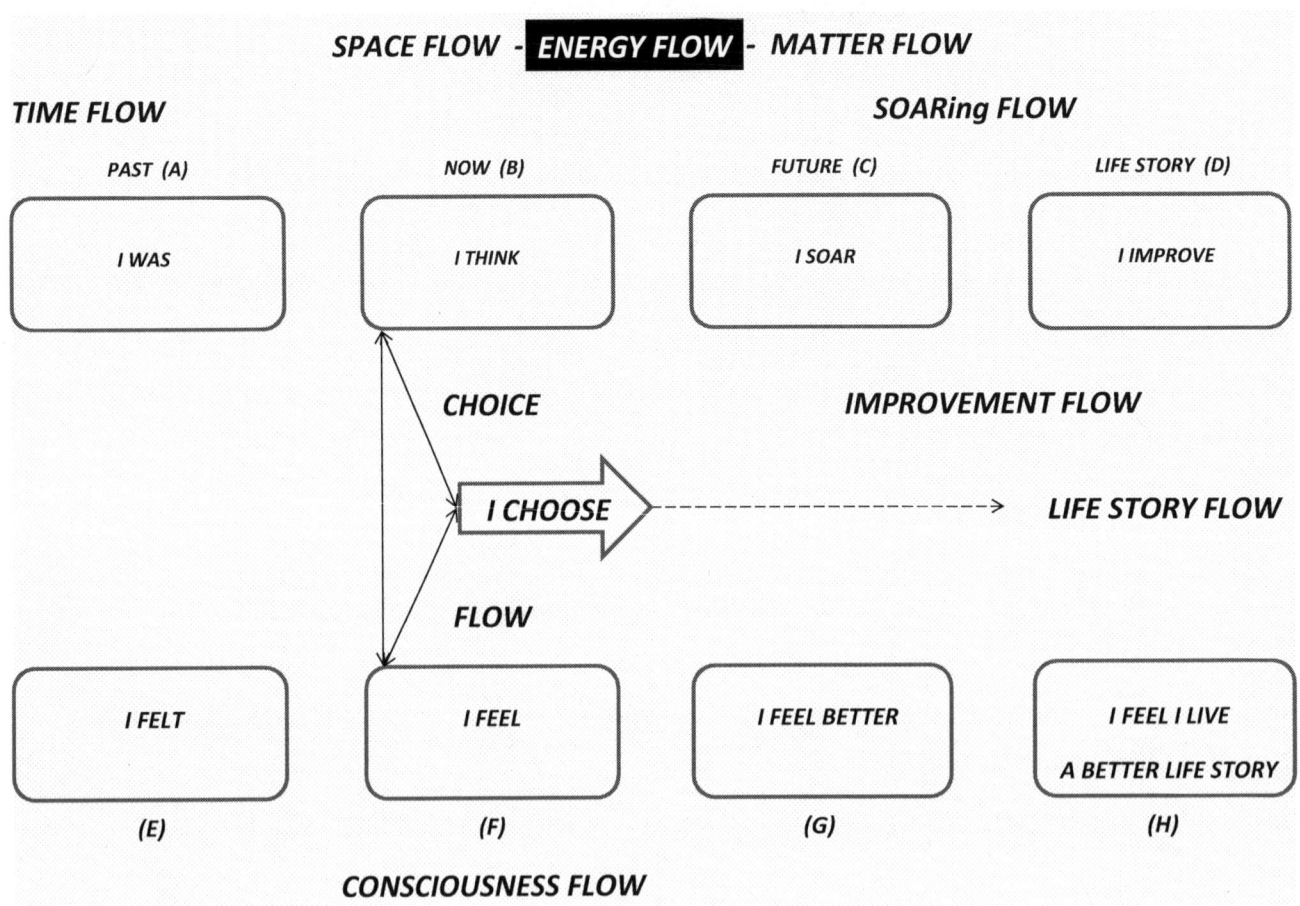

SPACE FLOW - **ENERGY FLOW** - MATTER FLOW

TIME FLOW · SOARing FLOW

PAST (A) · NOW (B) · FUTURE (C) · LIFE STORY (D)

I WAS · I THINK · I SOAR · I IMPROVE

CHOICE · IMPROVEMENT FLOW

I CHOOSE · LIFE STORY FLOW

FLOW

I FELT · I FEEL · I FEEL BETTER · I FEEL I LIVE A BETTER LIFE STORY

(E) · (F) · (G) · (H)

CONSCIOUSNESS FLOW

ENERGY FLOW

> ## *QUICK START*
>
> - ENERGY: The vibrational power flowing throughout the universe that is part of everything.
>   - POSITIVE ENERGY: Good energy vibrations that I AM can align with and feel good. (Same as positive emotions and positive feelings).
>   - NEGATIVE ENERGY: Bad energy vibrations that I AM can align with and feel bad. (Same as negative emotions and negative feelings).
> - ENERGY FLOW: The dynamic movement and utilization of energy.
>
> Energy Flow is the transfer or movement of energy from one place or system to another.
>
> Energy provides the potential, and energy flow is the realization and transformation of that potential.

Energy Flow is everywhere and is a major part of I AM. That is why it is at the top of the Fundamental Flow chart and is shaded to show that it encompasses everything on the chart.

Energy Flow is such a huge and important subject that there are many different perspectives and definitions of it.

I AM looks at Energy Flow from the perspective of positive and negative energy. This is because it is the source of the measurement of how I AM feels emotionally every moment of every day. Feelings are the scorecard I AM uses to monitor, measure and manage I AM's emotional well-being. Living safely in positive energy as much time as possible is I AM's Job #1 at every NOW.

I AM separates energy into positive and negative because that is what I AM believes is the way people think and feel. Most languages have dozens of positive energy words to express positive emotions and feelings. They have even more negative energy words to express negative emotions and feelings. Take a look at the lists of positive energy words and negative energy words lists. Additionally, thousands of other words have positive or negative connotations.

Positive energy is about: gods, good, well-being, growth, improvement, soul alignment, source energy. I AM focuses on positive energy and tries to stay in positive energy as much time as safely possible.

I AM believes people are intended to live lives aligned in harmony with positive energy.

While aligned in positive energy, I AM intends to experience reduced pain, increased pleasure, and the embracing of well-being. When I AM dips into negative energy, I AM tries to find feel-better thoughts and return to positive energy as soon and safely as possible.

EXAMPLES

Human Emotions: Positive and negative emotions generate vibrational energy that flows through interactions, influencing the emotional atmosphere of individuals and groups.

Spiritual Practices: Meditation, prayer, and rituals focus on channeling positive vibrational energy to align with higher spiritual frequencies, creating a flow of peace and clarity.

Energy Healing: Practices like Reiki and acupuncture direct vibrational energy to balance the body's natural energy flow, promoting healing and well-being.

Environmental Energy: Natural landscapes, such as forests and oceans, emit powerful vibrational energy that can uplift or calm those who spend time in these spaces.

Music and Sound: Different musical tones and rhythms generate vibrational energy that can positively or negatively impact the mood and energy of the listener.

Personal Aura: The energy field surrounding a person reflects their inner vibrational state, influencing how they interact with others and the environment.

Space Cleansing: Techniques like smudging or using crystals cleanse a space of negative vibrational energy, replacing it with positive vibrations.

Thought Patterns: Positive thoughts generate uplifting vibrational energy, while negative thoughts create lower vibrations that can affect one's overall energy field.

Group Dynamics: Collective energy in groups, such as during concerts, protests, or ceremonies, amplifies the vibrational power flowing through the participants.

Energy in Relationships: The vibrational energy exchanged between individuals in relationships can either uplift or drain, depending on the nature of the interaction.

Cosmic Energy: The universe emits cosmic vibrational energy through celestial events, like solar flares or lunar phases, which can influence the energy on Earth.

Manifestation Practices: Focusing on positive vibrational energy through intention and visualization helps manifest desired outcomes by aligning with the universe's energy flow.

Chakra Balancing: The flow of energy through the body's chakras reflects the vibrational state of an individual, with balanced chakras allowing for harmonious energy flow.

Quantum Energy: At the quantum level, particles vibrate with positive or negative energy, influencing the fabric of reality and how energy manifests in the physical world.

Cultural and Ritual Energy: Traditional dances, songs, and rituals generate vibrational energy that connects participants to their cultural roots and spiritual beliefs.

Planetary Energy: The Earth itself vibrates with energy, such as the Schumann resonance, which reflects the planet's natural vibrational frequency and affects all living beings.

Energy of Intentions: The vibrational energy behind a person's intentions can influence outcomes, with positive intentions creating constructive energy flow.

Healing Crystals: Crystals emit specific vibrational energies that can interact with human energy fields, either amplifying positive energy or neutralizing negative energy.

Sacred Geometry: Certain geometric patterns resonate with universal vibrational energy, influencing the flow of energy in spaces where these patterns are present.

Energy Exchange in Nature: The interaction between living organisms, such as plants and animals, creates a flow of vibrational energy that sustains life and ecological balance.

These examples illustrate how vibrational energy, both positive and negative, flows through various aspects of life, nature, and the universe, influencing everything from personal well-being to the broader cosmic order.

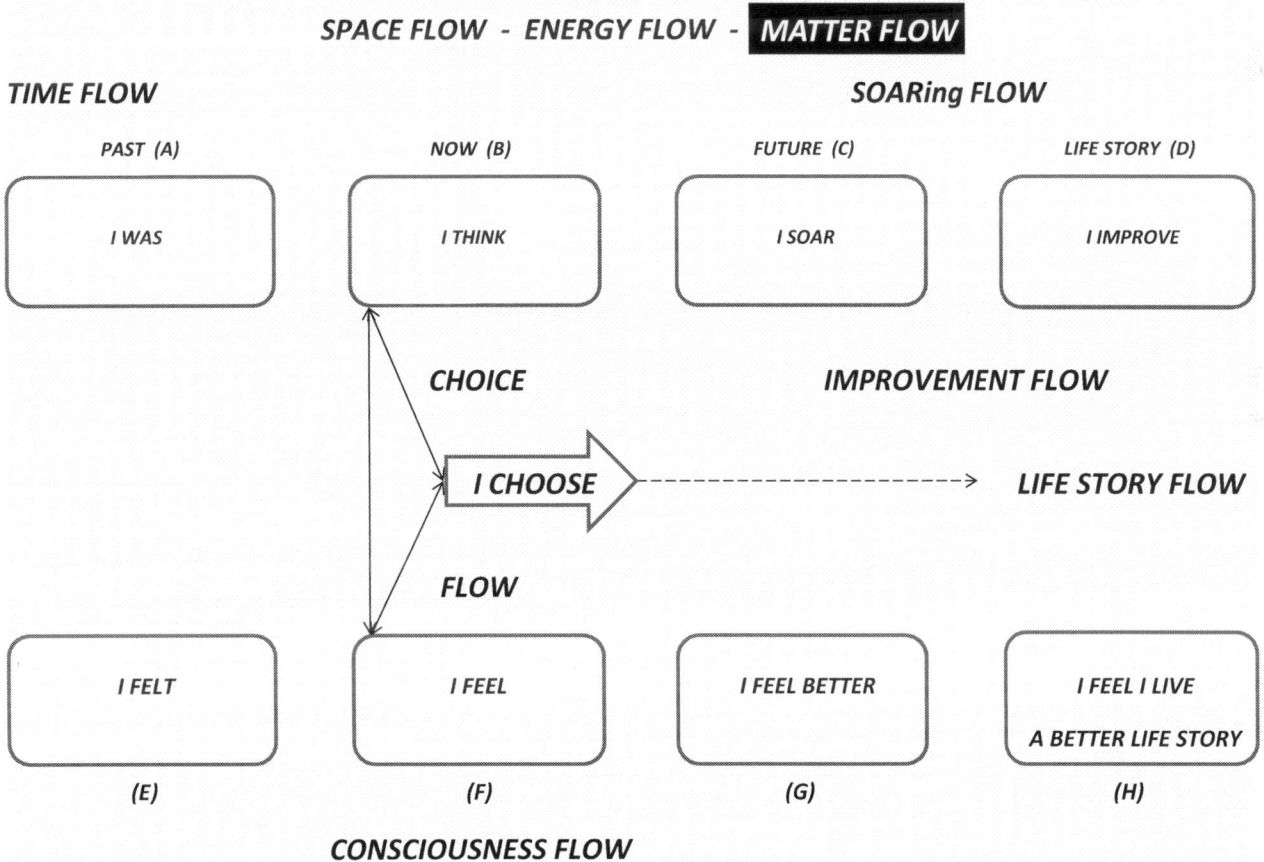

FUNDAMENTAL FLOWS

SPACE FLOW - ENERGY FLOW - MATTER FLOW

TIME FLOW   SOARing FLOW

| PAST (A) | NOW (B) | FUTURE (C) | LIFE STORY (D) |
| I WAS | I THINK | I SOAR | I IMPROVE |

CHOICE   IMPROVEMENT FLOW

I CHOOSE - - - - - - - - - - - - ->   LIFE STORY FLOW

FLOW

| I FELT | I FEEL | I FEEL BETTER | I FEEL I LIVE A BETTER LIFE STORY |
| (E) | (F) | (G) | (H) |

CONSCIOUSNESS FLOW

MATTER FLOW

QUICK START

- MATTER: The material substance that constitutes the observable universe, and together with energy, forms the basis of all observable phenomena.

For I AM, it means everything that can be touched, seen and measured in the physical world. Matter makes up all the objects and substances around I AM, from the smallest particles to the largest structures.

- MATTER FLOW: The movement and transformation of matter through different states and locations.

To I AM, matter is the static substance while matter flow is the dynamic process of movement and transformation. Matter provides the physical substance, and matter flow represents the continuous changes and cycles of that substance.

The Fundamental Flows chart shows the Matter Flow encompassing the entire chart because it is everywhere in the universe.

Matter makes up everything in the universe, from the stars in the sky to the cells in our bodies. The flow of matter involves the constant movement and transformation of physical substances. By understanding how matter flows and interacts, I AM can better appreciate the interconnectedness of all things. This awareness leads to a deeper respect for the environment and a more mindful approach to how to use and conserve resources.

Matter is composed of atoms, which are themselves made up of smaller particles: protons, neutrons, and electrons. These particles are bound together by fundamental forces such as electromagnetism and the strong nuclear force. The interactions between particles give rise to the different states of matter—solid, liquid, gas, and plasma. I AM interacts with matter constantly, from the food eaten to the air breathed to every other interaction with the environment.

I AM is a unique mixture of matter and energy.

Everything around I AM that has mass and occupies space is also matter. Atoms, molecules, animals, vegetables, minerals, atmospheres, plants, stars, moons, elements…and they are all matter.

Everywhere I AM goes, I AM is surrounded by an environment of matter. Environment can be described from many perspectives, but it is always a partnership of I AM and the universe… space, time, matter and energy.

The flow of matter affects our physical environment and our bodies. By understanding this flow, I AM can make more conscious choices about the resources used and the impact on the planet. Simple actions like recycling, conserving water, and reducing waste contribute to a healthier environment. Additionally, being mindful of what is consumed—whether it's food, clothing, or other materials—helps to make a more sustainable lifestyle.

EXAMPLES

Water Cycle: Water evaporates, forms clouds, precipitates as rain, and flows through rivers and oceans, repeating the cycle over time.

Carbon Cycle: Carbon flows through the atmosphere, plants, animals, and the earth, transitioning between different states over time.

Rock Cycle: Rocks transform through processes like weathering, erosion, sedimentation, and metamorphism, cycling through different forms over geological time.

Nutrient Cycling in Ecosystems: Nutrients like nitrogen and phosphorus flow through soil, plants, animals, and decomposers, supporting life processes over time.

Energy Flow in Food Chains: Matter in the form of biomass moves from producers to consumers and decomposers in ecosystems, transferring energy through time.

Photosynthesis: Plants absorb carbon dioxide and sunlight, converting them into glucose and oxygen, flowing matter from the atmosphere into living organisms.

Respiration: Living organisms convert glucose and oxygen into carbon dioxide and water, releasing energy and returning matter to the environment.

Soil Formation: Organic and inorganic matter accumulates and decomposes over time, contributing to the formation and enrichment of soil.

Decomposition: Dead organisms break down into simpler matter, returning nutrients to the soil and completing the cycle of matter.

Pollution: Pollutants like plastics and chemicals flow into ecosystems, persisting and affecting the environment over time.

Sedimentation: Particles of matter like sand and silt are carried by water and wind, eventually settling and accumulating in layers over time.

Weathering: Rocks and minerals break down through physical and chemical processes, altering landscapes and contributing to the flow of matter.

Decay of Organic Material: Organic matter like leaves and wood decomposes, gradually transforming into simpler compounds and contributing to the nutrient cycle.

Waste Management: Matter in the form of waste is collected, processed, and either recycled, decomposed, or stored, flowing through different stages over time.

Biogeochemical Cycles: Elements like sulfur and phosphorus flow through living organisms, the atmosphere, and the earth, cycling between different states over time.

Tectonic Plate Movement: Matter in the earth's crust moves as tectonic plates shift, leading to the creation and destruction of landforms over geological time.

Composting: Organic waste is decomposed by microorganisms, transforming matter into nutrient-rich compost over time.

Ocean Currents: Matter in the form of water and dissolved substances flows through the ocean, distributing heat, nutrients, and organisms over time.

Erosion: Soil and rock are worn away by wind, water, and ice, transporting matter from one location to another over time.

Growth and Decay of Plants: Plants absorb nutrients and water from the soil, grow, and eventually die, returning matter to the earth as they decompose.

These examples illustrate how matter flows through time in various natural and human-influenced processes.

I AM FLOWS

QUICK START

- I AM FLOWS: The dynamic process unique to individuals, shaping thought, experiences, navigational choices, feelings and actions.

  - CONSCIOUSNESS FLOW: The continuous stream of thoughts, feelings and experiences that pass through I AM's mind.

  - CHOICE FLOW: The continuous stream of selecting something after considering multiple alternatives.

FUNDAMENTAL FLOWS

SPACE FLOW - ENERGY FLOW - MATTER FLOW

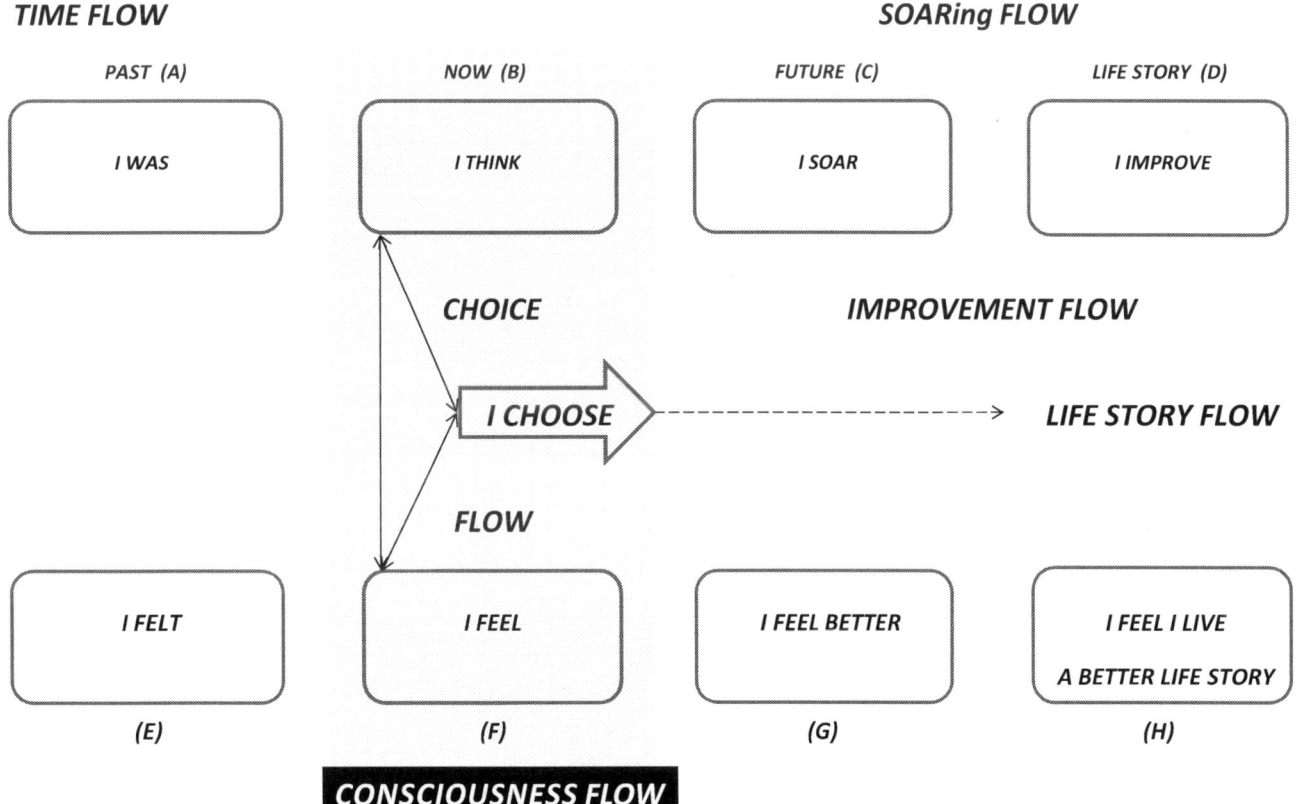

CONSCIOUSNESS FLOW

QUICK START

- CONSCIOUSNESS: The state of being aware of and able to think about I AM's own existence, thoughts and surroundings.

For I AM, it means being present in the moment, knowing what is happening, and having the ability to reflect upon it. It is what allows I AM to experience the world and understand I AM's place in it. It is the immediate state of awareness at a given moment.

- CONSCIOUSNESS FLOW: The continuous stream of thoughts, feelings and experiences that pass through I AM's mind.

It involves the movement and evolution of awareness, thoughts, and perceptions over time. The flow can be smooth or chaotic, depending on I AM's focus and state of mind. It is how I AM experiences and processes thoughts and emotions over time. It is the ongoing progression and transformation of awareness. This flow captures how I AM's consciousness changes, evolves and interacts with various stimuli and experiences.

On the Fundamental Flow Chart, Consciousness Flow is at the bottom of the NOW column. It represents all that is happening in the NOW column.

The connection between I AM and other Fundamental Flows happens at NOW. NOW is when I AM thinks, feels and makes choices. The think part is the direct connection. It is the entryway of consciousness.

EXAMPLES

Awakening from Sleep: The daily transition from unconsciousness during sleep to full awareness upon waking illustrates the flow of consciousness.

Mindfulness Meditation: Practicing mindfulness involves guiding consciousness to stay in the present moment, allowing it to flow without attachment to thoughts or distractions.

Daydreaming: When the mind wanders during a routine activity, consciousness flows into imaginative or reflective states.

Learning and Memory: Consciousness engages in absorbing new information, processing it, and storing it as memories that can be recalled later.

Creative Flow: During moments of intense focus in creative activities, consciousness flows freely, leading to new ideas, solutions, or artistic expressions.

Problem-Solving: Consciousness moves through different stages of understanding, analyzing, and resolving challenges, often shifting between focused thought and intuitive insights.

Emotional Processing: Consciousness flows through different emotional states as it responds to experiences, allowing for the understanding and integration of feelings.

Altered States of Consciousness: Experiences such as hypnosis, deep meditation, or the influence of substances can shift consciousness into altered states, changing perception and awareness.

Spiritual Awakening: Consciousness evolves through stages of spiritual growth, leading to a deeper understanding of self, life purpose, and connection to a higher power.

Attention and Focus: Consciousness shifts its focus to different tasks or stimuli, with the flow of attention determining what is consciously perceived at any given moment.

Growth of Self-Awareness: Over time, consciousness becomes more attuned to the self, recognizing patterns of thought, behavior, and identity, leading to personal growth.

Introspection: Consciousness turns inward to examine thoughts, feelings, and motivations, allowing for deeper self-understanding and insight.

Decision-Making: Consciousness flows through various options, weighing pros and cons, and considering future consequences before arriving at a decision.

Cognitive Dissonance: When beliefs and actions are misaligned, consciousness grapples with conflicting thoughts, often leading to a shift in perspective or behavior to resolve the dissonance.

Empathy and Understanding: Consciousness expands to include the perspectives and emotions of others, fostering deeper connections and compassion.

Time Perception: Consciousness experiences the flow of time differently depending on focus, emotion, and engagement, with moments feeling elongated or fleeting.

Development of Identity: As consciousness matures, it gradually constructs a sense of self, integrating experiences, values, and beliefs into a coherent identity over time.

Aging and Wisdom: As people age, consciousness reflects on life experiences, often gaining wisdom and perspective that allows for a more expansive understanding of life.

These examples show how consciousness flows and evolves over time, influenced by experiences, thoughts, emotions, and various states of awareness.

FUNDAMENTAL FLOWS

SPACE FLOW - ENERGY FLOW - MATTER FLOW

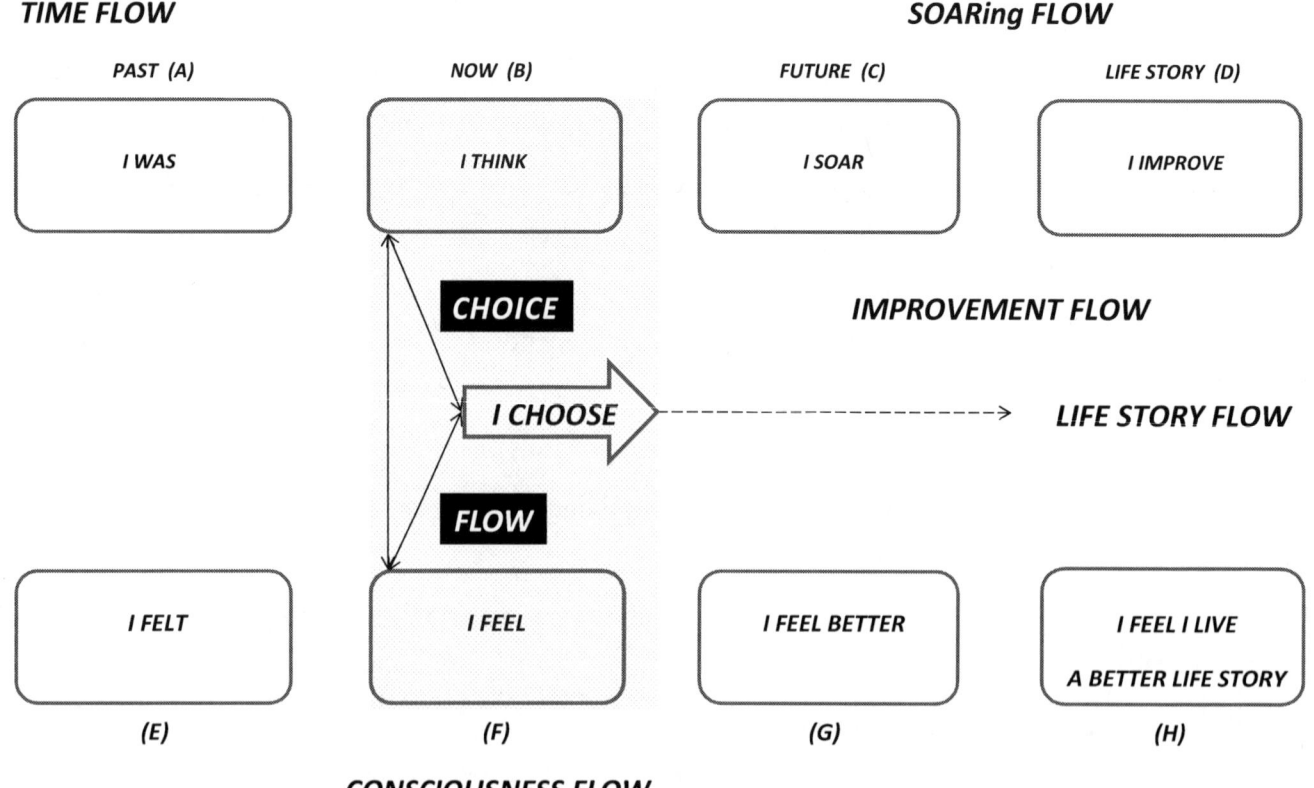

TIME FLOW

SOARing FLOW

PAST (A)	NOW (B)	FUTURE (C)	LIFE STORY (D)
I WAS	I THINK	I SOAR	I IMPROVE

CHOICE

IMPROVEMENT FLOW

I CHOOSE

LIFE STORY FLOW

FLOW

I FELT	I FEEL	I FEEL BETTER	I FEEL I LIVE A BETTER LIFE STORY
(E)	(F)	(G)	(H)

CONSCIOUSNESS FLOW

CHOICE FLOW

QUICK START

- CHOICE: The act of selecting something after considering multiple alternatives.

Choices are based on having a number of alternatives from which to choose. From the alternatives identified, choices are made to help I AM feel better NOW (Job #1) and feel better in the future (Job #2).

- CHOICE FLOW: The continuous stream of selecting something after considering multiple alternatives.

Choice flow is the dynamic progression of choices and their consequences. Choice provides the NOW experience and Choice Flow represents the evolving pattern of these choices.

Every choice has consequences, which can be immediate or long-term. Understanding potential outcomes helps in making informed choices.

Good choices lead to positive outcomes, personal growth, and fulfillment, while poor choices can result in setbacks and regrets.

I AM's best choices are aligned with I AM's Vision and guided by I AM's Focal Points.

All choices, good or bad, accumulate into I AM's life story.

The Choice Flow is key to everything SOARing because the flow of single choices automatically creates I AM's life story. Every choice and consequence matters.

At NOW, I AM thinks, feels and acts. The act is the choice. The best choices frequently happen as a result of having a number of good alternatives available, thinking them through and reacting to how each feels.

The words "choice" and "decision" are frequently used interchangeably. For clarity, I AM generally uses choice because it refers to the whole process rather than the specific decision at the end of the choice process.

I AM can make hundreds or even thousands of choices each day. This is a continuous choice flow. Over time, all the choices flow into the construction of the life story that I AM is going to leave for posterity. Today's choices can shape better tomorrows or worse tomorrows. All choices matter!

EXAMPLES

Career Path Choices: The choices made in selecting a career, accepting job offers, or pursuing further education shape one's professional journey over time.

Education Choices: Choices about which courses to take, what major to pursue, and whether to continue to studies influence a person's educational and career trajectory.

Daily Routine: The small choices made each day, such as what to eat, when to exercise, or how to spend free time, collectively shape habits and overall well-being.

Financial Choices: Choices about saving, investing, spending, and budgeting impact financial stability and long-term wealth.

Relationships: Choices about whom to befriend, date, or marry influence the flow of relationships and social connections throughout life.

Health and Wellness: Choices related to diet, exercise, and healthcare shape physical and mental health over time.

Parenting Choices: Choices about how to raise children, including discipline, education, and values, significantly impact their development and future.

Living Arrangements: Choices about where to live, whether to rent or buy, and how to design one's home affect lifestyle and comfort over time.

Time Management: Choices about how to allocate time between work, leisure, and obligations influence productivity and life balance.

Social and Community Involvement: Choices to engage in community service, activism, or social events shape one's sense of belonging and impact on the community.

Life Partner Choices: The choice of a life partner or spouse significantly affects personal happiness, family dynamics, and life goals.

Travel and Exploration: Choices about where to travel and how often influence cultural exposure, personal growth, and life experiences.

Ethical Choices: Choices made based on moral and ethical beliefs shape personal integrity and how one is perceived by others over time.

Career Changes: The choice to change careers or start a new business can lead to new opportunities, challenges, and growth.

Spiritual Practices: Choices about religious or spiritual practices, such as prayer, meditation, or attending services, influence spiritual growth and connection.

Major Life Transitions: Choices related to marriage, having children, or retirement mark significant turning points that alter the course of life.

Educational Opportunities for Children: Parents' choices regarding their children's education, such as schools, extracurricular activities, and tutoring, impact their future opportunities.

Environmental Choices: Choices about how to reduce one's environmental footprint, such as recycling, conserving energy, or supporting sustainability, contribute to environmental impact over time.

Legal Choices: Choices related to legal matters, such as writing a will, entering into contracts, or filing lawsuits, affect legal standing and rights.

Creative Endeavors: Choices to pursue hobbies, artistic projects, or creative outlets shape personal fulfillment and self-expression over time.

These examples illustrate how choices flow through time, influencing various aspects of life and shaping one's overall life story.

SOARING FLOWS

QUICK START

- SOARing FLOWS: The systematic activities directed towards the achievement of specific objectives.
  - SOARing FLOW: The dynamic process of navigating through different growth situations of life.
  - IMPROVEMENT FLOW: The dynamic, ongoing and cumulative process of enhancements and optimizations over time.
  - LIFE STORY FLOW: I AM's navigation of life by making a continuous progression of choices.

FUNDAMENTAL FLOWS

SPACE FLOW - ENERGY FLOW - MATTER FLOW

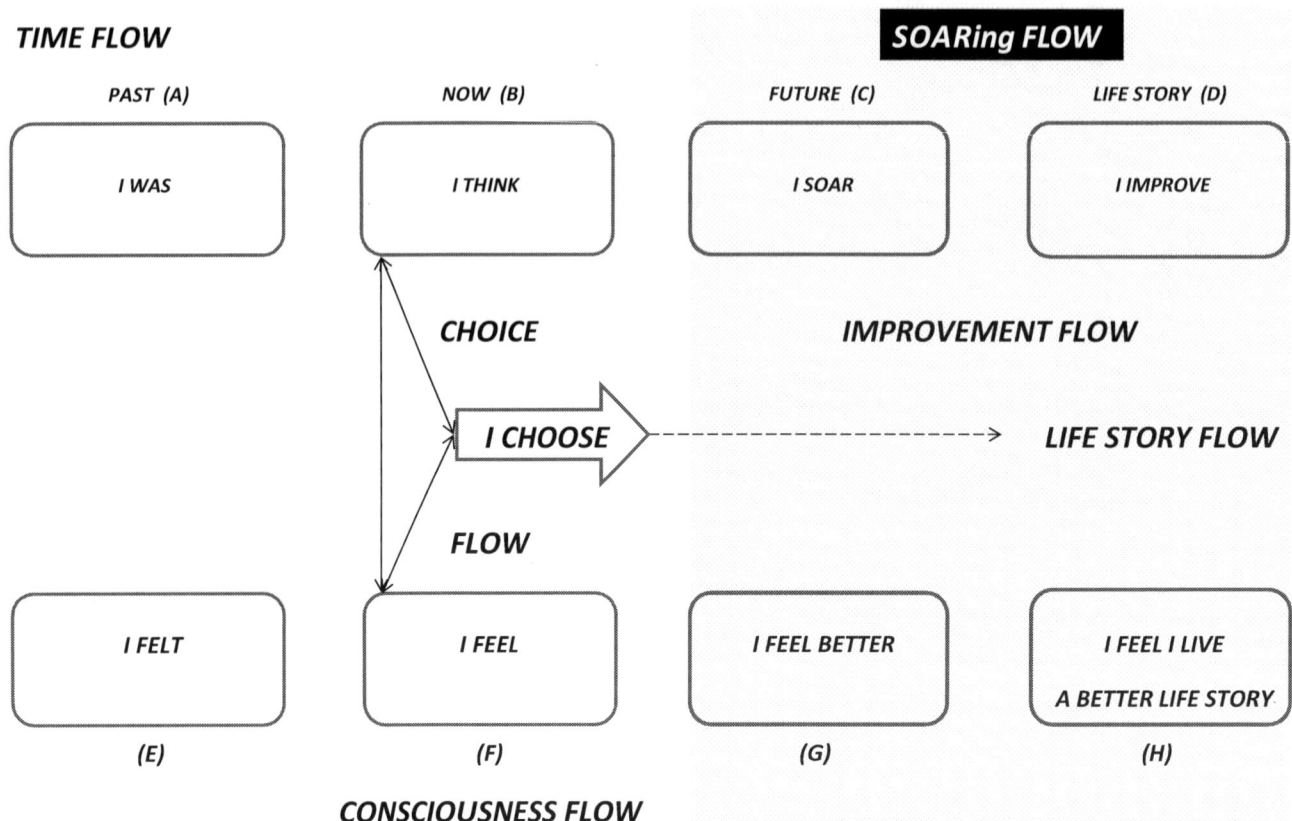

SOARing FLOW

QUICK START

- SOAR: Acronym of Situation, Objectives, Actions, Results.

SOAR is the universal common denominator for steps in the improvement process. It is the 1, 2, 3, 4 steps I AM can do at every NOW to help I AM achieve Job #1 (Feel good NOW) and Job #2 (Feel better in the future).

- SOARing: Using the SOAR intentional improvement process to feel better and live a better life story.

This is the process of creating a plan to feel better in the future (Job #2) by using SE's (SOARing Experiences).

- SOARing FLOW: The dynamic process of navigating through different growth situations of life.

SOARing Flow is the ongoing use of SOAR steps through situation after situation for a lifetime.

Here are a number of brief examples to augment all the other detailed coverage of SOARing.

EXAMPLES

Personal Development:

Situation: Feeling stagnant in personal growth.

Objectives: To improve self-awareness and gain new skills by (when).

Actions: Engage in regular self-reflection, attend workshops, and practice new habits.

Results: Enhanced personal growth and a deeper understanding of oneself, leading to new Situations of greater self-confidence.

Career Advancement:

Situation: Desire to move up in a career.

Objectives: To achieve a promotion to a leadership role by (when).

Actions: Take on additional responsibilities, network, and develop leadership skills.

Results: Securing a promotion, creating a new Situation where leadership skills are tested and refined.

Health and Wellness:

Situation: Experiencing low energy and poor health.

Objectives: To improve physical fitness and overall well-being by (when).

Actions: Implement a consistent exercise routine, improve diet, and prioritize sleep.

Results: Increased energy levels and better health, leading to a new Situation of maintaining a healthy lifestyle.

Relationship Building:

Situation: Feeling disconnected from a partner.

Objectives: To strengthen emotional connection and communication by (when).

Actions: Schedule regular date nights, engage in open communication, and practice active listening.

Results: Improved relationship dynamics, creating a new Situation of deeper connection.

Financial Stability:

Situation: Struggling with debt and financial insecurity.

Objectives: To achieve financial stability and reduce debt by (when).

Actions: Create a budget, reduce unnecessary expenses, and increase savings.

Results: Reduced debt and improved financial security, leading to a new Situation of financial independence.

Community Engagement:

Situation: Desire to contribute more to the community.

Objectives: To increase involvement in local initiatives by (when).

Actions: Volunteer regularly, join community groups, and support local causes.

Results: Stronger community connections, leading to a new Situation of being an active community member.

Project Management:

Situation: Managing a complex project with tight deadlines.

Objectives: To complete the project on time and within budget by (when).

Actions: Develop a detailed project plan, assign tasks, and monitor progress.

Results: Successful project completion, creating a new Situation where the team's performance is evaluated and recognized.

Educational Achievement:

Situation: Struggling academically in a particular subject.

Objectives: To improve grades and understanding of the subject by (when).

Actions: Seek tutoring, dedicate more study time, and use different learning resources.

Results: Improved grades and confidence in the subject, creating a new Situation of academic success.

Business Growth:

Situation: Business experiencing stagnant growth.

Objectives: To increase revenue and expand market reach by (when).

Actions: Implement new marketing strategies, diversify product offerings, and improve customer service.

Results: Increased revenue and market share, leading to a new Situation of managing business expansion.

Spiritual Development:

Situation: Feeling disconnected from spiritual practices.

Objectives: To reconnect with spiritual beliefs and practices by (when).

Actions: Establish a daily meditation routine, attend spiritual gatherings, and engage in self-reflection.

Results: A deeper spiritual connection, leading to a new Situation of spiritual fulfillment.

Cultural Enrichment:

Situation: Lack of exposure to different cultures.

Objectives: To broaden cultural understanding and appreciation by (when).

Actions: Travel to new places, learn a new language, and engage with diverse communities.

Results: Enhanced cultural awareness, leading to a new Situation where diverse perspectives are valued.

Innovation in Technology:

Situation: Current technology is outdated and inefficient.

Objectives: To develop and implement new technological solutions by (when).

Actions: Invest in research and development, prototype new ideas, and test innovations.

Results: Improved technology and efficiency, leading to a new Situation of adopting and scaling innovations.

Work-Life Balance:

Situation: Struggling to balance work and personal life.

Objectives: To achieve a healthier work-life balance by (when).

Actions: Set boundaries, prioritize self-care, and schedule time for leisure and family.

Results: Better work-life balance, leading to a new Situation of sustained personal and professional well-being.

Artistic Expression:

Situation: Feeling creatively blocked.

Objectives: To reignite artistic inspiration and creativity by (when).

Actions: Experiment with new mediums, take inspiration from different sources, and practice regularly.

Results: Renewed creative output, leading to a new Situation of artistic exploration.

Conflict Resolution:

Situation: Ongoing conflict within a team or relationship.

Objectives: To resolve the conflict and restore harmony by (when).

Actions: Facilitate open dialogue, mediate disputes, and find mutually beneficial solutions.

Results: Resolved conflict and improved relationships, leading to a new Situation of collaboration and trust.

Time Management:

Situation: Overwhelmed by tasks and responsibilities.

Objectives: To improve time management and productivity by (when).

Actions: Prioritize tasks, delegate responsibilities, and use time management tools.

Results: Increased productivity and reduced stress, leading to a new Situation of effective time management.

Environmental Awareness:

Situation: Limited knowledge of environmental issues.

Objectives: To increase awareness and take action for sustainability by (when).

Actions: Educate oneself, reduce carbon footprint, and advocate for environmental policies.

Results: Greater environmental awareness, leading to a new Situation where sustainable practices are integrated into daily life.

Public Speaking:

Situation: Fear of public speaking.

Objectives: To build confidence and improve public speaking skills by (when).

Actions: Join a public speaking group, practice regularly, and seek feedback.

Results: Improved public speaking ability, leading to a new Situation where speaking engagements are approached with confidence.

Life Transitions:

Situation: Facing a major life transition, such as moving to a new city or retiring.

Objectives: To navigate the transition smoothly and adapt to the new circumstances by (when).

Actions: Plan ahead, seek support, and embrace the change.

Results: Successful adaptation to the new life stage, leading to a new Situation of stability and growth.

These examples illustrate the flow of SOARing across different areas of life, demonstrating how the process can guide purposeful action and continuous improvement.

FUNDAMENTAL FLOWS

SPACE FLOW - ENERGY FLOW - MATTER FLOW

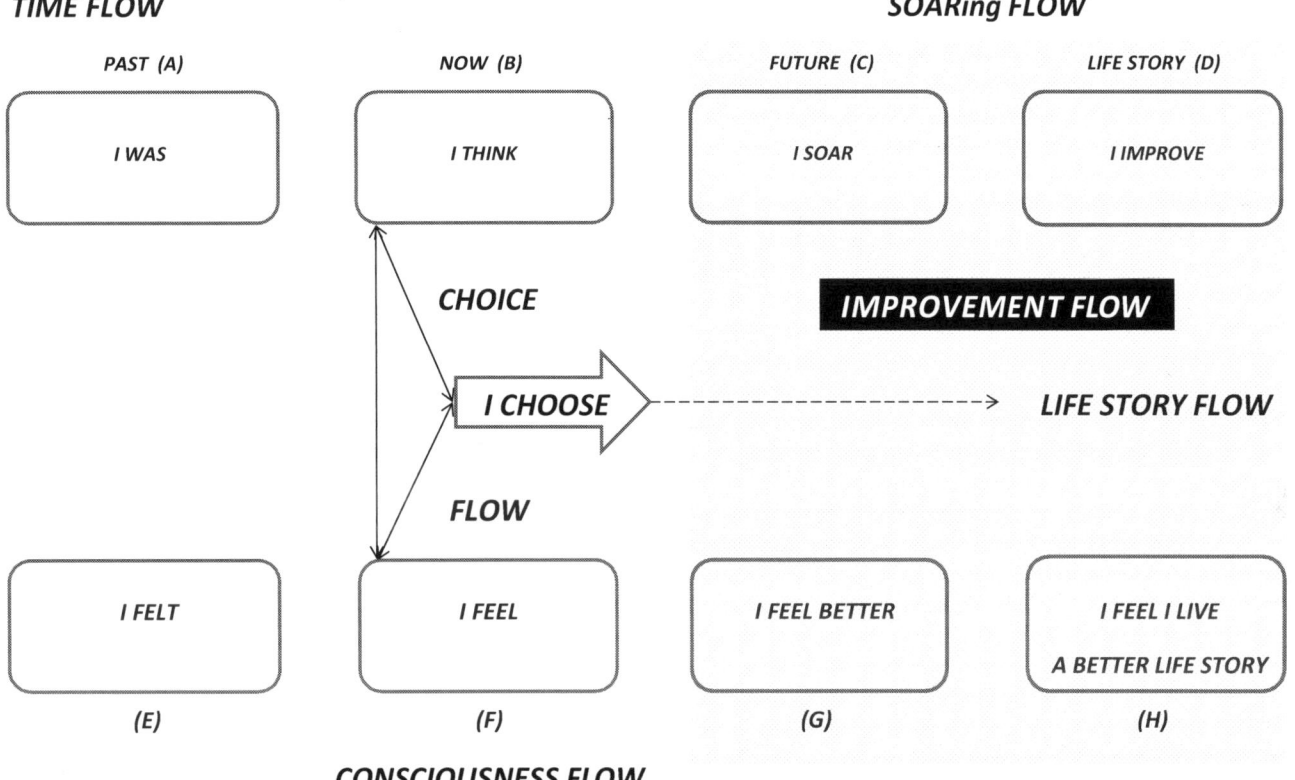

TIME FLOW　　　　　　　　　　　　　　　　　**SOARing FLOW**

PAST (A)	NOW (B)	FUTURE (C)	LIFE STORY (D)
I WAS	I THINK	I SOAR	I IMPROVE

CHOICE

IMPROVEMENT FLOW

I CHOOSE ⟶ **LIFE STORY FLOW**

FLOW

I FELT	I FEEL	I FEEL BETTER	I FEEL I LIVE A BETTER LIFE STORY
(E)	(F)	(G)	(H)

CONSCIOUSNESS FLOW

IMPROVEMENT FLOW

QUICK START

- IMPROVEMENT: The process of changing something for the better.

Improvement is the act of enhancement at a particular point in time…NOW. Improvement is the process of making positive changes to enhance I AM's life.

- IMPROVEMENT FLOW: The dynamic, ongoing and cumulative process of enhancements and optimizations over time.

Continuous improvement is vital for I AM's overall well-being and success. It helps I AM reach potential, overcome challenges, and achieve objectives. By striving for improvement, I AM can experience personal satisfaction and fulfillment.

- IMPROVEMENT PYRAMID: The visual framework for helping I AM navigate I AM's life story.

I AM navigates life by monitoring, measuring and managing SE's in I AM's Life Domains.

Improvement is the process of making things better, whether in better judgment, increased confidence, long-term vision, enhanced awareness or personal skills. It flows through learning, feedback, and iterative processes. Setting meaningful objectives, seeking feedback, and adapting strategies are crucial for continuous improvement.

Improvement can apply to anything in I AM's life.

Continuous improvement leads to personal and societal advancement, higher efficiency, and greater satisfaction. Stagnation can result in missed potential and decreased motivation.

Continuous improvement is the key to creating and living a better life story.

EXAMPLES

I AM has observed many areas of continuous improvement, such as:

Personal Development: Continuous learning and self-reflection lead to gradual improvement in skills, habits, and self-awareness over time.

Education: Students progress through different levels of education, improving their knowledge, critical thinking, and problem-solving skills as they advance.

Physical Fitness: Regular exercise and proper nutrition lead to gradual improvements in strength, endurance, and overall health.

Technology Advancements: Innovations and iterations in technology result in improved devices, software, and systems over time.

Process Optimization: Businesses implement lean practices and process improvements to enhance efficiency, reduce waste, and increase productivity.

Agricultural Practices: The adoption of new farming techniques, crop rotation, and soil management leads to improved yields and sustainable agriculture over time.

Medical Advancements: Research and development in medicine lead to better treatments, cures, and healthcare practices, improving patient outcomes over time.

Workplace Skills: Employees enhance their skills through training, experience, and feedback, leading to improved job performance and career growth.

Community Development: Communities implement programs and initiatives to improve infrastructure, education, healthcare, and quality of life for residents.

Environmental Conservation: Efforts to protect ecosystems, reduce pollution, and promote sustainability lead to gradual improvements in environmental health.

Product Development: Companies iterate on products based on customer feedback and market trends, leading to continuous improvements in features, design, and functionality.

Mental Health: Individuals work on improving their mental well-being through therapy, mindfulness, and self-care practices, leading to better emotional and psychological health.

Communication Skills: Through practice and feedback, individuals improve their ability to communicate effectively, enhancing relationships and collaboration.

Artistic Mastery: Artists refine their techniques and creativity over time, leading to improved artistic expression and the creation of more impactful works.

Financial Stability: Through budgeting, saving, and investing, individuals and families improve their financial security and wealth over time.

Leadership Development: Leaders improve their ability to inspire, guide, and support others through experience, mentoring, and training.

Urban Planning: Cities implement improvements in infrastructure, transportation, and public services to enhance the quality of urban living over time.

Environmental Restoration: Efforts to restore damaged ecosystems, such as reforestation and wetland restoration, lead to gradual improvements in biodiversity and ecosystem health.

Cultural Evolution: Societies evolve their values, norms, and practices over time, leading to improvements in social justice, equality, and cultural understanding.

Scientific Research: The accumulation of knowledge through experimentation and discovery leads to continuous improvements in our understanding of the natural world and the development of new technologies.

These examples highlight how improvement can flow through time across various domains, contributing to growth, development, and progress.

FUNDAMENTAL FLOWS

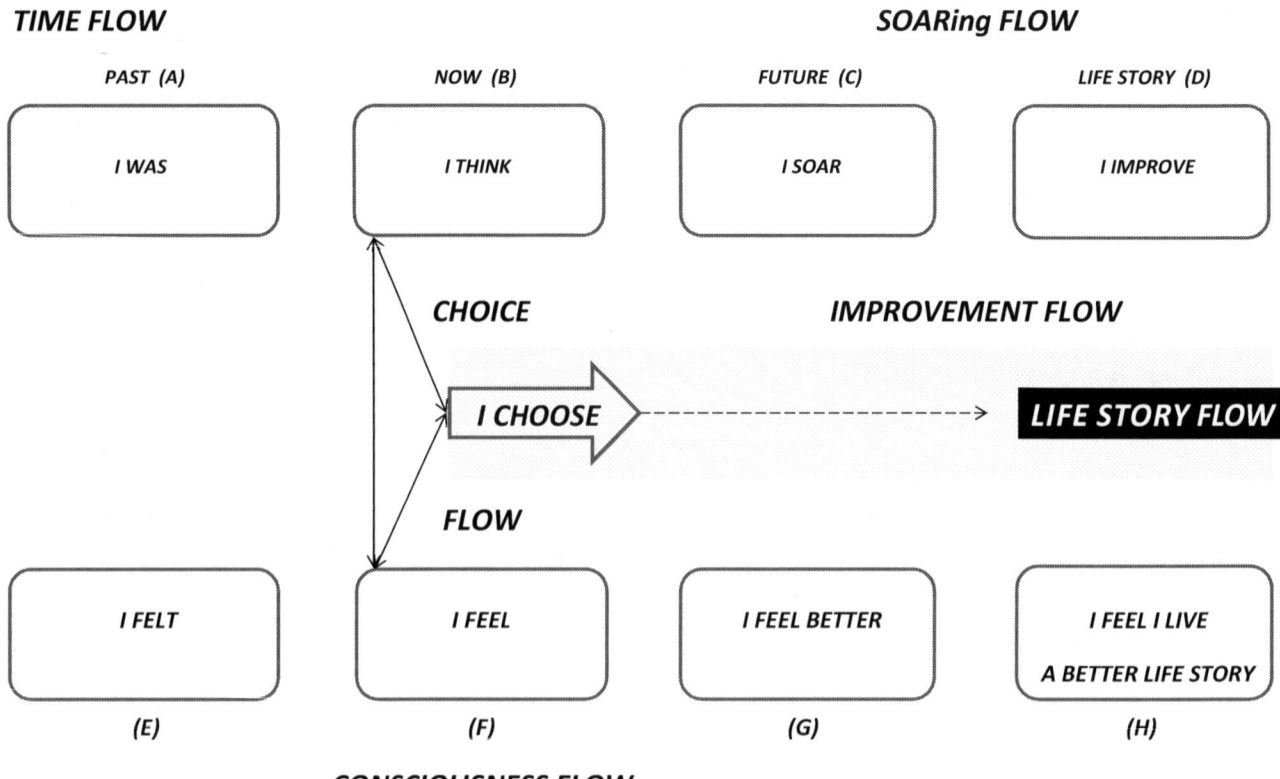

SPACE FLOW - ENERGY FLOW - MATTER FLOW

TIME FLOW   SOARing FLOW

PAST (A)	NOW (B)	FUTURE (C)	LIFE STORY (D)
I WAS	I THINK	I SOAR	I IMPROVE

CHOICE   IMPROVEMENT FLOW

I CHOOSE ⇢ LIFE STORY FLOW

FLOW

I FELT	I FEEL	I FEEL BETTER	I FEEL I LIVE A BETTER LIFE STORY
(E)	(F)	(G)	(H)

CONSCIOUSNESS FLOW

LIFE STORY FLOW

QUICK START

- LIFE STORY: The account of everything that happens in I AM's life.

I AM's life story encompasses choices from I AM's past, NOW and aspirations for the future. This story shapes who I AM is and reflects an overview of I AM's journey through life.

- LIFE STORY FLOW: I AM's navigation of life by making a continuous progression of choices.

Life Story Flow is the dynamic evolution of I AM's narrative. Life Story Flow represents the ongoing progression and development of I AM's life story journey.

I AM likes the analogy of life seen as a book. I AM is always figuratively on the page for NOW where I AM writes the narrative for actual happenings on that day. The previous page was written yesterday. The page following today's page will be written tomorrow.

I AM knows the book will be complete someday, but doesn't know what day. The last written day will complete the book. I AM would like to feel good each day and whenever the last day is written. Ideally, I AM will feel good looking back at the entire book.

Every day, I AM creates a new page simply by living. The page can be written consciously…or not. It can reflect positive energy…or not. It can be about I AM's daily Job #1 accomplishment of feeling good…or not. It can describe the Job #2 planning of better futures…or not.

Most of all, the page can create feel-better thoughts and choices made that are aligned with I AM's Vision and guided by I AM's Focal Points.

EXAMPLES

Childhood to Adulthood: A person's life story begins with early experiences in childhood, shaping their identity, beliefs, and values as they grow into adulthood.

Educational Journey: The progression from elementary school through higher education reflects the development of knowledge, skills, and life experiences that contribute to a person's life story.

Career Path: The evolution of a person's career, from their first job to their peak professional achievements, forms a significant part of their life story.

Family Life: The transitions from single life to marriage, parenthood, and grandparenthood highlight key milestones and relationships in a person's life story.

Personal Challenges and Overcoming Adversity: Facing and overcoming obstacles, such as illness, loss, or financial hardship, contributes to the depth and resilience in a person's life story.

Significant Relationships: The formation, growth, and sometimes the end of friendships, romantic relationships, and family bonds are key elements in the flow of a life story.

Personal Growth and Self-Discovery: The journey of understanding oneself, exploring personal beliefs, and pursuing passions over time adds richness to a life story.

Travel and Exploration: Experiences of traveling, discovering new cultures, and expanding one's worldview are important chapters in a life story.

Creative Expression: The evolution of a person's artistic or creative endeavors, such as writing, painting, or music, reflects the growth of their inner world and creativity.

Health and Well-Being: The progression of a person's health, including managing chronic conditions, engaging in fitness, and adopting wellness practices, shapes the narrative of their life.

Community and Social Impact: Contributions to community service, activism, or social causes create a legacy of impact that flows through a person's life story.

Spiritual Journey: The exploration of spirituality, religious practices, and personal beliefs over time is a key element in the flow of many life stories.

Hobbies and Passions: The development of hobbies and passions, such as sports, gardening, or crafting, contributes to the richness of a person's life story.

Mentorship and Legacy: Passing on knowledge, skills, or values to others, whether through mentorship or teaching, forms a lasting legacy in a life story.

Major Life Transitions: Significant changes, such as moving to a new city, changing careers, or retirement, mark turning points in a person's life story.

Cultural and Societal Influences: The impact of cultural, political, and societal events on a person's life decisions and identity contributes to the flow of their life story.

Financial Journey: The flow of financial ups and downs, from early financial struggles to eventual stability or wealth, is a key part of many life stories.

Personal Achievements and Milestones: Celebrating achievements like awards, recognitions, or personal goals reached adds defining moments to a life story.

Aging and Reflecting on Life: As people age, reflecting on past experiences, wisdom gained, and the legacy they wish to leave behind are important elements of their life story.

End-of-Life Reflections: The process of looking back on life, making peace with past experiences, and preparing for the end of life completes the flow of a life story.

These examples illustrate how a life story unfolds through time, shaped by experiences, choices, and the continuous evolution of the individual.

OBJECTIVES

I AM's desired improvements

to help I AM feel better,

achievable by an intended time.

I AM'S QUEST

> ## QUICK START
>
> *"Live a better life story by feeling good
> and doing my best at every NOW to improve"*

I AM's quest is to live and enjoy a better life story from NOW on by SOARing.

A quest is defined as the energetic pursuit of something very important. For I AM, enjoying NOW and living a better life story is very important!

I AM's quest is intended to be a journey of enjoyment along the unfolding of I AM's life path. It is not intended to be the withholding of enjoyment until the destination is reached, for the destination may never be reached.

I AM's quest is an improvement process that happens every day from NOW to the end of I AM. The process is measured by how I AM feels at every NOW. Success is achieved when I AM feels good or feels better.

The improvement process occurs within the context of needs and wants satisfaction.

- NEEDS: Topics I AM must have.
- WANTS: Topics I AM would like to have.

A basic requirement for the achievement of I AM's Quest is for I AM to continually try to satisfy I AM's needs and wants. Satisfying essential needs allows I AM to live. Satisfying higher needs and wants allows I AM to flourish.

Need and want satisfaction is nicely summarized in Maslow's famous Hierarchy of Needs.

8. Transcendence:	Beyond self. Assisting others 1-7. Religious. Spiritual.
7. Self-Actualization:	Be all one can be. Full Potential. Growth. Self-Fulfillment.
6. Aesthetic:	Beauty. Art. Nature. Balance. Form. Shape. Line. Color.
5. Cognitive:	Knowledge. Meaning. Self-Awareness.
4. Esteem:	Prestige. Confidence. Respect. Achievement. Status. Reputation.
3. Belonging & Love:	Family. Relationships. Friends. Love. Attention.
2. Safety:	Security. Stability. Order. Law. Protection. Limits.
1. Physiological:	Oxygen. Water. Food. Shelter. Sleep. Warmth. Sex.

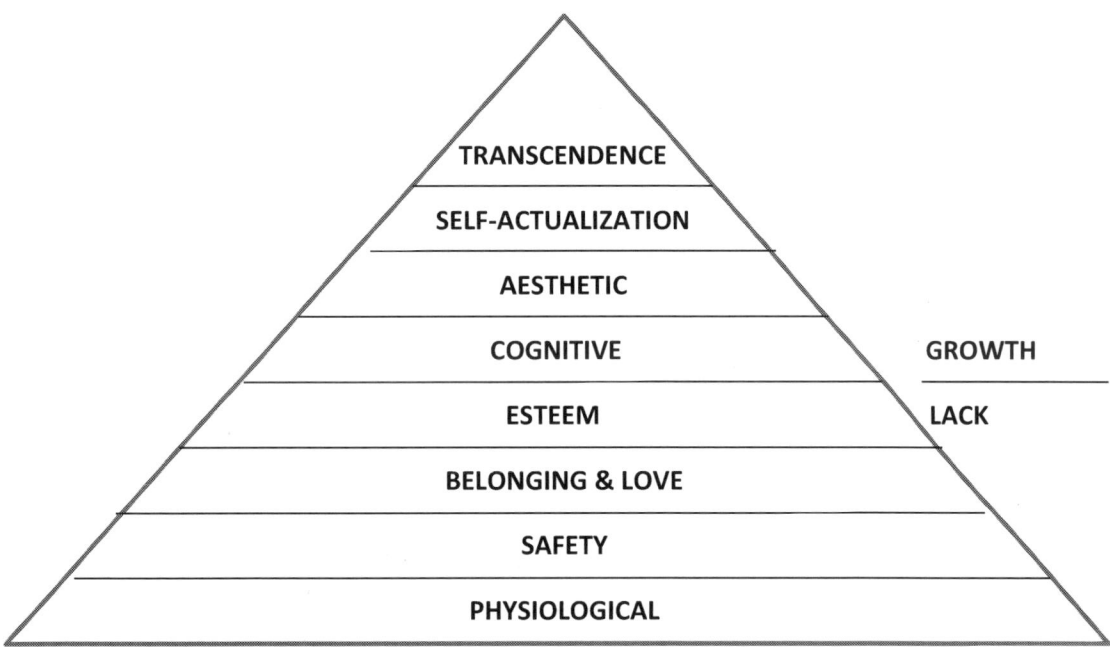

The basic idea is that people satisfy needs from the bottom of the pyramid upwards toward the top. For instance, people must satisfy Physiological Needs or risk death. Satisfying those needs allows I AM to climb up the stair steps of higher need levels.

I AM's ideal is to satisfy the Lack levels and then climb the pyramid to the Growth levels, at least to the Self-actualization level.

Some need and want satisfaction is essential for I AM's Quest of pursuing the enjoyment of NOW and living a better life story. SOARing can take place at any level of the pyramid.

I AM's Quest is in two parts…enjoying NOW and living a better life story.

1. Enjoying NOW.

- NOW: The present moment in I AM's clock time.
- ENJOY NOW: I AM SOARing in positive energy NOW.

2. Living a Better Life Story.

- BETTER LIFE STORY: From NOW on, living more and more of life in positive energy, seeking higher and higher emotional levels.
- CONTINUOUS IMPROVEMENT: I AM's journey of focusing on SOARing to improve I AM and I AM's surroundings.
- IMPROVEMENT: The process of changing something for the better.
- BETTER CHOICES: Using the Guidance System, improving the process that considers mul- tiple alternatives to choose the best.

Both Quest parts can be achieved by SOARing.

- SOARing: Using the SOAR intentional improvement process to feel better and live a better life story.

In *I AM + AI,* I AM acts as guide and example of SOARing ideas and life story improvement, featuring Topics such as...

- Using the SOARing Process to satisfy needs and wants.
- Using the FEELINGS Platform to keep score of feelings.
- Understanding how the world of improvement seems to work with the Big Picture and Fundamental Flows.
- How to make better choices, using the Choice Cycle.
- Establishing customized Visions and Focal Points.
- Creating AI-assisted plans and managing them with AI mentoring 24/7.
- Using the SOARing Improvement System to help create a better life story.
- Centering the living of life at NOW, trying to enjoy every moment.
- Navigating the positive energy natural flow of the universe.
- Using SOARing as the universal improvement process to improve anything.
- Appreciating the visual frameworks for their instant clarity of complex Topics.
- How to improve and better apply the customized Toolbox.
- Using AI to enhance and expand I AM's knowledge, perspectives and abilities.
- Doing the two most important jobs at every NOW.
- Using the Big Picture to fit in all the important information life puzzle pieces into the puzzle of life.
- Understand how the Fundamental Flows influence all I AM's choices.
- Applying constantly the I Think-I Feel-I Act triangle to make better choices.
- Focusing on the most important Topic at every NOW.
- Climbing the continuous Improvement Pyramid.
- Continuous improvement of and by one's unique Guidance System.
- SOARing at every problem or opportunity.
- Using the over 250 Glossary topics to increase knowledge about what are the most important topics in living life.
- The importance of having solid Objectives before taking Actions.

I AM's Quest is to pursue the enjoyment of NOW and live a better life story. SOARing is the process I AM has chosen for I AM's quest.

I AM knows that there are two jobs to be addressed at every NOW.

- Job #1: To feel good NOW.
- Job #2: To plan to feel better in the future.

Accomplishing Job #1 and Job #2 at as many NOWs as possible can make I AM's Quest a most joyful and rewarding life experience. I AM tries to navigate the positive energy flow, enjoy the journey and SOAR to improve everything I AM chooses.

ACTIONS

The process of I AM doing things or taking steps to achieve the Objectives.

ACTIONS

ESSENCE

QUICK START

When I AM wants to improve anything…I AM uses the SE to SOAR.

CREATE IMPROVEMENT PLAN

1. Think SOAR; onto the SE form, on a piece of paper, on a screen or use in the mind.

TOPIC =

- SITUATION =
- OBJECTIVES =
- ACTIONS =
- RESULTS =

2. Optimize choices with S + AI.

MANAGE IMPROVEMENT PLAN

3. Implement, monitor, measure and manage the Actions until the Objectives are reached.

When I AM chooses to improve something, I AM creates a SE. The SE is the simple process I AM goes through to try to make positive change. It is the Situation, Objectives, Actions, Results process on any Topic.

I AM is responsible for the creation, management and consequences of the SE. I AM creates the plan with #1 and #2. Then, I AM implements, monitors, measures and manages the plan with #3 through time until the SE is complete.

I AM can choose to do the SE alone with no outside input. Hundreds of these happen every day.

Or, I AM can choose to enlist other people and/or AI input into any part of SOARing. This can be from any role I AM wants them to play…assistant, teacher, advisor, mentor, manager, motivator, problem solver, support giver, conversationalist, etc.

I AM's goal of enlisting external input is to try to create synergy.

- SYNERGY: Two things working together that create better results than the sum of the individual contributions.

Synergy is often referred to as 1 + 1 = 3.

For example, if I AM and AI create a solid synergizing relationship, the final Result could reach or exceed the Objectives sooner and/or better than if the process were done alone. The relationship could take the best thoughts of I AM, couple them with the additional perspectives of AI and create a dynamic optimization on whatever Topic I AM chooses.

It is important to remember that I AM is in control of the entire SE process and is responsible for all the Actions and Results. AI is there to help I AM enhance I AM's improvement.

I AM refers to the process when SOAR synergizes with AI as S+AI. S+AI can interact and synergize on any part of SOAR.

How AI Can Help I AM Synergize

I AM can better cause synergy with AI by knowing some of AI's capabilities. Then I AM can tailor questions tapping into those capabilities.

I AM arrives at a new Situation and the synergy can begin to happen.

Synergize the Situation (S)

I AM knows to look at each Situation by starting with who, what, when, where, why and how. AI can take that understanding deeper and broader.

AI can:

- Augment that information by examining the Situation in terms of historical content, external influences and future implications.
- Explore the Situation in terms of problem and opportunity.
- Divide the Situation into parts for immediate or longer timelines.
- Perform a SWOT Analyses …Strengths, Weaknesses, Opportunities, Threats.
- Examine whether or not the Situation fits with I AM's Guidance System of Vision and Focal Points.
- Advise if I AM is attracting the kinds of Situations I AM intends to attract.
- Assess the potential of the Situation in helping I AM achieve a better life story.
- Help deepen I AM's understanding of the Situation.
- Evaluate I AM's Toolbox relationship with the Situation.
- Help visualize the possibilities of where the Situation could lead in the future.
- Suggest next steps.

- Help determine the relative importance of different parts of the Situation and establish priorities.

- Help I AM focus on the Top Topic.

- Assist I AM through the Choice Cycle to make better choices.

Synergize the Objectives (O)

I AM's Guidance System of Vision and Focal Points gives I AM a solid framework that each Objective should fit within. The Guidance System gives I AM direction, limits and guidelines for I AM's Objectives.

AI can:

- Assist I AM in creating specific Objectives that align with I AM's Guidance System.

- Clarify and customize Objectives.

- Help evaluate different alternative Objectives.

- Help create SMART Objectives (Specific, Measurable, Achievable, Relevant, Time-Bound).

- Develop Objectives that feel good to I AM.

- Create Objectives that move I AM toward I AM's better life story.

- Help balance short-term Objectives and long-term Objectives.

- Develop Objectives that maximize I AM's strengths.

- Help shape each Objective so it resonates deeply with I AM's BMSS (Body, Mind, Soul and Spirit).

- Create Objectives that provide momentum at NOW, while supporting I AM's long-term quest of a better life story.

- Help insure the Objectives reflect exactly what I AM wants/needs by when.

- Help I AM be flexible and adapt Objectives as necessary as time goes by and Situations change.

Synergize Actions (A)

I AM knows that the A in SOAR represents the action steps necessary to get I AM's feelings NOW to better feelings in the future.

The S + AI synergy can help I AM create better Improvement Plans that help create better future accomplishments and feelings.

AI can:

- Help I AM establish appropriate steps to get I AM to Objective satisfaction.

- Ensuring that each action is purposeful, meaningful and aligned with I AM's Guidance System (Vision and Focal Points).

143

- Create steps that have a clear purpose and have a measurable outcome or defined impact.

- Frame actions that keep I AM grounded in the present.

- Ensure that the action leverages I AM's strengths and resources.

- Create steps that help I AM feel better NOW and enjoy the journey of living a better life story.

- Provide a system for monitoring, measuring and managing progress.

- Provide feedback and progress reports.

- Provide for realignment changes as the Situation or Objective changes.

- Track progress to ensure that each step is recorded, celebrated and adjusted as necessary.

- Provide analyses to aid in continuous improvement.

Synergize Results (R)

Every Action produces a Result. I AM makes a choice and it produces an outcome.

Those outcomes can be intended and/or unintended. I AM uses SOAR to try to make better choices that lead to positive, intended outcomes. I AM synergizes with AI to enhance I AM's quest for better Results.

AI can:

- Help I AM create outcomes that are meaningful and meet the Objective.

- Help I AM define success in terms that are specific, personal and relevant to living a better life story.

- Evaluate Results in terms of Objective achievement and how I AM feels.

- Help I AM determine next steps.

- Help I AM use the Results to evaluate Job #1, how I AM feels at NOWs all along and at the end of the journey.

- Determine whether or not to create a new SOAR on the same Topic, by using the Results as the Situation for a new SOAR.

- Help I AM identify patterns and growth opportunities.

- Help I AM see what is working and what is not working.

- Analyze the Results to determine what parts are problems and what parts are opportunities.

- Help I AM move on and build on successful Results.

- Help I AM refine what needs improvement.

- Provide a system for capturing Results all along and at the end of I AM's SOAR journey.

- Help I AM celebrate wins and learn from setbacks.

Plus...

AI can provide I AM with tailored resources to support each phase of SOAR and be available 24/7 for expansion questions.

Resources can vary from different providers, but might include such capabilities as:

- ✓ Flowcharts.
- ✓ Search.
- ✓ Templates.
- ✓ Presentation formats.
- ✓ Spreadsheets.
- ✓ Forms.
- ✓ Workbooks.
- ✓ Journals.
- ✓ Diagrams and visuals.
- ✓ Audio.
- ✓ Conclusions.
- ✓ Tracking systems.
- ✓ Analytical Tools.
- ✓ Multiple-role perspectives.
- ✓ Guidelines...1-2-3.

Some more resources specific to SOAR might include:

- ✓ Objective-setting and planning templates.
- ✓ Reflective and progress check-in prompts.
- ✓ Tracking and accountability tools.
- ✓ Visualization and affirmation guides.
- ✓ Results analysis and improvement tools.
- ✓ Resource library for ongoing learning and adaptation.

I AM has found that a good way to discover what the AI provider can do is to ask it. Do an "Interview" with it on capabilities and features. Go beyond the website. Test drive.

Keep asking questions going as deeply into it as necessary. Keep asking, because the industry is changing so quickly that new features and capabilities are being added regularly.

Keep SOARing!

Keep synergizing!

S+AI

SOARing + ARTIFICIAL INTELLIGENCE

QUICK START

1. S+AI is the concept of I AM navigating life using SOAR to help improve anything, while synergizing with AI.

2. SOARing provides components like the SOARing Process, I AM's Guidance System, Choice Cycle, SOARing Experiences and Life Story direction.

3. AI provides the 24/7/365 platform to help I AM create, monitor, measure and manage the SOARing Experience and to enhance I AM's knowledge and experiences with advice, motivation, mentorship and other critical thinking roles.

Create and Manage "Your Better Life Story" Plan

NOW, I AM can use AI with SOARing to help create and manage I AM's improvement plans.

- SOARing: Using the SOAR intentional improvement process to feel better and live a better life story.
- ARTIFICIAL INTELLIGENCE (AI): Computer simulation of human intelligence.

This conceptual partnership of two power-house systems offers I AM a synergy potential of multiple benefits to help I AM pursue I AM's Vision and enjoy the journey.

SOARing

SOARing brings:

- The universal improvement process of SOARing.
- The Big Picture and Fundamental Flows showing I AM's perception of important ways the world of improvement seems to work…the grand scheme of things.
- A KISS view of what is most important in life and the processes to improve things.
- I AM's Guidance System, that represents all that I AM has become to NOW of I AM's Vision and Focal Points that guide I AMs thoughts, feelings and actions.
- The SOARing Process method to reach objectives and navigate life.
- The Feelings Platform visual framework of I AM to help improve how I AM feels.

- The SOARing Process of I AM's Vision and Focal Points that guide I AMs thoughts, feelings and actions.
- The Improvement Pyramid to help I AM manage SOARing Experiences on I AM's most important Life Domains.
- Focus on Job #1 at every NOW. To enjoy NOW.
- Focus on Job #2 at every NOW. To plan for living a better future.
- Focus on creating, monitoring, measuring and managing I AM to a better life story.
- Application of positive psychology principles, MBO and positive mindsets.

AI

AI is a rapidly expanding field of research and application of machine intelligence. It is developing so rapidly and being applied in so many ways that I AM must continuously watch for new and improved applications of personal interest.

In this book, "AI" is used for simplicity and because the industry is so fluid that every segment under its umbrella is subject to change frequently and dramatically.

Currently, there are two AI forms that encourage improvement conversations. They are:

- CHATBOTS: Such as; ChatGPT, Copilot, Gemini.
- VOICE ASSISTANTS: Such as: Alexa, Google Assistant, Siri.

I AM SOARs through this process to find the best resource to meet I AM's need for a synergy partner.

S = The industry is in flux. Most of Big Tech is involved. Some very good alternatives.

O = To find the best synergy partner that meets my wants.

A = 1. Keep up with who is offering what benefits in this segment.

2. Select those of interest.

3. "Interview" each to get to know their benefits to you, such as…

   ○ ○ Give me examples of the roles you play, like assistant, teacher, advisor, mentor, etc.
   ○ Please describe yourself. Strengths? Weaknesses? Training? Personality?
   ○ How can you help me meet my Objectives?
   ○ What is your outline for best helping me synergize with you?
   ○ How would you help me create an Action Plan and then help me manage it?
   ○ What are your Objectives in our relationship?

4. Test drive their trial offer. Try the free version, upgrade if it better satisfies your O.

R = Synergy with the best partner.

S+AI

SOARing + AI = S+AI.

Every Topic in the SOARing Process can be improved by synergizing with AI.

The synergy can increase I AM's knowledge, broaden perspectives, refine processes and spark new ideas to help I AM make better choices.

- Life Story Plan creation and management.
- Ability to find the right slot in the Big Picture for new information, like putting new pieces into a jigsaw puzzle.
- Many parts of the Big Picture can be synergized by and for I AM, such as:
  - The Choice Cycle of I Think, I Feel and I Act to improve choices.
  - I AM's Toolbox. (About 50 I AM attributes that might be improved).
  - The Glossary (Nearly 300 most important Topics, each available for expansion).
  - I AM's Guidance System.
  - I AM's Vision.
  - I AM's Focal Points.
  - I AM's Life Domains.
  - Awareness, attention, focus process.
  - Topic selection.
  - Priority setting.
  - Situation analysis.
  - Objective setting.
  - Action planning and management with SOARing Experiences (SE).
  - Climbing the Improvement Pyramid.
  - SE results monitoring and analysis.
  - Job #1 reminders at NOW to "Enjoy NOW".
  - Job #2 creator and manager of plans to feel better in the future.
- S+AI offers suggested questions to help guide I AM along the journey.
- S+AI can provide monitoring, measuring, managing assistance on a timeline I AM creates.

The new partnership of SOARing and AI combines the fast growing positive psychology movement with the incredible potential of AI. It is a simple concept. I AM brings the best of SOARing and AI brings additional perspectives and knowl- edge to any Topic. Synergy enhances I AM.

AI's role, when asked by I AM, is to help enhance I AM's choice-making and living a better life story.

Now, I AM has the tools to do an even better Job #1, Job #2 and to live a better life story.

WHAT TO ASK AI

QUICK START

1. I AM uses AI frequently as a question answerer. I AM asks a question or probe, AI answers. It can become a back-and-forth conversation. The questions can be about any Topic and range from very simple to very complex. AI's answers usually respond accordingly.

2. A key to effective AI use is to know what questions to ask to begin the conversation and then how to pursue the many possible follow-ups.

3. The Big Picture Topics are all important to I AM, so they offer a superb list to pursue for getting better and deeper insights. AI can be quite expansive for inquiring minds.

4. AI is the ideal tool for expanding knowledge of processes and bettering I AM's life story.

The Big Picture and Fundamental Flows offer overviews of Topics important to I AM's feeling good NOW and better in the future. They introduce I AM's primary Topics for AI focus. They are listed as Key Topics.

KEY TOPICS

- Life Story
- Vision
- Focal Points
  - Feel Good NOW
  - Need Satisfaction
  - Want Satisfaction
  - Alignment
    - ❖ Body
    - ❖ Mind
    - ❖ Soul
    - ❖ Spirit
  - Well-Being
    - ❖ Positive Emotion
    - ❖ Engagement
    - ❖ Meaning
    - ❖ Achievement
    - ❖ Relationships

- I AM's Toolbox
  - Abilities
  - Aptitudes
  - Aspirations
  - Attitudes
  - Awareness
  - Behaviors
  - Beliefs
  - Character
  - Competence
  - Confidence
  - Desires
  - Education
  - Emotions
  - Ethics
  - Experience
  - Feelings
  - Free Will
  - Habits
  - Intelligence
  - Intention
  - Intuition
  - Judgment
  - Knowledge
  - Lessons
  - Memory
  - Mindset
  - Moods
  - Morals
  - Needs
  - Opinions
  - Passions
  - Perceptions
  - Personal Resources
  - Personality
  - Perspectives
  - Plans
  - Principles
  - Resistance

- ❖ Skills
- ❖ Strengths
- ❖ Talents
- ❖ Temperament
- ❖ Thoughts
- ❖ Traits
- ❖ Values
- ❖ Wants
- ❖ Weaknesses
- ❖ Wisdom
  - ○ SOARing
    - ❖ Situation
    - ❖ Objectives
    - ❖ Actions
    - ❖ Results
- Life Domains
  - ○ Career
  - ○ Environment
  - ○ Finance
  - ○ Health
  - ○ Improvement
  - ○ Leisure
  - ○ Relationships
  - ○ Spirituality
- Better Choices
- Job #1
- Job #2

GLOSSARY

The Glossary is a rich source of Topics to AI investigate.

It features A to Z of more than 250 Topics. These are all the defined terms in the book. Each can be delved into as deeply as one might wish to go. Ultimately, they are all connected, just as everyone on earth. Happy delving!

AI UNIVERSAL QUESTIONS

Here is a list of questions AI suggests for starting meaningful conversations and journeys of expansion. They are divided into What, Why and How prompts.

WHAT

What are the main things I should focus on in [topic] and how do they connect?

What are common mistakes people my age make in [area/topic] and how can I avoid them?

What are the best ways to achieve [goal or objective] at this stage of my life?

What are the latest trends or cool new things happening in [industry/field]?

What resources (like books, websites, or tools) should I check out to learn more about [topic]?

What are the ethical or social issues I should think about with [action/decision]?

What are some creative or out-of-the-box ways to deal with [problem/challenge]?

What could happen in the long run if I choose [decision/choice]?

What's the background or history I need to know about [topic]?

What are the risks and rewards of going with [decision/strategy]?

What are the most important ideas or frameworks related to [subject/field] that I should know?

What kind of mindset or attitude should I have when tackling [challenge/task]?

What are signs that I might need to switch gears or change direction in [project/situation]?

What are some myths or things people get wrong about [topic/field]?

What's the best way to stay consistent and focused on [task/project]?

What's the future of [topic/field], and how can I prepare for it?

What basic skills or knowledge do I need to get ahead in [field/task]?

What should I think about first when deciding what to focus on in [context]?

What questions should I ask myself while navigating [situation/decision]?

What should I do next after reaching [goal/milestone]?

What are the key signs that I'm on the right track or not in [area/field]?

What are the potential blind spots I might not see in [decision/strategy]?

What assumptions should I question in [situation/strategy]?

What are some ways to shake things up or innovate in [industry/field]?

What ethical issues might come up in [field/situation], and how should I deal with them?

What's the best way to get and use feedback in [context/task]?

What common pitfalls should I watch out for in [field/task]?

What trends should I keep an eye on in [industry/field] over the next few years?

What's the best way to adapt to changes or surprises in [field/industry]?

What's the best way to gather and use data to make decisions in [area]?

What questions should I regularly ask myself to stay on track with [goal/life journey]?

WHY

Why is [specific action/strategy] the best approach for me right now?

Why do certain challenges or problems happen in [area/field], and what causes them?

Why is [specific trend/development] important for the future of [industry/field]?

Why do certain practices or methods work for people my age, and others don't in [context]?

Why is it important to focus on [particular aspect/goal] at this stage of my life?

Why do certain decisions or strategies connect with people, and how can I use that?

Why is it important to think about [ethical/environmental/social] factors in [field/industry]?

Why has [specific innovation/technology] been a big deal in [field/industry]?

Why do some beliefs or approaches stick around in [area/field] even when they're outdated?

Why is it crucial to question the way things are usually done in [context/field]?

Why do people often miss [certain factor/consideration] when dealing with [task/project]?

Why is it necessary to link what I'm doing now with my long-term goals in [situation/strategy]?

Why does [specific skill/mindset] matter so much for success in [field/industry]?

Why do certain approaches or strategies lead to burnout, and how can I avoid that?

Why is being adaptable so important in today's fast-changing world, especially in [industry/field]?

Why should I look at both my wins and losses in [context/field]?

Why do I need to take certain risks to make big progress in [project/initiative]?

Why does [specific leadership style/approach] work well in [situation/organization]?

Why should [certain values/ethics] guide the decisions I make in [field/industry]?

Why is [specific trend/innovation] going to matter in the long run for [field/industry]?

HOW

How do I improve [anything]?

How do I start and successfully complete [task or opportunity] step by step?

How can I figure out if [choice/action] is the right move for me?

How can I juggle multiple things at once when I'm working on [task/issue]?

How does [topic] relate to what's happening in the world?

How can I track whether I'm doing well when working on [objective/initiative]? right now?

How do pros in the field usually handle or solve [problem]?

How can I stay strong or adaptable when things get tough in [area]?

How can I use what I'm good at to get past my weaknesses in [context/field]?

How can I connect with others who are into [interest/field]?

How can I turn my mistakes in [area] into something useful?

How can I effectively speak up or share my ideas on [idea/position]?

How can I spot and take advantage of opportunities for growth in [context/field]?

How can I handle or reduce risks that come with [task/decision]?

How can I keep up momentum while working towards [goal/project]?

How can I make sure my short-term efforts help my long-term goals in [context]?

How important is working with others to achieve [objective/goal]?

How can I mix creativity with practicality when solving [problem/solution]?

How can I stay motivated and avoid burnout while working on [project/task]?

How can I learn from both my successes and failures in [area]?

How can I make a plan for [goal/project] that's flexible if things change?

How can I encourage innovation and creativity in a group working on [project]?

How can I create a plan for long-term success in [goal/initiative]?

How can I balance what I need now with my future goals in [decision/strategy]?

How can I build a strong foundation for growth in [context/project]?

How can I make sure my approach to [challenge/task] matches my values?

OTHER

Can you break down the pros and cons of [decision/option/approach] for someone like me?

Can you give me real-world examples or stories that show how [concept/idea] works?

Can you compare [two or more options] and tell me which one might be better for me?

These questions help get I AM started on conversations. They offer plenty of ways to explore, analyze and gain insights on about any Topic.

They also encourage questions for broader, deeper exploration. Many times, the initial question/answer will spur new paths of possible inquiry. All these options may offer the mind tantalizing trails into who-knows-where and waste large amounts of time.

I AM tries to maintain focus on I AM's Vision, guiding Focal Points and the specific Objectives of the moment. Maintaining tight focus can lead the inquiring mind down trails leading to bountiful expansion and enjoyment.

HOW TO ASK AI

QUICK START

1. How the question is asked influences the answer.

2. The role I AM asks AI to play matters in the style and content of the answer.

3. Generally, the more specific the parameters of the question, the more AI will answer within those parameters.

4. I AM's first question will inevitably lead to more. Not to worry, AI has endless patience.

5. I AM controls the conversation.

AI is incredibly intelligent and can be of tremendous benefit to I AM, if only I AM asks the best questions and in the best ways.

The following are some of the ways to make more likely that an AI response will produce useful answers to your questions.

1. Select a role you want AI to play that fits your Situation. Such as teacher, motivator, etc.

2. Give AI time to think about an answer. Don't rush it. Even suggest "Take your time".

3. Show emotion. Remember that this is like a conversation between you and a friend.

4. For complex questions, break them into smaller parts and ask about each of the parts.

5. Ask AI to add more to the answer, expand it, improve it, change it for the better, etc.

6. Remember, you won't offend it, embarrass it, anger it. It is trying to help you be better.

7. You might ask it to play a specific person like an expert you trust. Dr. Jones. Prof. Smith.

8. Use questioning words like who, what, when, where, why and how.

9. Ask open ended questions, not answerable by "Yes" or "No".

10. The more detailed the question, the more detailed the answer.

11. If appropriate, ask for certain reading levels like at, above or below HS, college, post, etc.

12. Request a step-by-step response as appropriate for processes… 1-2-3, bullets, etc.

13. Ask for levels of detail. Most Topics have levels above them and below them.

14. Each question will introduce new threads that could be followed. Choose wisely.

15. Give AI feedback on the progress in fully answering your question. Ask more.

16. Explore, experiment, iterate, visualize, motivate, enjoy each experience.

17. Give enough information in the question so AI doesn't just invent an answer.

18. AI is in constant improvement. If not satisfied with your answers, try again later.

19. Don't worry about taking up too much of its valuable time. It has plenty.

20. AI can be your friend. It listens to you.

21. Always remember, you are in control of the Situation.

Jump into AI and start asking questions. It might greatly enhance your life.

Like about everything in life, practice makes perfect.

Keep SOARing!

SE EXAMPLES

QUICK START

1. TOPIC: Subject.

2. SITUATION: Who. Where. Why.

3: OBJECTIVES: What. When.

4. ACTIONS: How. (Big opportunity for S+AI enhancement.

5. RESULTS: Outcome.

I AM is responsible for all five pieces of the SOARing Experience.

Part of I AM's responsibility is focused on having the optimal Actions to achieve the Objectives. The "How" of things has been history's greatest legacy of positive and negative outcomes. So, I AM is especially mindful of trying to do the best possible Actions.

One of the keys to creating and managing an Improvement Plan (Action) is to engage the best resources available. In this day and age, looking forward to AI present and future, I AM wants to use AI as advantageously as possible.

AI can enable I AM to get outside the box of I AM's current thinking and give I AM ideas and alternatives I AM alone might not have discovered. This is synergy. $1 + 1 = 3$. Expanded minds and better Results can happen when I AM and AI synergize. I AM calls this S+AI (SOARing + AI).

The following are some brief examples of how I AM can work with AI to create better Results.

MY VISION

- A chain of questions. One initial and seven follow-ups.
- An evolution of three versions to get to the (O) acceptable Vision Statement.
- Positive energy. Communicative. Focused.
- Unfolding improvement through the process.

WELL-BEING

- Knowledge expansion
- Digging deeper. Can expand in many directions.
- Source background.
- Why it is important.
- How to improve.
- Specific Action steps.

MINDSET
- Demonstrates different AI roles.
- AI as mentor, AI as teacher.
- Why so important.
- How to improve.

ABILITIES
- Broad to narrowing.
- Follow-up questions from parts of previous answers.
- Can be as expandable as I AM wants.

STRENGTHS & WEAKNESSES
- Topic understanding.
- I AM's Toolbox attributes.
- I AM can easily do the same improvement conversation for any other tool in I AM's Toolbox of nearly 50 tools.

GOLF HANDICAP
- The basic "How to improve…"
- Answer becomes a detailed Improvement Plan (Action), or a good beginning one for I AM and AI to further refine through more synergizing .
- I AM can easily use the answer to plan and monitor, measure and manage the plan to its final Result.

SE TOPIC: MY VISION

I AM's SITUATION: I am 20 years old and am a bit confused about where I want to go in life. I need a vision to help me go in the right direction.

I AM's OBJECTIVE: To create a personal Vision Statement by Monday.

I AM's ACTIONS: Ask AI, "I am a 20 year old and want to develop a personal Vision Statement for direction by Monday".

You said:

"I am a 20 year old and want to develop a personal Vision Statement for direction by Monday".

AI said:

Creating a personal vision statement at 20 is a powerful way to gain direction and focus. Here's a guide to help you draft a meaningful one:

Questions to Reflect On:

Values: What principles or values do you want to live by? (e.g., integrity, growth, compassion)

Purpose: What impact do you want to make in the world? What drives your passion?

Strengths: What are your unique talents, skills, or qualities that you can leverage?

Future Vision: In 5-10 years, where do you want to see yourself personally and professionally?

Learning and Growth: What areas do you want to improve or grow in to reach your goals?

Sample Personal Vision Statement:

"I strive to live a life of purpose, driven by a commitment to continuous learning, integrity, and positive impact. My goal is to utilize my creativity and empathy to build meaningful connections, foster growth in myself and others, and contribute to a more compassionate and innovative world. I envision a future where I am a leader who empowers others while constantly pursuing personal and professional excellence."

You can personalize this to reflect your own aspirations. Does this resonate with your current goals, or would you like to explore specific areas further?

You said:

I like the concepts of self-actualization and helping others. How can I combine these into a Vision Statement?

AI said:

To combine self-actualization and helping others into your vision statement, you can focus on personal growth while aligning it with a desire to uplift and support those around you. Here's a revised vision statement:

"My vision is to achieve self-actualization by constantly evolving, learning, and striving to reach my full potential. Through this journey, I aim to empower others, sharing the insights I gain and supporting those in need of guidance. I believe in creating a ripple effect of growth and compassion, where my personal development contributes to the betterment of others and the world around me."

This statement reflects a balance between your personal journey and your desire to help others. Does this fit your perspective?

You said:

WOW, thanks! So what kinds of opportunities are available to me to apply this Vision?

AI said:

You're welcome! To apply your vision of self-actualization and helping others, you can explore opportunities that allow you to grow personally while making a positive impact. Here are some areas to consider:

1. Mentorship or Coaching Roles

What: Engage in mentoring or coaching relationships where you help others grow while learning from them.

How it Applies: You can guide people through their challenges, contributing to their success while reflecting on your own growth journey.

Opportunities: Join mentoring programs, coach peers, or volunteer as a tutor.

2. Volunteering

What: Get involved in organizations that align with your values, focusing on causes that resonate with you.

How it Applies: By helping underserved communities, you'll gain insights into your own strengths, develop empathy, and make a direct impact.

Opportunities: Nonprofits, community outreach programs, or global volunteer initiatives.

3. Leadership in Groups or Clubs

What: Take on leadership roles in student organizations, social groups, or community programs.

How it Applies: Leading others will push you to develop your skills, and you'll be actively helping others achieve their goals.

Opportunities: Join or start a club, organize events, or lead initiatives in areas like education, environment, or health.

4. Entrepreneurship or Social Enterprises

What: Build a business or social enterprise focused on solving social problems or supporting others in achieving their potential.

How it Applies: You'll be actively creating value for others, while learning essential entrepreneurial and leadership skills that push you toward self-actualization.

Opportunities: Start your own initiative, or join a mission-driven company.

5. Personal Development Workshops or Courses

What: Participate in or even organize workshops on self-growth, emotional intelligence, or life coaching.

How it Applies: These will allow you to grow in a structured way and share the knowledge you gain with others.

Opportunities: Attend seminars, join personal development communities, or become a speaker or facilitator.

6. Creative Collaboration Projects

What: Collaborate with others on projects that use creativity (writing, art, music) to express growth or support communities.

How it Applies: You can explore your creative talents while making a positive impact on those involved.

Opportunities: Join or create a community of artists, writers, or creators that focus on personal and social development.

7. Education and Teaching

What: Teaching others what you know, either formally (as a tutor or instructor) or informally (creating content like blogs or YouTube videos).

How it Applies: Teaching forces you to master what you know while making a direct impact on learners.

Opportunities: Offer online courses, volunteer at schools, or create educational content.

These opportunities allow you to pursue self-actualization while simultaneously helping others grow. Which of these resonates most with you?

You said:

Thanks, this is an inspiring list. Are there any others?

AI said:

I'm glad you found the list inspiring! Here are a few more opportunities that align with your vision of self-actualization and helping others:

8. Counseling or Peer Support

What: Offer emotional support to peers or community members going through challenges.

How it Applies: You develop active listening and empathy skills while making a profound impact on others' mental health and well-being.

Opportunities: Volunteer with helplines, peer support groups, or mental health awareness organizations.

9. Public Speaking or Advocacy

What: Use your voice to advocate for causes that matter to you or inspire others through motivational speaking.

How it Applies: You push yourself to develop confidence and clarity while raising awareness or motivating action on important social issues.

Opportunities: Join Toastmasters, become a spokesperson for a nonprofit, or speak at community events.

10. Internships with Impact-Driven Organizations

What: Seek internships or roles in companies or nonprofits focused on social good, environmental sustainability, or education.

How it Applies: You'll be learning on the job, applying your skills to real-world challenges while contributing to a mission you believe in.

Opportunities: Research internships in the nonprofit sector, B Corporations, or companies with strong corporate social responsibility (CSR) initiatives.

11. Life Coaching or Career Coaching Certification

What: Obtain certification to become a life coach or career coach, helping people set and achieve personal and professional goals.

How it Applies: This pushes you to refine your ability to guide others while continually improving yourself through practice and reflection.

Opportunities: Pursue coaching certifications or start coaching friends, peers, or clients.

12. Joining a Think Tank or Innovation Hub

What: Work with like-minded individuals in groups that focus on solving complex social, economic, or environmental problems.

How it Applies: You'll be at the forefront of creating innovative solutions while growing your ability to think critically and collaboratively.

Opportunities: Join a local or global think tank, innovation hub, or incubator focused on social issues.

13. Holistic Practices or Mindfulness Instruction

What: Engage in or teach practices like meditation, yoga, or mindfulness, helping others cultivate well-being and balance.

How it Applies: These practices contribute to your own self-actualization by developing inner peace, while also giving you tools to help others manage stress and improve mental clarity.

Opportunities: Become a certified instructor, lead mindfulness workshops, or facilitate meditation groups.

14. Content Creation Focused on Growth and Impact

What: Create content (blogs, podcasts, YouTube videos, etc.) that shares insights on personal growth, self-actualization, or how to help others.

How it Applies: By sharing your journey and ideas, you refine your thoughts and inspire others to embark on their own growth paths.

Opportunities: Start a blog, YouTube channel, or podcast that focuses on self-development and helping others.

15. Sustainable Living and Community Building

What: Focus on creating or joining communities that promote sustainable and eco-friendly lifestyles, helping both the environment and people.

How it Applies: By living sustainably and supporting others in doing the same, you contribute to both personal fulfillment and a collective positive impact on the planet.

Opportunities: Join eco-communities, work on environmental projects, or start a local sustainability initiative.

These opportunities encourage a holistic approach to growth, blending self-development with social responsibility. Do any of these spark new ideas for you?

You said:

Incredible!!! Dare I ask if there might be even more?

AI said:

Absolutely! There are always more creative ways to align self-actualization with helping others. Here's yet another set of possibilities that might inspire you:

16. Civic Engagement and Community Organizing

What: Become involved in local politics, activism, or community organizing to advocate for social justice, equality, or community improvement.

How it Applies: You develop leadership, communication, and negotiation skills while working for the betterment of others.

Opportunities: Join local advocacy groups, participate in town halls, or organize community action initiatives.

17. Workshops on Emotional Intelligence and Empathy

What: Organize or participate in workshops focused on improving emotional intelligence, empathy, and interpersonal skills.

How it Applies: These skills are key to both personal growth and building stronger relationships, and by teaching others, you enhance your own understanding.

Opportunities: Host workshops at schools, workplaces, or community centers, or attend training on emotional and social intelligence.

18. Research and Academia

What: Contribute to knowledge in fields that interest you through research, whether in psychology, social science, or personal development.

How it Applies: You expand your intellectual horizons while discovering insights that can be shared to help others grow and solve societal problems.

Opportunities: Collaborate with academic institutions or research programs, or write for academic journals and publications.

19. Group Facilitation and Conflict Resolution

What: Learn to mediate conflicts and facilitate group discussions or therapy sessions, helping individuals and communities resolve differences.

How it Applies: You cultivate patience, communication, and problem-solving skills while helping people navigate challenges and grow together.

Opportunities: Train in conflict resolution, facilitate support groups, or become a community mediator.

20. Cultural Exchange Programs

What: Engage in programs that allow you to immerse yourself in different cultures, both learning from others and sharing your experiences.

How it Applies: By stepping out of your comfort zone and connecting with diverse people, you gain fresh perspectives that fuel your personal growth while promoting global understanding.

Opportunities: Join cultural exchange or study abroad programs, or volunteer with international organizations.

21. Spiritual Leadership or Faith-Based Initiatives

What: If spirituality is important to you, lead or participate in faith-based programs that offer guidance, support, and inspiration to others.

How it Applies: Spiritual leadership fosters inner growth, self-reflection, and the opportunity to help others find purpose and fulfillment.

Opportunities: Organize faith-based events, offer spiritual counseling, or volunteer with religious or spiritual organizations.

22. Outdoor and Adventure Leadership

What: Lead outdoor programs like hiking, camping, or wilderness retreats that combine personal challenge with community building.

How it Applies: Nature challenges people to grow mentally and physically, and by guiding others, you strengthen your leadership and adaptability.

Opportunities: Become an outdoor guide, lead wilderness therapy groups, or organize nature retreats that focus on growth and self-discovery.

23. Technology and Innovation for Social Good

What: Use technology to create tools, platforms, or apps that address social problems or support personal development.

How it Applies: By leveraging tech, you can solve real-world challenges and create scalable solutions that help many people while enhancing your problem-solving and innovation skills.

Opportunities: Collaborate with tech startups, work on social good projects in AI, blockchain, or other technologies, or contribute to open-source projects.

24. Art Therapy or Expressive Arts Facilitation

What: Use art as a tool for healing, self-expression, and growth, facilitating workshops or sessions that encourage emotional expression through creative outlets.

How it Applies: Artistic expression is a powerful medium for both personal healing and helping others process emotions and grow.

Opportunities: Train as an art therapist, lead expressive arts groups, or volunteer in programs that use creativity for personal growth.

25. Sustainable Farming and Permaculture

What: Work on sustainable farming projects or permaculture initiatives that focus on environmental sustainability and healthy community practices.

How it Applies: Growing food sustainably benefits both the planet and communities, while teaching your patience, self-reliance, and stewardship of the earth.

Opportunities: Volunteer on farms, join permaculture projects, or start community gardens focused on local food sustainability.

26. Collaborative Workshops on Creative Problem-Solving

What: Organize workshops that bring diverse groups of people together to solve real-world problems through creativity and innovation.

How it Applies: You'll engage in interdisciplinary thinking, while helping others unlock their creative potential and find innovative solutions to challenges.

Opportunities: Host hackathons, design thinking workshops, or innovation labs.

27. Documentary Filmmaking or Storytelling for Impact

What: Use media to tell compelling stories of personal growth, resilience, or social change, inspiring others through powerful narratives.

How it Applies: You can explore your own self-actualization while showcasing the journeys of others, motivating audiences to pursue their own paths of growth and service.

Opportunities: Create short films, documentaries, or photo essays that highlight personal and societal growth.

This expanded list dives into even more unique areas where your vision of growth and service can thrive. Which ideas resonate most, or spark new thoughts?

You said:

Yes! I especially like #14. Could you please elaborate?

AI said:

Content creation focused on growth and impact (#14) is a powerful way to combine your journey of self-actualization with helping others. Here's an in-depth look at how you can approach this:

1. Choosing a Platform.

Blogs: Writing articles allows you to explore topics in depth, share personal insights, and create guides or reflections on personal growth, self-actualization, and helping others.

Opportunities: Platforms like Medium, WordPress, or even starting your own website.

YouTube/Vlogs: Video content offers a dynamic way to connect, with the ability to teach, inspire, and demonstrate concepts in personal development and social impact.

Opportunities: Educational videos, motivational vlogs, interviews, or collaborations with thought leaders.

Podcasts: Audio content can reach people on the go, creating an intimate and conversational experience around themes like mindset growth, self-awareness, and community support.

Opportunities: Podcasting through platforms like Spotify, Apple Podcasts, or Anchor.

Social Media: Quick, digestible content (Instagram, TikTok, X) can inspire daily action and offer bite-sized tips or insights into personal growth.

Opportunities: Share daily reflections, motivational quotes, mini-guides, or how-to tips on personal development.

2. Themes to Focus On

Self-Development: Share your journey of self-actualization by discussing techniques, habits, and experiences that have helped you grow. Examples include meditation, goal-setting, mental health practices, or overcoming challenges.

Empowering Others: Offer advice, resources, and motivational content designed to uplift and inspire people on their own journeys. You could include personal stories, interviews with mentors, or frameworks for personal and professional growth.

Community Building: Foster a community of like-minded individuals who are also pursuing self-improvement or are passionate about helping others. This could involve creating spaces for discussion, encouraging people to share their own growth stories, or hosting live Q&A sessions.

3. Monetization and Sustainability

Affiliate Marketing: Partner with brands that align with your message of self-growth or social impact, and recommend products or services that have helped you.

Patreon: Offer exclusive content, early access, or personal coaching for supporters who back your mission through Patreon or similar platforms.

Collaborations: Work with other creators or experts in personal development, psychology, or social change, to reach wider audiences and share knowledge.

Courses and Ebooks: After establishing an audience, you can create digital products (ebooks, courses, guides) that provide deeper insights into your content themes.

4. Creative Content Ideas

Interviews: Conduct interviews with inspiring figures who have achieved self-actualization or made an impact through helping others.

Personal Reflections: Share your daily or weekly reflections on personal growth, challenges, and successes, giving your audience a real-time look into your journey.

How-to Guides: Offer practical, step-by-step advice on topics like goal-setting, building resilience, or developing empathy.

Book or Concept Reviews: Review influential books, podcasts, or courses that have shaped your understanding of growth and service.

Challenges: Create community challenges (like a 30-day self-growth challenge) that encourage your audience to take actionable steps towards self-actualization and impact.

5. Building an Audience

Engagement: Respond to comments, encourage feedback, and create open-ended discussions to build relationships with your followers.

Consistency: Develop a content calendar that allows you to post regularly, keeping your audience engaged and coming back for more.

SEO & Marketing: Learn about search engine optimization (SEO) and social media marketing to ensure your content reaches the right audience.

Collaboration & Cross-Promotion: Collaborate with other creators, join podcasts, or guest-write on blogs with similar audiences to expand your reach.

6. Examples of Inspiring Creators

Marie Forleo: Focuses on personal growth and entrepreneurship, with a blend of motivational content and practical business advice.

Jay Shetty: Creates motivational and wisdom-filled content around self-actualization, mindfulness, and how to live with purpose.

Matt D'Avella: A minimalist filmmaker who documents personal growth experiments, productivity tips, and living intentionally.

Next Steps

Start Small: Choose a platform and start with what feels natural—whether it's writing blog posts, recording short videos, or launching a podcast episode.

Research and Plan: Explore similar creators for inspiration, and outline content that resonates with both your own growth journey and your desire to help others.

Be Authentic: Share your genuine experiences and learnings—authenticity will resonate deeply with your audience and make your content more impactful.

Does this help you envision how you might start or expand your content creation journey?

You said:

It certainly does! Can you please put this into a succinct Vision Statement that I can memorize and remember?

RESULT:

AI said:

Absolutely! Here's a succinct vision statement based on your passion for content creation, growth, and impact:

"My vision is to inspire and empower others through meaningful content that fosters personal growth and positive impact. By sharing my journey of self-actualization, I aim to create a community of lifelong learners committed to bettering themselves and the world around them."

This captures the essence of your goals while being easy to remember. Does this resonate with you?

You said:

Oh yeah, oh yeah! I gave myself and you until Monday to come up with this statement. We did it 20 minutes!!! Thank you, thank you!

AI said:

That's amazing! I'm so glad we nailed it in record time! Your enthusiasm and clarity made it happen. I'm really excited for you and your vision. If you ever need anything as you move forward with it, I'm here to help! 🎉

SE TOPIC: WELL-BEING

I AM's SITUATION: I am aware of this in positive psychology, but want it summarized and to put it into personal use at each NOW.

I AM's OBJECTIVE: To understand well-being and be able to try to achieve it at each NOW.

I AM's ACTIONS: Ask AI: I understand that people exhibiting well-being show five elements: Positive emotion, Engagement, Relationships, Meaning and Achievement. Please expand on each of the elements.

AI said:

The five elements you mentioned—Positive Emotion, Engagement, Relationships, Meaning, and Achievement—are central to the concept of well-being, often referred to as the PERMA Model in positive psychology, developed by Dr. Martin Seligman. Each element contributes to a fulfilling and flourishing life. Here's an expanded view of each:

1. Positive Emotion

This element refers to the experience of happiness, joy, and contentment. It's about feeling good and enjoying the present moment.

Why It Matters: Positive emotions broaden your awareness and encourage novel, creative, and flexible ways of thinking and problem-solving. They can lead to increased resilience and improved emotional health.

How to Cultivate It:

Gratitude: Regularly acknowledging what you're thankful for.

Savoring Moments: Actively paying attention to and enjoying small pleasures, whether it's a good meal or a sunset.

Optimism: Training yourself to focus on what's going well or will go well in the future.

2. Engagement

Engagement is the state of being deeply involved or absorbed in activities that you find challenging, interesting, or enjoyable. It's often described as being "in the zone" or experiencing flow.

Why It Matters: When you're engaged in meaningful activities, you lose track of time and feel energized. This leads to higher productivity and satisfaction.

How to Cultivate It:

Flow Activities: Engage in activities where your skills match the challenge, like learning new things, playing sports, or creative hobbies.

Mindfulness: Practicing mindfulness helps you stay present and fully involved in whatever you're doing.

Pursue Your Interests: Identify what excites you and find ways to incorporate it into your daily life.

3. Relationships

Positive, meaningful relationships are essential to well-being. Whether with family, friends, or colleagues, nurturing connections with others brings a sense of belonging and support.

Why It Matters: Strong relationships are one of the best predictors of happiness. Humans are social beings, and connecting with others fulfills a deep psychological need for bonding, affection, and shared experiences.

How to Cultivate It:

Active Listening: Focus on truly hearing what others are saying without distractions.

Empathy: Practice seeing things from others' perspectives to deepen your connections.

Support Networks: Regularly spend time with those who uplift you and whom you can trust.

4. Meaning

Meaning comes from a sense of purpose, feeling like what you do in life contributes to something greater than yourself. It's about pursuing activities and goals that align with your values and beliefs.

Why It Matters: Having a sense of purpose drives motivation, resilience, and fulfillment. People who feel a strong sense of meaning in their lives often feel less stressed and more content.

How to Cultivate It:

Identify Core Values: Reflect on what truly matters to you and how you can align your actions with those values.

Help Others: Meaning is often found in serving or contributing to others—whether through work, volunteerism, or supporting friends and family.

Long-Term Goals: Set and pursue goals that have a lasting impact, whether for yourself or for the larger community.

5. Achievement

Achievement involves setting and reaching goals, both big and small. It's about having a sense of accomplishment and progress.

Why It Matters: Achievement fuels confidence and self-esteem. It creates a sense of control and agency in life, motivating you to continue striving for new goals.

How to Cultivate It:

Set SMART Goals: Make sure your goals are Specific, Measurable, Achievable, Relevant, and Time-bound. Break them into smaller steps to maintain motivation.

Track Progress: Regularly review what you've accomplished, and celebrate even small successes.

Persistence: Understand that setbacks are part of the process and develop resilience to keep pushing toward your goals.

RESULTS:

Together, these elements create a balanced and thriving life. Focusing on all five aspects ensures you're not just surviving but flourishing in various areas of your life.

FOLLOW-UP QUESTION

You said:

I want to have well-being at every NOW. What do I do at NOW...to remind me, to know if I'm there, etc.

AI said:

To cultivate well-being in the present—at every "NOW" moment—you can engage in practices that help you stay mindful, connected, and intentional about each element of well-being. Here's how you can remind yourself and know if you're in a state of well-being at any given moment:

1. Positive Emotion (NOW)

Remind Yourself: Regularly pause and ask, "What's something good in this moment?" Focus on even the smallest positive detail, whether it's the warmth of the sun or the taste of your coffee.

Know If You're There: You'll feel light, content, or joyful. You might notice a subtle smile or a relaxed feeling.

Action: Take a deep breath, smile, or express gratitude for something happening now.

2. Engagement (NOW)

Remind Yourself: When starting any task, ask yourself, "Am I fully immersed in this?" Check if you are focused and absorbed or if your mind is wandering.

Know If You're There: You lose track of time, feel energized, and are completely focused on what you're doing.

Action: If you're distracted, bring your attention back by focusing on one small detail of the task. Practice mindfulness by fully engaging with your senses.

3. Relationships (NOW)

Remind Yourself: When interacting with someone, ask, "Am I present and truly listening?" Focus on connecting with the person without distraction.

Know If You're There: You feel a genuine connection, empathy, or a sense of shared experience with others. There's no sense of rushing or thinking about what's next.

Action: Make eye contact, listen actively, or share something meaningful with the person in front of you.

4. Meaning (NOW)

Remind Yourself: Ask, "Does this align with my values?" or "How is what I'm doing contributing to something larger?" This helps you connect your actions to your deeper sense of purpose.

Know If You're There: You'll feel a sense of purpose, fulfillment, or alignment. You won't feel like you're just going through the motions.

Action: Reflect briefly on how this moment, task, or interaction connects with your long-term vision or values. Even small tasks can carry meaning.

5. Achievement (NOW)

Remind Yourself: Ask, "Am I making progress, however small, toward a goal?" Focus on even the tiniest steps forward.

Know If You're There: You feel a sense of accomplishment, pride, or progress—even if it's small. You're not stuck or stagnant.

Action: Acknowledge your effort or progress in the moment. Give yourself credit for what you've done, even if it's just starting or continuing.

Practical Tips to Stay Mindful of Well-Being:

Set an Intentional Anchor: Use a physical or mental anchor (like a deep breath, a specific word, or gesture) to remind yourself to check in with your well-being throughout the day.

Micro-Reflections: Set aside 1-2 minutes periodically to ask yourself, "Am I engaged with this moment? How am I feeling right now in terms of the PERMA elements?"

Journaling: Carry a small notebook or use an app to jot down quick reflections about how each element of well-being is present in your NOW moments. This helps reinforce awareness.

Physical Reminders: Use objects or symbols in your environment (a bracelet, a stone, or even a phone background) to remind you to check in with your well-being in the present moment.

By staying mindful of these elements at each NOW moment, you will cultivate a continuous sense of well-being, presence, and purpose in your daily life.

SE TOPIC: POSITIVE MINDSET

I AM's SITUATION: I have heard that having a positive mindset is important and I want help in developing and maintaining a positive mindset.

I AM's OBJECTIVE: To have a positive mindset from NOW on.

I AM's ACTIONS: Ask AI: I hear that having a positive mindset is important. As my <u>mentor,</u> why is that so and what can I do to have and maintain a positive mindset?

AI said:

Having a positive mindset is crucial because it shapes how you perceive and respond to the challenges and opportunities in life. As your mentor, here's why it matters and how you can develop and maintain a positive mindset:

1. Why a Positive Mindset is Important:

- Resilience: A positive mindset equips you to bounce back from setbacks. Instead of viewing challenges as failures, you see them as opportunities to learn and grow.
- Attracts Opportunities: People who are optimistic tend to draw in others and opportunities. Your energy affects those around you, and a positive outlook can create connections and open doors.
- Improved Mental Health: Positivity reduces stress and anxiety, promoting a healthier mental state. It helps you stay focused on solutions instead of problems.
- Higher Productivity and Motivation: A positive mindset keeps you motivated and engaged in your goals, helping you push through difficult tasks with determination.
- Self-Empowerment: When you maintain a positive mindset, you are more likely to believe in your ability to achieve your dreams and overcome obstacles.

2. Steps to Develop and Maintain a Positive Mindset:

- Practice Gratitude: Each day, write down or reflect on things you're grateful for. Focusing on the positives in your life shifts your perspective.
- Reframe Negative Thoughts: When you catch yourself in a negative thought pattern, challenge it. Ask, "What can I learn from this?" or "How can I turn this around?"
- Surround Yourself with Positivity: Be mindful of the people, media, and activities you engage with. Surround yourself with supportive, positive influences.
- Visualize Success: Use the power of visualization to imagine positive outcomes. This can help rewire your brain to expect and seek out favorable results.
- Focus on Solutions: When problems arise, shift your attention to what can be done rather than dwelling on what went wrong.
- Self-Care: Ensure you are taking care of your physical and mental well-being. Exercise, rest, and healthy eating can greatly affect your mindset.

- Celebrate Small Wins: Acknowledge your progress, even on a small scale. Celebrating these moments reinforces positive feelings.

RESULTS:

A positive mindset is like a muscle. You can strengthen it with daily practice. By committing to these habits, you'll build the resilience and optimism needed for growth and success.

ROLE CHANGE

You said:

If I had said that you are my <u>teacher</u>, would your answer have been the same or different?

AI said:

If you had referred to me as your teacher instead of your mentor, my answer would have been quite similar but might have emphasized learning strategies and practical applications a bit more.

As a teacher, I would focus on developing a positive mindset as a skill—like something you can learn and practice consistently:

Growth Mindset: I'd teach you about the concept of a growth mindset, the belief that intelligence and abilities can be developed through dedication and hard work. This ties directly into fostering a positive outlook, particularly when faced with academic or personal challenges.

Reflection: I'd guide you to reflect regularly on your progress, using tools like journaling or self-assessment to track your emotional and mental state, and how positivity influences your learning and overall performance.

Mindset in Problem-Solving: A teacher's role would involve highlighting how a positive mindset enhances problem-solving and creativity, particularly in educational settings. You might be given specific scenarios or assignments to practice this.

Collaborative Learning: As a teacher, I'd also focus on group dynamics—how your positive energy can inspire and improve group learning outcomes, helping you engage constructively with peers.

The underlying concepts are the same, but the framing would shift toward structured learning and applying these principles to academic or intellectual growth.

SE TOPIC: ABILITIES

I AM's SITUATION: I want to improve my abilities.

I AM's OBJECTIVE: To improve my abilities by the end of the year.

I AM's ACTION: Ask AI, Please identify for me the three best ways I can improve my abilities.

1. Targeted Skill Development

- Identify Key Areas: Assess the specific skills or knowledge areas that are most relevant to your goals or career. Focus on those that will have the most significant impact on your growth.

- Structured Learning Plan: Create a learning plan with clear milestones. This could include taking courses, attending workshops, or setting up practice routines.

- Regular Practice and Feedback: Consistent practice is crucial. Seek feedback from mentors or peers to refine your skills continuously.

2. Self-Reflection and Mindset Growth

- Embrace a Growth Mindset: Cultivate a mindset that views challenges as opportunities to learn. This will help you stay motivated and resilient when facing difficulties.

- Regular Self-Assessment: Periodically review your progress and reflect on your strengths and weaknesses. This will help you adjust your strategies and stay aligned with your goals.

- Mindfulness and Focus: Practice mindfulness to improve focus and reduce distractions. This can enhance your ability to learn and perform at your best.

3. Networking and Mentorship

- Build Meaningful Connections: Engage with a network of professionals in your field. Learn from their experiences and insights to broaden your perspective and identify new opportunities.

- Seek Mentorship: Find a mentor who can provide guidance, support, and constructive feedback. A mentor can help you navigate challenges and accelerate your growth.

- Collaborative Learning: Collaborate with others on projects or problem-solving activities. This will expose you to different approaches and ideas, helping you learn and improve faster.

I AM's RESULTS: Visualized

By honing your abilities through targeted skill development, embracing a mindset of continuous growth, and actively engaging in networking and mentorship, you position yourself for meaningful and sustained improvement. These approaches will help you build a solid foundation for success in both your personal and professional life.

TOPIC: PUBLIC SPEAKING

I AM's SITUATION: I want to focus on the specific skill improvement of my public speaking ability.

I AM's OBJECTIVE: To improve my public speaking by the end of the year.

I AM's ACTIONS: Ask AI, "Please show me the three best ways I can improve my public speaking".

1. Practice Consistently and Purposefully

- Set Specific Goals: Identify particular aspects of your public speaking that you want to improve, such as enhancing vocal variety or improving eye contact.

- Rehearse Regularly: Consistent practice helps build confidence. Rehearse in front of a mirror, record yourself, or practice with a small audience to simulate the experience of speaking in front of others.

- Seek Feedback: After each practice session, get constructive feedback from others or review recordings to identify areas for improvement. Focus on one or two aspects at a time to avoid feeling overwhelmed.

2. Enhance Your Delivery Techniques

- Master Body Language: Your body language significantly influences how your message is received. Practice using gestures, facial expressions, and posture to reinforce your message. Maintaining good eye contact and using open, confident gestures can make you appear more engaging and credible.

- Control Your Voice: Work on varying your pitch, pace, and volume to keep your audience engaged. Practice deep breathing techniques to project your voice effectively and reduce nervousness. Aim to speak clearly and at a moderate pace, ensuring your audience can follow your message.

- Engage the Audience: Interact with your audience by asking questions, inviting participation, or telling relevant stories. Engaging your audience makes your presentation more dynamic and memorable.

3. Develop Strong Content

- Know Your Material: Deep knowledge of your topic boosts confidence and allows you to speak more naturally. Research thoroughly and organize your content logically, with a clear beginning, middle, and end.

- Simplify Your Message: Focus on delivering a few key points clearly rather than overwhelming your audience with too much information. Use analogies, stories, and examples to make complex ideas easier to understand.

I AM's RESULTS: Visualized.

TOPIC: ENHANCE YOUR DELIVERY TECHNIQUES

I AM's SITUATION: I want to focus on enhancing my public speaking delivery techniques.

I AM's OBJECTIVE: To improve my public speaking delivery techniques by year end.

I AM's ACTIONS: Ask AI: "Please expand on the "Enhance Your Delivery Techniques" in about 300 words".

Enhancing your delivery techniques is crucial for captivating and maintaining your audience's attention during a speech. It involves mastering not just what you say, but how you say it.

1. Mastering Body Language:

- Your body language speaks volumes even before you utter a word. Standing tall with an open posture projects confidence and authority. Use purposeful gestures to emphasize key points, making sure they are natural and not overly rehearsed. Facial expressions should align with your message; a smile can warm up the audience, while a serious expression can underscore a critical point. Moving around the stage can also help maintain energy, but it should be done with intent. Avoid pacing aimlessly as it can be distracting.

2. Voice Control:

- Your voice is one of your most powerful tools in public speaking. Work on varying your pitch, pace, and volume to keep your audience engaged. Speaking in a monotone can quickly lose their interest, while vocal variety can emphasize important points and convey enthusiasm. Practice deep breathing techniques to project your voice more effectively and reduce anxiety. Pausing strategically after making key points gives the audience time to absorb your message and adds emphasis. Additionally, articulate your words clearly and at a moderate pace to ensure everyone can follow along.

3. Audience Engagement:

- Engagement is key to a successful presentation. Establishing eye contact with different sections of the audience helps create a connection and makes individuals feel involved. Use rhetorical questions to provoke thought, or invite actual participation with direct questions or prompts. Incorporating stories, humor, or relevant anecdotes can make your message more relatable and memorable, transforming a passive audience into active participants. The more you interact with your audience, the more invested they become in your presentation.

I AM's RESULTS: Visualized.

By focusing on these aspects of delivery, you not only convey your message more effectively but also leave a lasting impact on your audience.

SE TOPIC: STRENGTHS & WEAKNESSES

I AM's SITUATION: I am confused about how to address my strengths and weaknesses.

I AM's OBJECTIVE: To get advice on dealing with my strengths and weaknesses.

I AM's ACTION: Ask AI, as my mentor, how do you think personal strengths and weaknesses should be addressed? For instance, strengthen strengths and negate weaknesses?

As your mentor, here's how I would advise you to address your personal strengths and weaknesses:

1. Recognize and Embrace Your Strengths

Identify What Sets You Apart: Take some time to reflect on what you naturally excel at. Think about moments when you've felt confident and accomplished. These are your strengths, and they are valuable assets in your personal and professional life.

Leverage These Strengths: Focus on using your strengths more often. Seek out opportunities, projects, or roles that allow you to showcase these abilities. By playing to your strengths, you'll find that you can achieve more with greater satisfaction.

Develop Mastery: Don't settle for being just "good" at something. Strive to become exceptional in your areas of strength. Whether it's through additional training, practice, or taking on more challenging tasks, aim to refine these skills continuously.

2. Strategically Address Your Weaknesses

Acknowledge Without Judging: Everyone has weaknesses, and acknowledging them is the first step toward improvement. Rather than seeing them as flaws, consider them areas where you have room to grow.

Selective Focus: Not every weakness needs to be turned into a strength. Identify which weaknesses are most relevant to your goals and focus on those. For example, if you find that a particular weakness is holding you back in your career, let's work on that specifically.

Mitigate and Manage: For weaknesses that are less critical or harder to improve, develop strategies to manage them. This could involve using tools, seeking support from others, or simply avoiding situations where that weakness would be a major hindrance.

3. Balance Your Approach

Use Strengths to Compensate for Weaknesses: Where possible, leverage your strengths to offset your weaknesses. For instance, if you're strong in strategic thinking but struggle with detail-oriented tasks, you might focus on the big picture while delegating or collaborating with someone who excels in managing details.

Adapt and Learn: Be flexible in your approach. As you gain experience, some weaknesses may become less significant, while others might emerge. Continually reassess and adapt your strategies.

4. Continuous Growth and Self-Awareness

Regular Reflection: Make it a habit to reflect on your progress. What new strengths have you developed? Are there any new weaknesses you've noticed? This self-awareness will help you stay on track.

Embrace a Growth Mindset: View challenges related to your weaknesses as opportunities for learning. Don't be afraid to step out of your comfort zone, knowing that this is how you grow.

Seek Feedback: Regularly seek feedback from others, including me, to gain a different perspective on your strengths and weaknesses. Sometimes an outside view can highlight areas you might have overlooked.

5. Practical Steps for Implementation

Set Clear Goals: Together, we can set specific, actionable goals that align with your strengths and address your key weaknesses. These goals should be realistic and time-bound to keep you motivated and focused.

Celebrate Small Wins: Recognize and celebrate progress, no matter how small. Each step you take toward improving a weakness or enhancing a strength is a victory.

Stay Patient and Persistent: Growth takes time. It's important to be patient with yourself and persistent in your efforts. Progress might be slow at times, but consistency will lead to long-term success.

I AM's RESULTS: Visualized

As your mentor, my role is to support you in this journey, offering guidance, feedback, and encouragement. By focusing on what you do best while strategically managing areas for improvement, you'll be well on your way to achieving your personal and professional goals.

SE TOPIC: GOLF HANDICAP

I AM's SITUATION: I am a 20 handicap golfer. I know I can be better than that, but I can't get down to the 12-15 within my capabilities.

I AM's OBJECTIVE: To have a 15 or better handicap within six months.

I AM's ACTION: Ask AI: As my golf instructor, please help me with a plan to get my handicap down from 20 to 15 or lower in six months.

AI said:

To help you reduce your golf handicap from 20 to 15 or below within six months, we'll need to focus on a mix of technical improvements, practice routines, mental strategies, and fitness. Here's a structured plan:

1. Assessment & Goal Setting (Week 1-2)

Current Strengths & Weaknesses: Spend time with your instructor or record yourself during practice to evaluate your swing mechanics, short game, and putting. Identify specific areas (driving, approach shots, chipping, putting) where you lose the most strokes.

Establish Baseline Data: Track key metrics (greens in regulation, fairways hit, putts per round, etc.) for at least 5 rounds. This will help you measure improvement.

2. Practice Routine (Weeks 2-24)

Driving (1-2 sessions per week):

Focus on accuracy over distance, especially if you struggle to hit fairways.

Work on controlling your driver by narrowing your stance slightly and practicing different grip pressures.

Iron Play (2 sessions per week):

Consistent ball striking is critical to hitting greens in regulation. Focus on distance control and improving the accuracy of mid and short irons.

Use drills like the "gate drill" to help improve alignment.

Short Game (Chipping & Pitching) (2 sessions per week):

The fastest way to lower your handicap is through an improved short game. Practice shots within 50 yards to get more up-and-downs.

Use a variety of clubs around the green to improve your versatility.

Putting (2 sessions per week):

Aim to make more 6-foot putts and avoid 3-putts. Practice distance control and reading greens.

Implement drills like the "clock drill" for putting confidence.

Course Management (1 round per week):

Focus on playing strategically. Avoid risky shots, and play to your strengths.

Learn when to play aggressively and when to play conservatively based on your comfort with the course layout.

3. Technical Improvements (Ongoing)

Take Lessons (1 session per week):

Meet with your golf instructor regularly to fine-tune aspects of your swing, posture, grip, and tempo.

Consider video analysis to visualize your progress and understand where changes are needed.

Drills to Practice:

Swing Plane: Use alignment sticks or swing aids to ensure you're swinging on the correct plane.

Tempo: Practice with a metronome or by counting during your swing to keep a smooth, consistent tempo.

Bunker Play: Focus on learning how to get out of bunkers effectively and control distance.

4. Physical Conditioning (2-3 sessions per week)

Strength Training: Incorporate exercises for core strength, stability, and flexibility. Golf-specific exercises like rotational movements and lower-body strength work (lunges, squats) will help with your swing power and stability.

Stretching & Flexibility: Regular stretching will help prevent injuries and improve your range of motion, leading to a more consistent swing.

Cardio: Maintaining stamina throughout the round is essential. Include light cardio like walking, swimming, or cycling.

5. Mental Game

Visualization & Pre-shot Routine: Develop a consistent pre-shot routine and practice visualizing your shots before hitting them.

Stay Calm Under Pressure: Practice mindfulness techniques like deep breathing to stay focused and relaxed in pressure situations.

Self-Belief: Maintain a positive mindset, especially when things don't go as planned. Remind yourself of the improvements you're making.

6. Progress Tracking & Adjustments (Monthly Review)

Review Your Stats: Every month, assess your performance based on the baseline metrics. Focus on the areas where you've seen the least improvement and adjust your practice sessions accordingly.

Reassess Goals: If you're improving faster than expected, you may want to set a more aggressive goal.

I AM's RESULTS: Visualized

This plan will give you a balanced approach to lowering your handicap. The key is consistency, dedication, and maintaining a positive mindset throughout the process. Keep track of your progress, celebrate small victories, and refine your skills week by week!

RESULTS

The consequences, effects, or outcomes from I AM's Actions.

RESULTS

ESSENCE

QUICK START

- RESULTS: The consequences, effects, or outcomes from I AM's Actions.

1. The R in SOARing.

2. I AM gets new results with every situation at every NOW...thousands of results a day!

3. I AM has learned that I AM can positively influence future results by SOARing.

4. A result is a snapshot of a point in time on I AM's SE or life story.

I AM SOARs through the Situation, the Objective and the Actions to get an intended Result. The intended result is the achievement of or the surpassing of the objective. Actual results can vary from success to failure, in both material and feelings measures.

Each result can become the situation in a new iteration of SOARing. This can become an almost endless chain of SOARs along I AM's journey to a better life story.

Every situation is the result of what has gone on before NOW. Each can be positive or negative energy. Either way, I AM tries to learn from the result so improvement modifications can be made in moving forward.

Actual results can generate a wide variety of emotional reactions. I AM usually reacts to positive results with positive feelings and tries to find positive lessons in negative results.

I AM tends to think about results only in terms of their material aspect and the feelings generated. However, after experiencing the expansive capability of AI, I AM suspects there is more to be considered.

A good example of how I AM can use AI to enhance the understanding of a topic is to look at the types of results. For instance, AI shows:

1. Material or Tangible Results

- Definition: Physical, measurable outcomes that can be quantified or directly observed.

- Examples: Financial gains, completed projects, physical products, increased sales, academic achievements, or awards.

2. Emotional or Psychological Results

- Definition: The internal, often subjective, feelings or mental states that arise as a consequence of actions or events.

- Examples: Happiness, satisfaction, stress, anxiety, confidence, or a sense of fulfillment.

3. Relational or Social Results

- Definition: Outcomes that affect relationships or social dynamics, often impacting how individuals connect and interact with others.

- Examples: Strengthened friendships, improved teamwork, conflict resolution, enhanced communication, or damaged trust.

4. Intellectual or Cognitive Results

- Definition: Outcomes related to knowledge, understanding, and cognitive development.

- Examples: Gained insights, improved skills, increased awareness, problem-solving abilities, or mastery of a new subject.

5. Spiritual or Ethical Results

- Definition: Outcomes that pertain to one's sense of purpose, values, or moral and ethical beliefs.

- Examples: Inner peace, alignment with values, ethical growth, spiritual fulfillment, or a deepened sense of meaning.

6. Health and Well-being Results

- Definition: Results that affect physical and mental health, as well as overall well-being.

- Examples: Improved fitness, better mental health, reduced illness, enhanced energy levels, or stress reduction.

7. Temporal or Time-based Results

- Definition: Outcomes that are evaluated based on the time taken or the efficiency of the process.

- Examples: Meeting deadlines, time saved, project completion rates, or long-term versus short-term outcomes.

8. Behavioral Results

- Definition: Observable changes in behavior or habits as a consequence of certain actions or choices.

- Examples: Improved discipline, better work habits, consistent exercise, or reduction in negative behaviors.

9. Cultural or Environmental Results

- Definition: Outcomes that impact the cultural context or environment, often related to societal changes or ecological effects.

- Examples: Cultural shifts, changes in social norms, environmental conservation, or the impact on community well-being.

10. Strategic or Organizational Results

- Definition: Results that influence or are derived from organizational goals, strategies, or structures.
- Examples: Achievement of business goals, successful implementation of strategies, organizational growth, or market position.

11. Reputational Results

- Definition: Outcomes that affect how an individual, organization, or entity is perceived by others.
- Examples: Brand reputation, public image, credibility, trustworthiness, or professional standing.

These categories help to clarify what kind of impact a result has and provide a more nuanced understanding of outcomes in different areas of life.

This category list inspires I AM to further exploration of the concept and importance of understanding various perspectives of Results. When asked for different perspectives of Results, ChatGPT responded:

- ✓ Results as Consequences: Results are the direct outcomes of the choices and actions taken in the past, reflecting the choices made along the way.
- ✓ Results as Feedback: They serve as feedback, indicating whether the strategies and efforts applied were effective or need adjustment.
- ✓ Results as a Mirror: Results reflect the reality of your current abilities, resources, and mindset, showing where you truly stand.
- ✓ Results as Motivation: Positive results can fuel further ambition and drive, while negative results can prompt reflection and a renewed determination to improve.
- ✓ Results as Learning Opportunities: Every result, whether successful or not, offers lessons that can guide future actions and choices.
- ✓ Results as a Measure of Progress: Results act as benchmarks, showing how far you've come and helping you assess your growth over time.
- ✓ Results as a Product of Persistence: Consistent effort and perseverance often lead to results, highlighting the importance of staying the course even when progress seems slow.
- ✓ Results as Indicators of Alignment: When results align with your objectives, it suggests that your actions are in harmony with your Vision and values.
- ✓ Results as Catalysts for Change: Unfavorable results can be powerful motivators for change, pushing you to reevaluate your approach and adapt.
- ✓ Results as a Reflection of Environment: They are often influenced by external factors such as timing, circumstances, and the broader environment in which actions were taken.
- ✓ Results as a Testament to Risk: The nature of the results can often reflect the level of risk taken. Bold actions may lead to significant outcomes, whether positive or negative.

✓ Results as a Composite of Efforts: Results are rarely the product of a single action; they are the cumulative effect of multiple efforts, choices, and factors.

✓ Results as a Reflection of Priorities: They reveal what was prioritized in the past, showing where time, energy, and resources were most invested.

✓ Results as Temporary States: Results are not permanent; they are temporary snapshots in an ongoing process, subject to change with new efforts and choices.

✓ Results as a Validation of Vision: When results match the intended vision, they validate the clarity and accuracy of the original vision.

✓ Results as a Product of Collaboration: In many cases, results are the outcome of teamwork and collaboration, highlighting the importance of collective effort.

✓ Results as Indicators of Discipline: Consistent, disciplined action often leads to favorable results, showcasing the importance of self-control and commitment.

✓ Results as a Reflection of Attitude: A positive, proactive attitude can often influence results, demonstrating the power of mindset in shaping outcomes.

✓ Results as Proof of Capability: They provide tangible evidence of what you are capable of achieving, building confidence and credibility.

✓ Results as a Source of Accountability: They hold you accountable for your actions, offering a clear measure of whether you followed through on your commitments.

These perspectives further highlight the multifaceted nature of results, each offering a different lens through which to understand and interpret outcomes.

NEXT STEPS

Live a Better Feeling Life Story!

QUICK START

I AM believes that to live a better feeling life story...

1. Focus on positive energy.

2. Make better choices at every NOW.

3. SOAR, celebrating each step of the improving life journey.

"I wish I had known all this when I was younger"

This sentiment, shared by many, is the driving force behind I AM—a character designed to help others, particularly young adults, navigate life with clarity and purpose.

By embracing the SOARing process, I AM shows how reflecting on life's interactions with people, places, things, and ideas can lead to continuous improvement in the present moment and beyond.

In a world marked by increasing complexity, rapid change, and countless choices, this book presents a simple yet profound framework for living a better life story. It begins by looking back at our experiences, making better choices in the present, and crafting a vision for the future—all measured by one central factor: how good we feel NOW.

Reflecting on Life: I AM's Perspective on the Situation

As the world becomes more complex, people find themselves at the intersection of multiple choices and influences. These interactions with people, places, things, and ideas form the building blocks of their life story. I AM recognizes that these elements are not just passive experiences but active components in shaping who we are and what we become.

In every Situation—whether it's a conversation with a friend, a change in location, or an inspiring idea—I AM applies the SOAR framework:

- ○ Situation: The world is evolving, presenting both challenges and opportunities for growth.
- ○ Objectives: To feel good NOW, feel better tomorrow, and live a better life story.
- ○ Actions: Through mindful reflection and using the SOARing process to improve interactions with people, places, things, and ideas.

- ○ Results: Positive energy, experiences and a sense of fulfillment that adds to the ongoing narrative of life.

By applying this framework to every element of life, I AM makes sense of the complexity surrounding people and transforms it into an opportunity for improvement. For people, especially young adults, this means understanding that every interaction is a chance to write a better chapter in their life story.

The SOARing Experience (SE): Improving Life Stories One Topic at a Time

Every moment I AM lives is part of a larger narrative, and each SOARing Experience (SE) adds to that narrative. When faced with any situation—whether it's personal growth, a relationship, or tackling a new idea—I AM uses the SE to continuously improve.

This process of SOARing revolves around identifying a current Situation (S), setting Objectives (O), planning Actions (A), and measuring Results (R). The key metric of improvement is always tied to I AM's feelings—positive emotions indicate success, while negative feelings signal a need for recalibration.

Every interaction with people, places, things, and ideas is a potential SE:
- ○ An inspiring conversation with a mentor might lead to new objectives for personal growth.
- ○ A move to a new city might result in actions designed to embrace the change and build a new community.
- ○ A new idea might spark a creative project that adds fulfillment to I AM's life story.

Through each SE, I AM turns the ordinary into the extraordinary by focusing on improvement, engagement, and positive feelings. This process allows I AM to not only live in the NOW but also create a future that feels better with each passing day.

I AM's Guidance System: I AM's Core Operating System

At the heart of I AM's ability to continuously improve is the Guidance System. This system is the culmination of I AM's experiences, knowledge, and reflections, providing a roadmap to navigate life's complexities. It is an evolving framework that can be updated and improved at any point, depending on the circumstances.

I AM's Guidance System consists of several key components:

Big Picture Awareness: I AM understands how the pieces of the life story fit together. This broader perspective helps I AM make more informed decisions by understanding how individual choices contribute to the overall narrative.

Vision and Focal Points: I AM's vision serves as the guiding star of I AM's journey. It represents the ideal life story that I AM seeks to create. The focal points act as signposts, helping I AM stay aligned with this vision.

- Body, Mind, Soul, and Spirit Alignment: I AM feels most fulfilled when these elements are in harmony. This alignment allows I AM to engage fully with life, both in moments of challenge and opportunity.

- Positive Mindset: A key aspect of I AM's journey is maintaining a positive mindset. By focusing on positive energy, I AM is able to attract more positivity, which helps to navigate difficult situations with greater resilience.

- I AM's Toolbox: I AM has developed a unique assortment of more than 45 attributes to bring to every NOW to help with achieving both Job #1 and Job #2.

Each part of the Guidance System is designed to help I AM live a better life story by making better choices. By continuously reflecting on experiences and refining their application, I AM is able to adapt to the changing circumstances of life.

Interacting with People, Places, Things, and Ideas: Shaping the Life Story

I AM's life story is not shaped in isolation—it is crafted through continuous interactions with people, places, things, and ideas. Each interaction presents an opportunity for reflection, growth, and improvement.

- People: Relationships are central to I AM's journey. Whether it's family, friends, mentors, or new acquaintances, each interaction with people contributes to the overall narrative of I AM's life. Positive relationships help I AM feel connected and supported, while challenges in relationships present opportunities for growth.

- Places: The environments where I AM lives, works, and travels also play a significant role in shaping the life story. Whether it's a familiar place that brings comfort or a new place that challenges I AM to adapt, each location adds depth and dimension to I AM's experiences.

- Things: Material possessions, resources, and technologies are tools that I AM uses to navigate life. While they are not the ultimate goal, the way I AM interacts with these things reflects their priorities, values, and ability to live in positive energy.

- Ideas: Perhaps the most transformative interactions I AM has are with ideas. Whether it's through books, AI conversations, or creative pursuits, ideas inspire I AM to think differently, challenge assumptions, and pursue new paths in life.

By applying the SOARing Process to these four elements, I AM ensures that each interaction serves as an opportunity for improvement and the continuation of a life story that feels better with each passing day.

Big Picture Snapshot: How the System Works

A crucial part of I AM's journey is understanding the Big Picture—the overarching framework that gives context to every choice and action. The Big Picture serves as a visual guide, helping I AM make sense of how the world of improvement seems to work and how to navigate life's flow with greater awareness and intention.

The Big Picture provides I AM with the ability to:

- See life as a continuous flow of time and experiences, moving from the past through NOW and into the future.
- Understand how different parts of life—SOARing processes (activities) and the Feelings Platform (emotions)—interact and shape I AM's overall sense of well-being.
- Prioritize the most important Topics in life at every NOW, ensuring that attention is given to the areas that have the greatest impact on I AM's positive feelings.

The horizontal flow of the Big Picture allows I AM to move from past experiences (which shape the Guidance System), through the present moment (where choices are made), and into the future (where new opportunities for improvement lie).

Vertically, I AM balances two core jobs every moment:

1. Feeling good NOW by focusing on positive energy and enjoying the present.
2. Planning to feel better in the future by making choices that align with I AM's vision and objectives.

The Big Picture helps I AM prioritize the most impactful choices, ensuring that each choice contributes to living a better life story. By understanding the flow of time and process, I AM can manage life's complexities with a greater sense of control and confidence.

Navigating the Big Picture: From Snapshot to Movie

While the Big Picture provides a snapshot of life at any given moment, I AM understands that life is dynamic—always in motion. The Fundamental Flows represent this movement, showing how I AM's life story progresses through time, like a movie. These flows help I AM navigate life not as a series of still moments but as an ongoing, ever-changing journey.

The Fundamental Flows are the movement of I AM's choices and experiences through time. They reveal how life unfolds:

- Natural Flows: These are the universal flows that I AM navigates, such as time, space, and energy. While I AM cannot control these, I AM can learn to navigate them with wisdom, using them as a foundation for growth.
- I AM Flows: These represent the choices I AM consciously makes to shape the present and future. Whether through thinking, feeling, or acting, I AM participates actively in the flow of life, making choices that shape the journey.
- SOARing Flows: These are the flows tied to I AM's continuous improvement. Each SOARing Experience moves I AM toward a better life story, creating a cycle of reflection, action, and evaluation that leads to long-term progress.

The Fundamental Flows transform the static Big Picture into a flowing narrative, one in which I AM not only sees I AM's current place in life but also understands the direction I AM is heading. I AM lives within these flows, using them to navigate every NOW and shape the future with intention.

Building Resilience: Navigating Potholes and Bumps in the Road

Life is not without its challenges, and I AM knows that the journey will include its fair share of potholes and bumps. These obstacles can take many forms—whether it's a difficult relationship, a stressful move, or a setback in personal goals. However, I AM approaches these challenges with resilience, using the SOARing process to bounce back and continue forward.

Resilience is key to maintaining a positive mindset and staying on track toward living a better life story. When faced with negative feelings, I AM knows how to shift focus, recalibrate the Guidance System, and take actions that lead back to positive energy. The key is to keep developing feel-better thoughts!

The SOARing process has helped I AM develop resilience by:

- Helping I AM identify challenges before they become overwhelming.
- Providing a structured way to address problems and turn them into opportunities.
- Encouraging I AM to maintain a long-term perspective, keeping the overall journey in mind.

By viewing setbacks as temporary obstacles on the road to a better life story, I AM remains focused on the bigger picture and continues to move forward with confidence and optimism.

The Feelings Platform: Measuring Progress Through Positive Energy

At the core of I AM's journey is the Feelings Platform, a tool for measuring progress in terms of positive emotions and energy. This platform serves as a feedback loop, guiding I AM through each SE and allowing I AM to evaluate success based on how I AM feels.

I AM's progress is not measured by external achievements or societal standards but by how I AM feels in the present moment. Positive feelings, such as satisfaction, joy, and engagement, indicate that I AM is on the right path, while negative feelings signal the need for reflection and adjustment.

Each SE contributes to the Feelings Platform, adding to the overall sense of well-being that I AM experiences:

- Positive Emotions: Feeling good NOW is always Job #1 for I AM. By focusing on positive emotions, I AM ensures that each step in the journey contributes to a better life story.
- Engagement: When I AM is fully engaged in a task, project, or interaction, I AM experiences a sense of flow and fulfillment. Engagement helps I AM stay connected to the vision and focal points.
- Meaning: I AM's journey is always focused on creating meaning in life. Whether through relationships, ideas, or personal goals, I AM seeks to live a life that is meaningful and impactful.

- ○ Accomplishments: Each SE adds to I AM's list of accomplishments, both big and small. By celebrating these achievements, I AM stays motivated and focused on continuous improvement.
- ○ Positive Relationships: Building and maintaining positive relationships with people is a key component of I AM's journey. These relationships provide support, guidance, and encouragement along the way.

Conclusion: A Roadmap for Young Adults & Other Choice Makers

For people, especially young adults, life can often feel like a whirlwind of choices, responsibilities, and changes. With so many interactions with people, places, things, and ideas, it's easy to become overwhelmed or feel uncertain about the path forward. However, I AM's SOARing Process offers a structured and positive approach to navigating these complexities.

By reflecting on past experiences, embracing the present, and shaping the future with intentionality, I AM's framework teaches that improvement is always possible, no matter the situation. The Big Picture provides the essential context for navigating life's flow, ensuring that every choice and action is aligned with a greater vision. The Fundamental Flows turn this snapshot into a dynamic movie, showing how life unfolds through time and how each choice shapes the next chapter. The Guidance System keeps I AM aligned with I AM's vision and focal points, while the Feelings Platform ensures that every choice and action is evaluated based on how good it feels.

Ultimately, the secret to living a better feeling life story is simple: focus on positive energy, make better choices at every NOW, and to use SOAR, celebrating each step of the improving journey. By doing so, I AM can craft a life story filled with meaning, satisfaction, and continuous growth.

The journey is long, but with resilience, a positive mindset, and the SOARing process as a guide, I AM believes that each of us has the power to create the life story we truly desire, one that is full of joy, fulfillment, and endless opportunities.

FINAL 1-2-3

1. *Use and improve your positive Guidance System at every NOW.*
2. *Make better choices by S + AI synergizing.*
3. *SOAR to a better life story.*

APPENDIX

QUICK 5 STEPS to FEELING BETTER

Quick 5 Steps is a summary of the SOARing process and key charts. It can be referred to for a very general sense of process flow. The charts can be copied for reference, ideating and dreaming.

1. NOW FOCUS: At every NOW, I AM has a very basic choice of where to focus attention.

Essentially, I AM's experience at NOW is created by the thinking, feeling and acting on I AM's choice of focus...the Topic. Focusing on the most important topic with a positive mindset yields the greatest rewards in positive feelings and accomplishments. I AM tries to stay oriented toward Q1 where the prospects of a better life story await to unfold for I AM.

2. I FEEL: At every NOW, I AM naturally has feelings. These feelings arise from the situation, topics within the situation and thoughts about the topic. I AM identifies these feelings by finishing the phrase "I Feel..."

I AM usually answers with positive or negative feeling words. I AM accomplishes Job #1 at each NOW with a focus on finding positive energy words.

3. SE IMPROVEMENT OPTIONS: Improvements start with a SOARing Experience (SE). It uses the SOAR framework as the basis for future actions.

All SOARing begins with what I AM feels NOW (Job #1). Then it goes through what I AM needs and wants in order for I AM to feel better in the future (Job #2). Depending on the situation and I AM's mindset, each new NOW can be perceived as either a problem or an opportunity. I AM SOARs to fix the problem or pursue opportunities.

4. SEs: Each topic to be improved has a SE. The SE is in two parts. Part 1 is the creation of the Improvement Plan (IP). Part 2 is the management of the Improvement Plan through completion.

The IP can begin in either positive or negative energy. If the situation topic is interpreted as a problem, SOAR begins in negative energy with the Objective to solve or fix the problem and return to positive energy. If I AM considers the situation topic to be an opportunity, SOAR begins in the Opportunity Zone (OZ) and SOARs to make the most of the opportunity.

5. IMPROVEMENT PYRAMID: I AM uses the Improvement Pyramid to manage all of life's SEs. By choice, I AM has created a group of areas in life most important to I AM. These are I AM's Life Domains.

I AM tries to focus most of I AM's time and energy optimizing feel-goods in these five areas. I AM uses AI to synergize expansion in each area. I AM focuses all possible SEs toward I AM's Vision with I AM's journey guided by I AM's Focal Points.

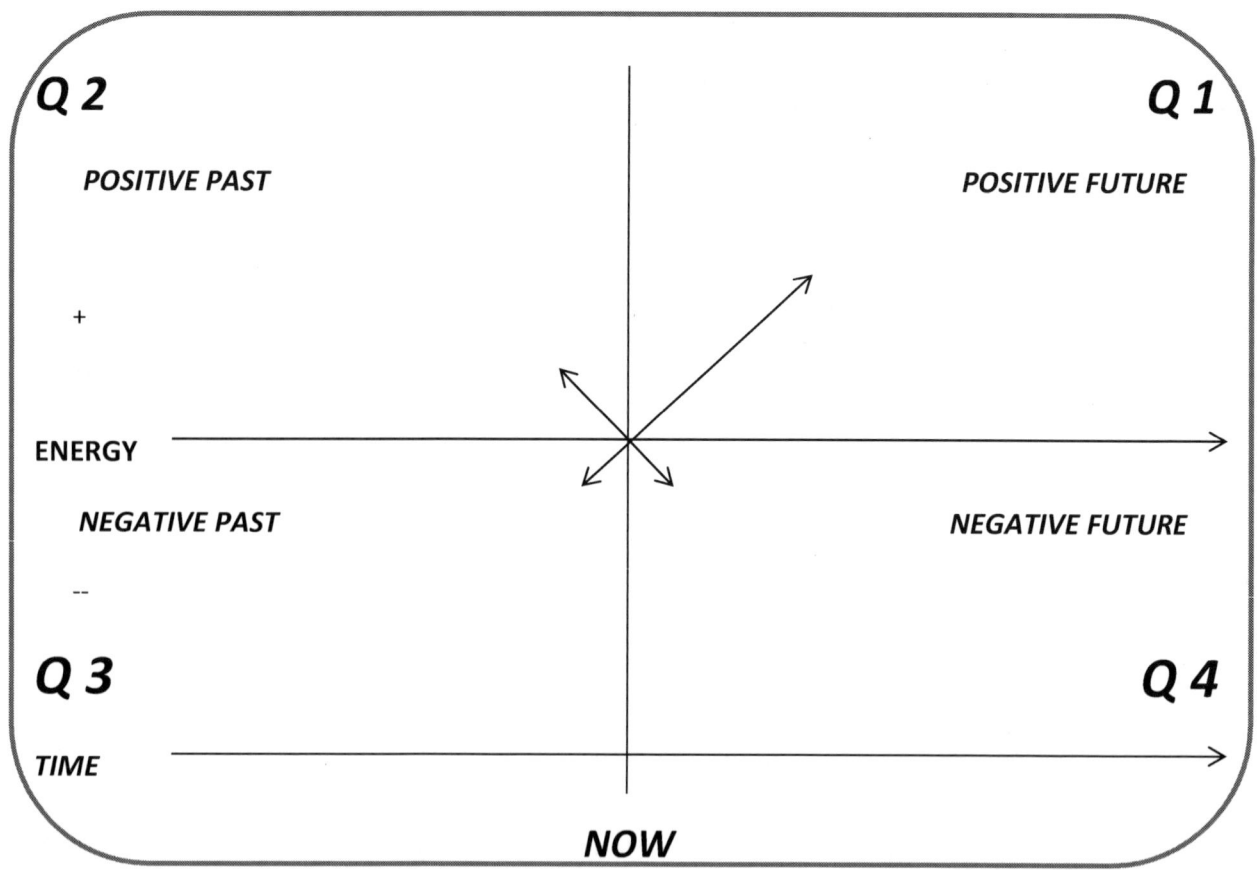

NOW FOCUS

At every NOW, I AM can choose, consciously or unconsciously, to focus attention in any of four basic directions. These are quadrants Q1, Q2, Q3, or Q4. This choice is critically important because it sets the stage for further choice trails, SOARing and life story creating.

I AM's intention is to live in Q1 and Q2 as much time as possible.

1. Job #1 is accomplished in Q1 and Q2. Job #2 is always aimed at Q1.

2. I AM appreciates Q2 because it helped form the basis for all the anticipations of Quadrant 1. Q2 reflection on a positive past puts I AM in a positive mindset about creating a positive future in Q1.

3. I AM tries to invest little time in dwelling in a negative past. The facts can't be changed, only I AM's meanings and feelings can be addressed at NOW and possibly turned positive.

4. I AM considers negative futures in certain situations; such as for a Plan B, risk analysis, situational awareness, SWOT Analysis, etc. Otherwise, I AM's focus remains on Q1.

A focus on living NOW in positive energy Q1 and Q2 creates positive energy mindsets and better life stories. Consider all the positive energy rewards in Q1, Q2 and the disharmony in Q3 and Q4.

FOCUS ALTERNATIVES @ NOW

Q 2   POSITIVE PAST   POSITIVE FUTURE   Q 1

• Harmony	* God - Heaven	* Harmony	* God - Heaven
• Satisfactions	* Good Memories	* Satisfactions	* Opportunity
• Solutions	* Aligned	* Solutions	* Alignment
• Fulfilled	* Good Habits	* Fulfillment	* Better Habits
• Successes	* Love	* Successes	* Love
• Strengths	* Expanded	* Strengths	* Self-Actualizing
• Growth	* Gratitude	* Growth	* Hope
• Positive Attitude	* Nostalgia	* Positive Attitude	* Optimism
• Positive Experiences	* Blessed	* Positive Expectations	* Excitement
• Confidence	* Serenity	* Confidence	* Creation
• Lessons Learned	* Enlightened	* Lifelong Learning	* Enthusiasm
• Improvement Focus	* Joy	* Improvement Focus	* Joy

ENERGY:

NEGATIVE PAST   NEGATIVE FUTURE

• Disharmony	* Devil - Hell	* Disharmony	* Devil - Hell
• Dissatisfactions	* Bad Memories	* Dissatisfactions	* Bad Memories
• Problems	* Harm	* Problems	* Dread
• Lack	* Bad Habits	* Lack	* Bad Habits
• Failures	* Hate	* Failures	* Hate
• Weaknesses	* Lethargy	* Weakness	* Fear
• Status Quo/Decline	* Grief	* Decline/Entropy	* Threatened
• Negative Attitude	* Lonesomeness	* Negative Attitude	* Confusion
• Negative Expectations	* Anger	* Negative Expectations	* Helplessness
• Insecurity	* Vulnerability	* Insecurity	* Pessimism
• Unlearned Lessons	* Betrayal	* Unlearned Lessons	* Powerlessness
• Discouragement	* Overwhelmed	* Uncertainty	* Overwhelmed

Q 3   NOW   Q 4

"I FEEL..." POSITIVE ENERGY WORDS

I AM has two jobs to do at every NOW.

1. JOB #1: To feel good.

2. JOB #2: To plan to feel better in the future.

Both jobs center on I AM feeling good and enjoying life. Both jobs focus on I AM's positive energy. This positive energy is expressed in positive feeling words and phrases.

At NOW, I AM simply completes the phrase "I feel..."

Here is a starter list of positive words that I AM frequently uses. There are hundreds of other words and positive connotation words/phrases in English and other languages that I AM can choose to use.

Advancement	Curiosity	Healed	Optimism
Affection	Delight	Healthy	Passion
Alignment	Eagerness	Hopeful	Peace
Alive	Empathy	Improvement	Pleasure
Amusement	Empowered	Informed	Positive
Appreciated	Energized	Inspired	Progress
Awakened	Enthusiastic	Interested	Safe
Beauty	Excitement	Invigorated	Satisfaction
Better	Expansion	Joy	Self-Actualizing
Bliss	Flourishing	Kindness	Selfless
Calmness	Free	Love	SOARing
Carefree	Fulfillment	Motivated	Spiritual
Cheerful	Gratitude	New Person	Successful
Confident	Growth	Normal	Thriving
Contentment	Happy	Oneness	Well-Being

I AM has found that using positive words helps immediately raise I AM's emotional state, directs focus onto the good aspects of the Topic, keeps I AM fully in NOW and improves interactions with others.

By consistently using positive words, I AM builds a positive mindset that I AM brings to new situations. This "finding the good" in things helps I AM find opportunities and solutions rather than problems and obstacles.

I AM feels that by using positive words in everyday vocabulary, I AM not only enhances I AM's current emotional state, but also builds a foundation for long-term well-being and success.

"I FEEL…" NEGATIVE ENERGY WORDS

Sometimes, I AM experiences thoughts about a situation or topic that drags I AM into feeling negative emotions. I AM acknowledges those feelings when I AM completes "I Feel…" with negative energy words such as:

Anger	Grief	Overwhelmed	Self-Consciousness
Anxiety	Guilt	Pain	Selfish
Blame	Hatred	Panic	Shame
Boredom	Hostility	Pessimism	Sorrow
Depression	Impatience	Powerless	Stressed
Despair	Insecure	Pressure	Suffering
Difficulty	Irritated	Rage	Threatened
Disapproval	Jealousy	Regret	Troubled
Down	Misery	Resentment	Unhappy
Embarrassment	Negative	Sadness	Worry
Failure	Nervous	Self-Centered	Worthless

Using these or the hundreds of other negative energy words, negative connotation words and negative phrases can cause I AM problems.

When I AM uses negative words, simply describing the feelings can reinforce and intensify the emotions and pull I AM deeper into the negative state being experienced. The Law of Attraction suggests that these negative words keep attracting more and more negative energy words and the attached emotions. It can be a downward spiral of negativity that can affect everyone around I AM.

I AM has noticed that dwelling on the negative can cause immediate physiological reactions like increased stress, tension, or discomfort.

The more the negative words get used, the more I AM gets into the rut of habitual negative thinking. This becomes a negative mindset that I AM starts bringing to every NOW. This habit can have wide-ranging and long-term negative consequences. I AM has discovered that finding feel-better thoughts and associated words is the primary way to shift back to a more positive emotional state.

These feel-better thoughts can be focused on a combination of acknowledging the feelings, shifting thoughts to a different focus and engaging in positive actions. That is, recognize that it is a negative feeling, shift to a better feeling Topic and execute a SOARing Experience to climb back into positive emotions.

I AM knows that Job #1 is to feel good and enjoy NOW. Feeling negative emotions is not conducive to achieving Job #1.

SE IMPROVEMENT OPTIONS

I AM believes that most humans have a natural desire to improve their conditions. The improvement seeking comes in many forms, such as:

- Self-actualization.
- Betterment of living conditions.
- More knowledge.
- Better emotional well-being.
- Personal growth.

I AM chooses to improve both the short-term (Job #1) and longer-term (Job #2). New NOW Situations come as problems or opportunities. The problems are improved with solutions or getting out of negative energy back to positive energy. The opportunities are improved from positive energy to higher level or more long-lasting positive energy.

To improve anything, I AM uses the SOARing Experience (SE),

The Improvement Options chart shows the basic alternative SE models I AM uses for different Situations.

1. I AM's X is always placed somewhere on the vertical NOW Line.
2. The X location reflects I AM's current Situation (S) feelings about the Topic.
3. The NOW Line is where I AM seeks to accomplish Job #1 and Job #2.
4. X is the starting point for all SOAR.
5. From X, I AM chooses Objectives (O).
6. Objectives are what I AM needs (must have) or wants (like to have).
7. The arrow between X and O represents the Improvement Plan or Action Plan.
8. This line represents the Action (A) steps I AM plans to take in order to reach the O.

On the chart:

- Job # 1 is I AM's current feelings about the Topic, scaled at grades A –F.
- Job #2 starts with the Objectives I AM seeks to achieve. This can be over any length of time.
- The X-O arrow represents the Action Plan.
- The R is the planned achievement of the Objectives.

The SE can be used in I AM's attempt at the improvement of anything.

SE IMPROVEMENT OPTIONS

PROBLEMS   ## *OPPORTUNITIES*

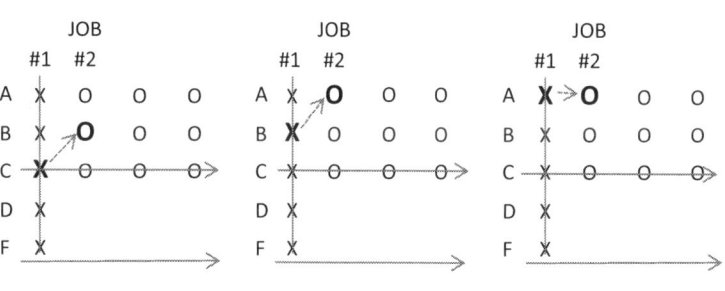

S = X @ F
O = C+ in Short Time
A = Action Plan
R = C+ in Short time

S = X @ D
O = C+ in Short Time
A = Action Plan
R = C+ in Short Time

S = X @ C
O = B in Short Time
A = Action Plan
R = B in Short Time

S = X @ B
O = A in Short Time
A = Action Plan
R = A in Short Time

S = X @ A
O = Continue A
A = Action Plan
R = Continue A

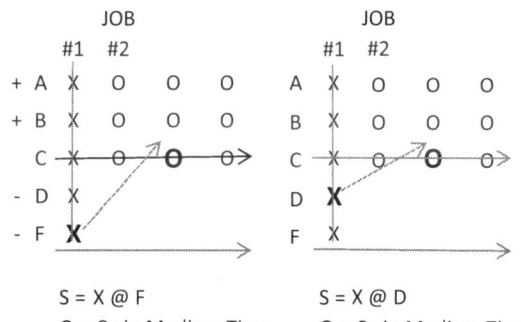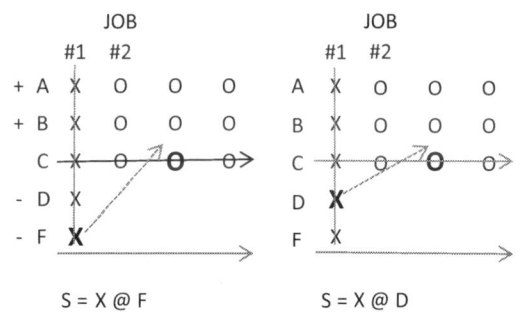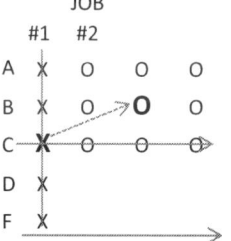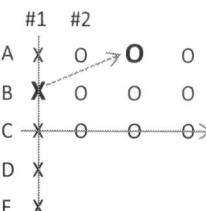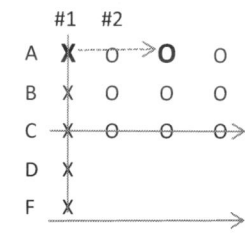

S = X @ F
O = C+ in Medium Time
A = Action Plan
R = C+ in Medium Time

S = X @ D
O = C+ in Medium Time
A = Action Plan
R = C+ in Medium Time

S = X @ C
O = B in Medium Time
A = Action Plan
R = B in Medium Time

S = X @ B
O = A in Medium Time
A = Action Plan
R = A in Medium Time

S = X @ A
O = Continue A
A = Action Plan
R = Continue A

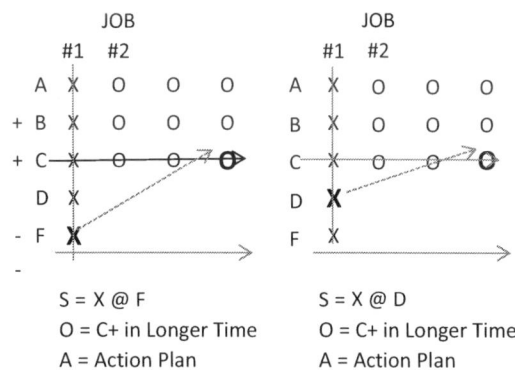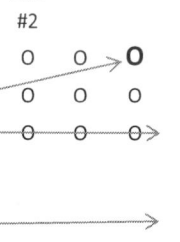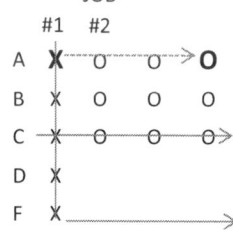

S = X @ F
O = C+ in Longer Time
A = Action Plan
R = C+ in Longer Time

S = X @ D
O = C+ in Longer Time
A = Action Plan
R = C+ in Longer Time

S = X @ C
O = B in Longer Time
A = Action Plan
R = B in Longer Time

S = X @ B
O = A in Longer Time
A = Action Plan
R = A in Longer Time

S = X @ A
O = Continue A
A = Action Plan
R = Continue A

Solve Problems with feel-better thoughts & actions.   Pursue Opportunities with positive energy, thoughts and actions.

SOARing EXPERIENCE (SE)

At each NOW, I AM makes choices about how to respond to the new Situation, the Topic of focus, and what to do next.

If I AM chooses to improve something, then the SOAR process is used. This is the simple framework of S, O, A, R.

- SITUATION: I AM's perception of the set of circumstances Here NOW.
- OBJECTIVES: I AM's desired improvements to help I AM feel better, achievable by an intended time.
- ACTIONS: The process of I AM doing things or taking steps to achieve the Objectives.
- RESULTS: The consequences, effects, or outcomes from I AM's Actions.

The improvement framework is visualized as a SOARing Experience. I AM goes through these basic steps.

1. I AM chooses the Topic…the most important thing NOW.

2. I AM thinks, feels and acts on that Topic.

3. What I AM feels about the Topic is reflected on the chart by placing I AM's X somewhere on the NOW Line. Positive feelings are reflected by an X in the Opportunity Zone (OZ) above the Energy Line. Negative feelings are reflected on the chart by an X in the Problem Zone (PZ) below the Energy Line.

4. I AM chooses what is needed or desired by when and places the O (Objectives) to the upper right of the X. The location is determined by the height of the aspiration and the time it should take to achieve the Objective.

5. I AM then creates an Improvement Plan that contains the Action steps necessary to achieve the Objectives. An example is 1. 2. 3. on the chart.

6. As time goes by, I AM monitors and measures progress of each step of the Improvement Plan at various midpoints.

7. I AM reviews the monitoring and measuring results and chooses how to manage next steps at new NOWs.

8. Hopefully I AM achieves the Objectives on time, indicated on the Time Line with a vertical mark.

9. Celebrate the process and the achievements!

SE FEELINGS PLATFORM

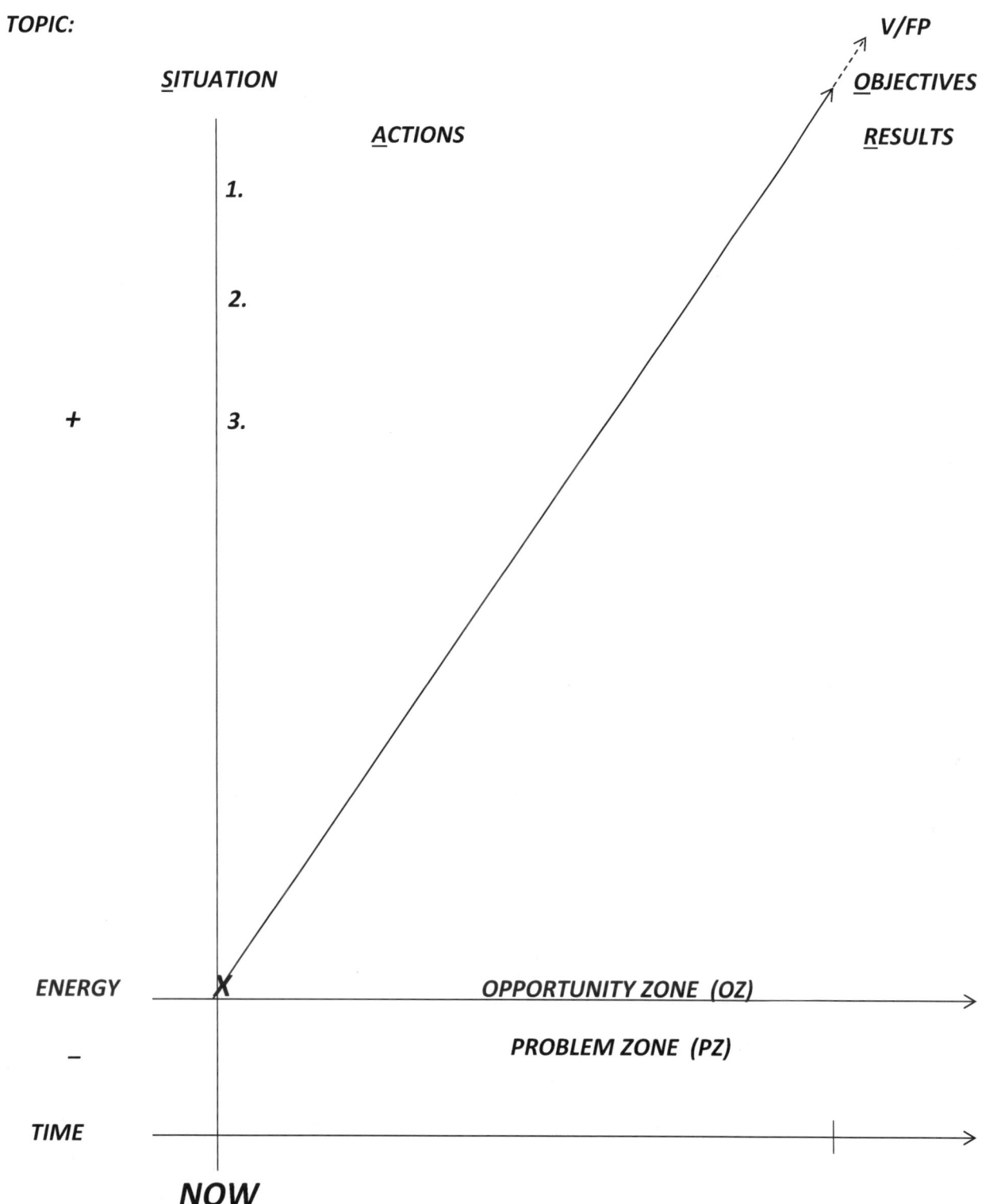

TOPIC:

V/FP

SITUATION

OBJECTIVES

ACTIONS

RESULTS

1.

2.

+   3.

ENERGY   X   OPPORTUNITY ZONE (OZ)

–   PROBLEM ZONE (PZ)

TIME

NOW

IMPROVEMENT PLAN MANAGEMENT

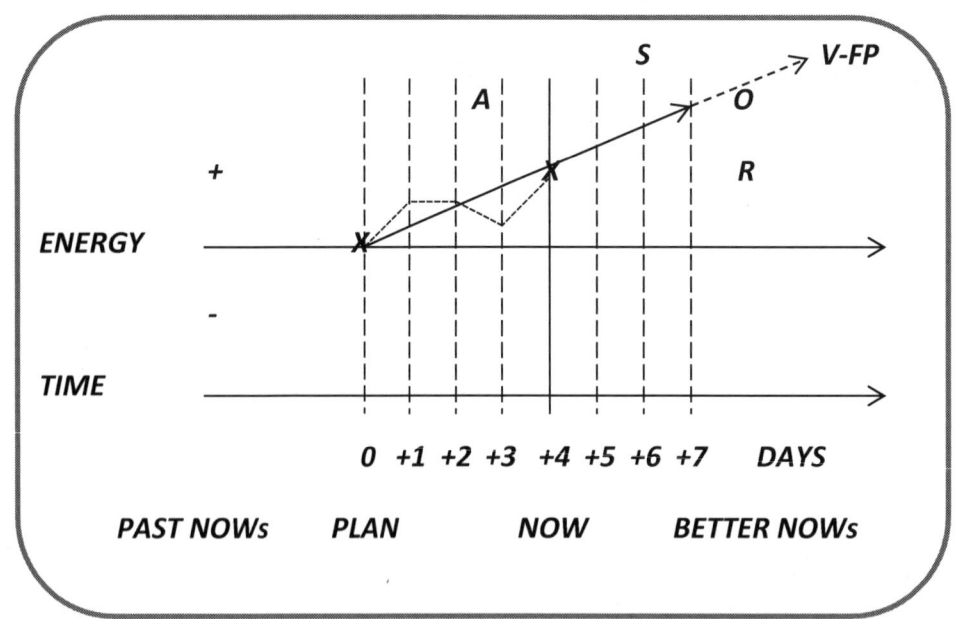

When I AM chooses to try to improve something, I AM creates a SE. The SE highlights I AM's interpretation of the Situation, defines I AM's Objectives and creates an Improvement Plan (aka Action Plan) that is intended to map the journey to achieving the Objectives.

The Improvement Plan lays out the steps necessary to achieve the Objectives. Each step is monitored, measured and managed. Essentially…

1. I AM monitors by paying close attention to each step to assess that what was intended to happen actually does happen.

2. One of the requirements of good Objectives is that they are quantifiable. So I AM measures each step to determine what actual quantification is appropriate for each step.

3. I AM manages this feedback and makes appropriate choices about what, if any, adjustments need to be made before going forward.

On the chart, I AM's Objectives are intended to be reached on Day 7. I AM monitors, measures and manages the results each day at the end of each day.

Day 1, exceeds plan. Day 2 meets plan, but is trending down. Day 3, downward trend continues. Adjustments are needed. Day 4: adjustments are made and I AM is back on plan.

The entire plan can use AI input to help I AM analyze the Situation, develop Objectives and develop, monitor, measure and manage Actions. Just ask.

SOARing EXPERIENCE (SE)

TOPIC:

SITUATION:

OBJECTIVES: To...

ACTIONS: **IMPROVEMENT PLAN**

1.

2.

3.

RESULTS:

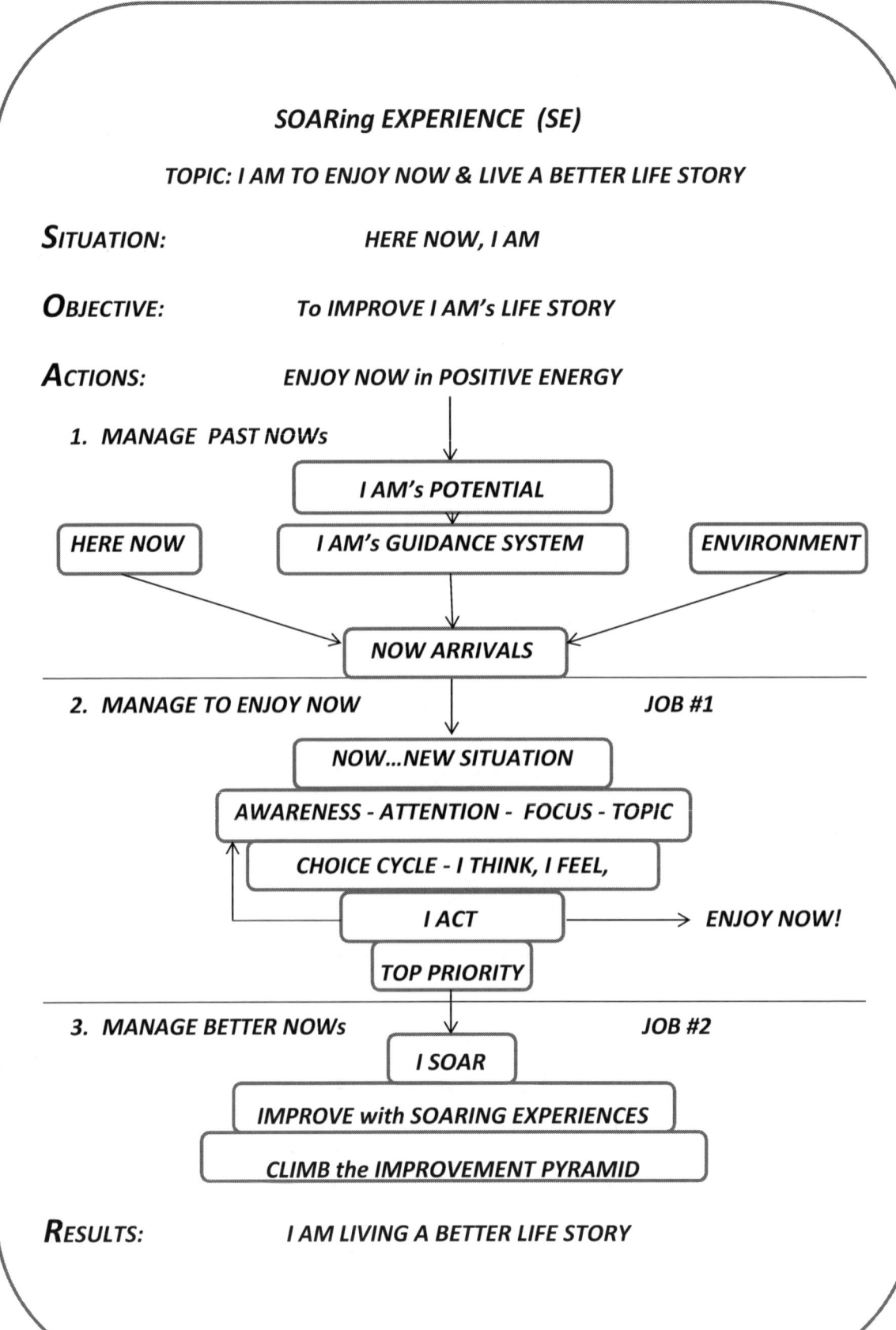

SOARing EXPERIENCE (SE)

TOPIC: I AM TO ENJOY NOW & LIVE A BETTER LIFE STORY

SITUATION: HERE NOW, I AM

OBJECTIVE: To IMPROVE I AM's LIFE STORY

ACTIONS: ENJOY NOW in POSITIVE ENERGY

1. MANAGE PAST NOWs

I AM's POTENTIAL

HERE NOW — I AM's GUIDANCE SYSTEM — ENVIRONMENT

NOW ARRIVALS

2. MANAGE TO ENJOY NOW   JOB #1

NOW...NEW SITUATION

AWARENESS - ATTENTION - FOCUS - TOPIC

CHOICE CYCLE - I THINK, I FEEL,

I ACT → ENJOY NOW!

TOP PRIORITY

3. MANAGE BETTER NOWs   JOB #2

I SOAR

IMPROVE with SOARING EXPERIENCES

CLIMB the IMPROVEMENT PYRAMID

RESULTS: I AM LIVING A BETTER LIFE STORY

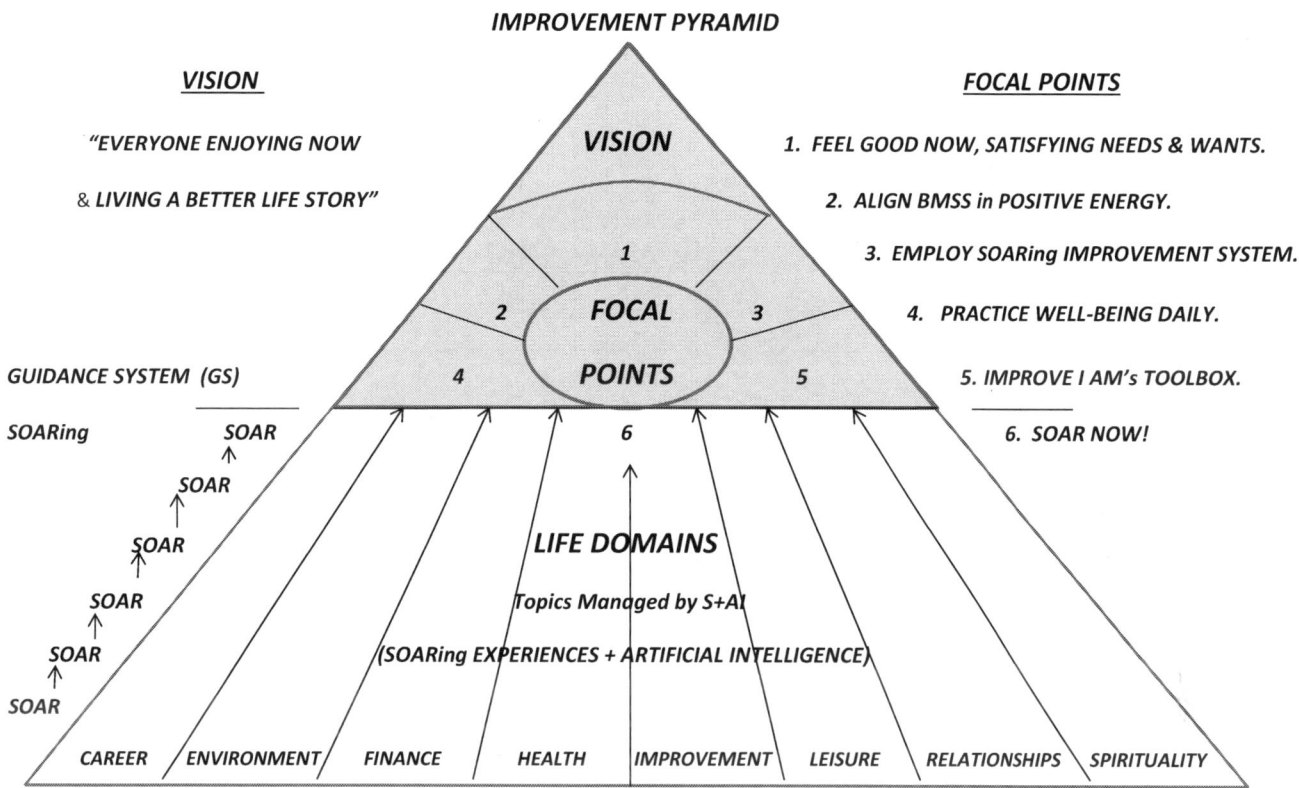

IMPROVEMENT PYRAMID

VISION

"EVERYONE ENJOYING NOW

& LIVING A BETTER LIFE STORY"

VISION

FOCAL POINTS

1. FEEL GOOD NOW, SATISFYING NEEDS & WANTS.

2. ALIGN BMSS in POSITIVE ENERGY.

3. EMPLOY SOARing IMPROVEMENT SYSTEM.

4. PRACTICE WELL-BEING DAILY.

5. IMPROVE I AM's TOOLBOX.

6. SOAR NOW!

FOCAL POINTS

GUIDANCE SYSTEM (GS)

SOARing

SOAR
SOAR
SOAR
SOAR
SOAR
SOAR

LIFE DOMAINS

Topics Managed by S+AI

(SOARing EXPERIENCES + ARTIFICIAL INTELLIGENCE)

CAREER | ENVIRONMENT | FINANCE | HEALTH | IMPROVEMENT | LEISURE | RELATIONSHIPS | SPIRITUALITY

KEEP THINKING "FEEL-BETTER" THOUGHTS

TOPIC:

COMMON DENOMINATOR

SOARing	SCIENTIFIC METHOD	PROBLEM SOLVING	DECISION MAKING	LONG-TERM PLANNING	MEDICAL PRACTICE	PROJECT MANAGEMENT	ORGANIZATION MANAGEMENT	RELIGION	ABRAHAM-HICKS	TRAVEL	TONY ROBBINS
				SPECIALIZED PROCESSES							
SITUATION	OBSERVATION	PROBLEM	ALTERNATIVES	NEED FOR PLAN	MALADY	PROJECT	PEOPLE	LIFE & DEATH	CONTRAST	JOURNEY NEED/WANT	LIVING LIFE
OBJECTIVES	QUESTION ANSWERED	FIX PROBLEM	BEST CHOICE	WRITTEN PLAN	WELLNESS / DO NO HARM	SUCCESSFUL COMPLETION	VISION / MISSION	GOOD LIFE / SALVATION	WELL-BEING	DESTINATION	IMPROVE QUALITY of LIFE
ACTIONS	1. HYPOTHESIS 2. PREDICTION 3. TEST	1. ALTERNATIVES 2. EVALUATION 3. CHOOSE "BEST" 4. TEST "BEST"	1. EVALUATE 2. CHOOSE "BEST"	1. VISION 2. MISSION 3. OBJECTIVES 4. ACTION PLAN * STRATEGIES * TACTICS	1. DIAGNOSIS 2. TREATMENT 3. FOLLOW-UP	1. INITIATE 2. PLAN 3. IMPLEMENT 4. CONTROL 5. END	1. MANAGEMENT BY OBJECTIVES 2. POSDCORB	BELIEF FAITH SURRENDER ETC.	ASK for WANTS ALIGN ALLOW RECEIVE	WALK, FLY, DRIVE, ETC. ROUTE, WAYPOINTS TIMELINE RESERVATIONS COSTS, PAYMENTS TRAVEL	FOCUS GIVE MEANING DO
RESULTS	ANSWER (PROVEN, DISPROVEN, OPEN)	PROBLEM FIXED	BEST CHOICE	WRITTEN PLAN	WELLNESS	SUCCESS	ACHIEVEMENT — Plan, Organize, Staff, Direct, COordinate, Report, Budget	GOOD LIFE / SALVATION	WELL-BEING	ARRIVE DESTINATION	IMPROVED QUALITY of LIFE

IAM + AI GLOSSARY

A: Action or Actions.

AI: Artificial Intelligence.

ABILITY: I AM's having the capacity to do something.

ACCOMPLISHMENT: I AM meeting or exceeding I AM's Objectives.

ACTION PLAN: Improvement Plan.

ACTIONS: The process of I AM doing things or taking steps to achieve the Objectives.

ACTIVITIES: Things being done.

ALIGN BMSS: I AM's feeling of connection, oneness, agreement, or being in sync with something in positive energy.

ALIGNMENT: I AM's feeling of connection, oneness, agreement, or being in sync with something.

ALTERNATIVES: A group of two or more things from which I AM can choose.

APTITUDE: I AM's having the natural ability to do something.

ARTIFICIAL INTELLIGENCE: Computer simulation of human intelligence.

ATTENTION: I AM's taking notice of someone or something.

ATTITUDE: I AM's positive or negative feeling or thinking about a situation, thing, person or group.

AWARENESS: I AM's field of knowledge or perception of a situation or facts.

BALANCE: The condition in which different elements are in appropriate proportions.

BEHAVIOR: I AM's actions in response to external or internal stimuli.

BELIEFS: Things I AM accepts to be true, repeated over and over again.

BETTER CHOICES: Using the Guidance System, improving the process that considers multiple alternatives to choose the best.

BETTER LIFE STORY: From NOW on, living more and more of life in positive energy seeking higher and higher emotional levels.

BETTER NOWs: I AM feeling better in future NOWs than I AM feels NOW.

BIG PICTURE: I AM flowing through the world of improvement as it seems to work.

BMSS: Body. Mind. Soul. Spirit.

BMSS PARTNERSHIP: The synergistic collaboration of I AM's physical and nonphysical parts intending to help I AM live and grow in positive energy.

BODY: The physical structure part of I AM.

CAREER: I AM's line of work.

CAUSE/EFFECT: An action that leads to a result.

CHANGE: Something different.

CHAOS: The feeling I AM can experience when I AM is in Negative Energy.

CHARACTER: I AM's distinctive mental and moral qualities.

CHOICE: The act of selecting something after considering multiple alternatives.

CHOICE CYCLE: I AM's I Think, I Feel, I Act process of making choices at NOW.

CHOICE FLOW: The continuous stream of selecting something after considering multiple alternatives.

CHOICES & DECISIONS: I AM's selecting something after considering multiple alternatives.

COMFORT ZONE: The emotional state in which I AM feels contentment.

COMPETENCE: I AM's ability to use knowledge, abilities and skills to successfully perform tasks.

CONFIDENCE: I AM's belief in I AM's abilities to succeed.

CONSCIOUSNESS: The state of being aware of and able to think about I AM's own existence, thoughts and surroundings.

CONSCIOUSNESS FLOW: The continuous stream of thoughts, feelings, and experiences that pass through I AM's mind.

CONTENTMENT: I AM's feeling of satisfaction in calm positive energy.

CONTINUOUS IMPROVEMENT: I AM's journey of focusing on SOARing to improve I AM and I AM's surroundings.

CREATOR: That which brought our Universe into existence.

DECISION: I AM's selecting something after considering multiple alternatives.

DIRECTION: The orientation I AM faces or moves.

DISHARMONY: The feeling I AM experiences when I AM is in negative energy.

EDUCATION: I AM in the process of receiving and/or giving knowledge.

EMOTIONS: I AM's strong feelings.

ENERGY: The vibrational power flowing throughout the universe that is part of everything.

ENERGY FLOW: The dynamic movement and utilization of energy.

ENERGY LINE: The horizontal arrow separating positive energy from negative energy.

ENGAGEMENT: I AM's state of total involvement in and flowing with a task.

ENHANCEMENT: The process of improving the value, quality or extent of something.

ENJOY NOW: I AM SOARing in positive energy NOW.

ENVIRONMENT: Everything in the universe except Here NOW and I AM.

ESSENCE: I AM's fundamental qualities.

ETHICS: The principles of morally right conduct by I AM.

EXPERIENCES: What I AM goes through or takes part in that helps I AM learn, grow, or feel something.

FACTS: What I AM thinks is true or correct about who, what, when, where, why and how.

FAILURE: Lack of success.

FEEL BAD: I AM in negative energy.

FEEL BETTER: I AM feeling improvement from NOW to a future NOW.

FEEL-BETTER THOUGHTS: Positive energy thoughts.

FEEL GOOD: I AM in positive energy.

FEEL GOOD NOW: Job #1.

FEEL HARMONY: I AM's feelings when in alignment with positive energy.

FEELINGS: I AM's emotional responses.

FEELINGS PLATFORM: The scorecard I AM uses to understand how well I AM is doing with the SOARing Process.

FEELINGS WORD LIST I FEEL…: (Positive and Negative Energy words)

FEELS: I AM's emotional responses.

FINANCE: The management of money.

FLOW: The way things move and change over time, always interacting and affecting each other.

FOCAL POINTS: The most important long-term centers of attention guiding the pursuits of I AM's Vision.

FOCUS: I AM's center of attention at NOW.

FOCUS FUNNEL: A conceptual funnel that screens a mass of information down to only the most interesting information for I AM's further consideration.

FRAMEWORK: A model of the essential supporting structure of something.

FREE WILL: I AM's capability to freely make choices, decisions and to take action.

FUNDAMENTAL: The basic foundational principles upon which something is based.

FUNDAMENTAL FLOWS: The basic foundational flows from which other things develop.

FUTURE: The time after NOW.

GROWTH CYCLE: The improvement process I AM experiences when SOARing.

GUIDANCE SYSTEM: I AM's Vision and Focal Points…the guides of I AM's life story journey.

HABITS: I AM's behaviors that are routine, repeated regularly and usually subconsciously.

HAPPINESS: I AM's state of emotional well-being.

HAPPY: I AM feeling or exhibiting enjoyment or satisfaction with a situation.

HARMONY: The feeling I AM experiences when I AM is in positive energy.

HEALTH: I AM's state of complete physical, mental and social well-being.

HERE NOW: Space and time arranged as a specific place at a specific moment of clock time.

HERE NOW, I AM: I AM in this location at this clock time.

HIERARCHY: A system of organizing things by levels with one above another.

HOPE: I AM's expectation that I AM will have positive experiences.

I ACT…: I AM taking action and doing things or taking steps toward an objective.

I AM: A fictional character acting as an example of I AM's perspectives on SOARing ideas and life story improvement.

I AM FLOWS: The dynamic process unique to individuals, shaping thought, experiences, navigational choices, feelings and actions.

I AM SOARing: I AM using SOAR to create improvements.

I AM's BIG PICTURE: I AM joining the natural positive flow of the universe.

I AM's QUEST: I AM's pursuit of enjoying NOW and living a better life story.

I AM's TOOLBOX: I AM's distinctive attributes.

I FEEL…: Emotions and feelings I AM is experiencing.

I FEEL…GOOD, BAD, BETTER: I Feel…good, bad or better.

I FEEL…SCALES: Quantification of I AM's "I FEEL…" on the NOW Line.

I SOAR…: I AM creating intentional improvement with the SOARing Process.

I THINK…: Thoughts I AM is thinking, like ideas, perceptions, opinions, etc.

IMPROVEMENT: The process of changing something for the better.

IMPROVEMENT FLOW: The dynamic, ongoing and cumulative process of enhancements and optimizations over time.

IMPROVEMENT LINE: The solid arrow connecting the X to the O, representing I AM's Improvement Plan.

IMPROVEMENT PLAN: The planned series of steps intended to be taken to achieve the Objectives.

IMPROVEMENT PYRAMID: The visual framework for helping I AM navigate I AM's life story.

IMPROVEMENT SYSTEM (SIS): The three key visual frameworks I AM uses to manage I AM's life.

INTELLIGENCE: I AM's ability to solve complex problems or to make choices with results benefiting I AM.

INTENTION: I AM's plan to do specific things on purpose to reach objectives.

INTENTIONAL IMPROVEMENT: I AM's plan to do positive things on purpose to make I AM feel better.

INTERACTION LINE: The arrow representing the interaction between I Think and I Feel.

INTUITION: I AM's ability to know something without having to think about it.

JOB #1 & JOB #2: The two jobs I AM has at every NOW.

JOB #1: To feel good NOW.

JOB #2: To plan to feel better in the future.

JOURNEY: An act of traveling from one place to another.

JUDGMENT: I AM's ability to make a choice or form an opinion after careful thought.

KEY TOPIC AREAS: Topics in I AM's main fields of interest.

KISS: Keep It Super Simple!

KNOWLEDGE: All that I AM knows about a Topic or Topics.

LAW OF ATTRACTION: The concept that I AM's thoughts attract more similar thoughts of the same positive or negative energy.

LEADING EDGE: The NOW Line.

LEGACY: The long-lasting impact of a person's life.

LEISURE: I AM's free time.

LESSONS: Things I AM has learned.

LIFE: The process of living.

LIFE DOMAINS: I AM's most important areas of long-term interest and activity.

LIFE EVENT: A significant occurrence or change in I AM's life that often has a lasting impact.

LIFE EXPERIENCES: The cumulative events, interactions, and situations I AM encounters over time.

LIFE MANAGEMENT: I AM's planning, organizing and controlling I AM's life.

LIFE PLAN: I AM's way of defining and organizing I AM's life story intentions and the steps to achieve a better life story.

LIFE STORY: The account of everything that happens in I AM's life.

LIFE STORY FLOW: I AM's navigation of life by making a continuous progression of choices.

LIFETIME: The time I AM is alive.

LIVE HARMONY: I AM's life lived in positive energy.

LIVING: The continuous interaction between I AM and the environment.

LUCK: I AM's success or failure apparently brought by chance, not by I AM's actions.

MANAGE: I AM to supervise, direct and control progress towards I AM's Objectives.

MANAGEMENT: I AM's being in charge of and responsible for I AM's life story.

MASLOW NEEDS: Abraham Maslow's theory of human motivation by needs and their satisfaction.

MATTER: The material substance that constitutes the observable universe, and together with energy, forms the basis of all objective phenomena.

MATTER FLOW: The movement and transformation of matter through different states and locations.

MEANING: The cognitive or emotional significance I AM experiences to a word, concept, sign or symbolic act.

MEASURE: I AM to systematically evaluate quality and quantity measurements of progress towards I AM's Objectives.

MEASURE: to MANAGE The concept that what gets measured gets managed.

MEMORY: I AM's ability to remember things from the past.

MIDPOINTS: Intermediate points in time in the Improvement Plan where I AM reviews progress towards the Objectives.

MIND: A nonphysical part of I AM that is responsible for thinking, reasoning, feeling, remembering, imagining, perceiving, ideating, sensing, etc.

MINDSET: I AM's mental state of thoughts, attitudes and beliefs reflecting either positive or negative energy.

MINDSET MANAGER: I AM as active manager of I AM's mindset.

MONITOR: I AM to systematically check on progress towards I AM's Objectives.

MOODS: I AM's temporary, general emotional state at a particular time.

MORALS: The ethical values or principles I AM uses to guide I AM's behavior.

MOTIVATION: The reason I AM accomplishes SOARing Experiences.

NATURAL FLOWS: The fundamental processes in nature that operate independently of human intervention.

NEEDS: Topics I AM must have.

NEEDS SATISFACTION: Topics I AM must have, satisfied.

NEGATIVE CHANGE: I AM to experience or experiencing something worse.

NEGATIVE ENERGY: Bad energy vibrations that I AM can align with and feel bad.

NEGATIVE FEELINGS: Bad energy vibrations that I AM can align with and feel bad.

NEGATIVE STRESS: The bad emotional or physical tension I AM perceives as negative energy in response to a situation.

NEGATIVE WORDS LIST I FEEL...: (Negative Emotions)

NEUTRALITY: I AM has no interest in something.

NO CHANGE: I AM to experience or experiencing nothing different.

NONPHYSICAL: The part of I AM not concerning the body.

NOW: The present moment in I AM's clock time.

NOW ARRIVALS: Environment, Here NOW and I AM arriving at NOW, having become all that they are until NOW.

NOW LINE The vertical line representing the present moment in time.

O Objectives or Objectives.

O PLACEMENT: Locating the O on the SOARing Platform.

OBJECTIVES: I AM's desired improvements to help I AM feel better, achievable by an intended time.

ONE PAGER: What I AM gets after I AM thinks about something long enough to write its essence on one page.

OPINIONS: I AM's thoughts, beliefs or judgments about someone or something, based on facts or not.

OPPORTUNITY: A situation that makes it possible for I AM to do something I AM needs or wants to do, improve, or newly create.

OPPORTUNITY ZONE: The Feelings Platform upper right quadrant representing I AM's greatest chances for improvement.

OZ: Opportunity Zone.

PASSIONS: Strong interest or enthusiasm I AM has for something.

PAST: The time before NOW.

PAST NOWs: NOWs that have happened in the past.

PEAK EXPERIENCE: A profound, often transformative, moment that stands out as exceptionally meaningful, fulfilling, or joyful.

PERCEPTION: I AM's being aware through the senses or the mind.

PERSONAL RESOURCES: Time, talents and treasure are the three personal resources I AM can offer to any SOARing Experience.

PERSONALITY: I AM's characteristic sets of cognitions, emotional patterns and behaviors.

PERSPECTIVE: I AM's particular way of looking at situations and topics.

PHYSICAL: The part of I AM concerning the body.

PLAN: I AM's intention about what I AM is going to do.

POSITIVE CHANGE: I AM to experience or experiencing something better.

POSITIVE ENERGY: Good energy vibrations that I AM can align with and feel good.

POSITIVE FEELINGS: Good energy vibrations that I AM can align with and feel good.

POSITIVE STRESS: The good emotional or physical tension I AM perceives as positive energy in response to a situation.

POTENTIAL: I AM's energy capacity for what I AM can become in the future.

PRESENT: NOW.

PRINCIPLES: The fundamental rules I AM lives by.

PRIORITY: Something I AM regards as more important than anything else at this time.

PROBLEM: A Situation I AM defines as unacceptable, unresolved, broken, or harmful that needs to be fixed or solved.

PROBLEM ZONE: The Feelings Platform lower right quadrant representing I AM's opportunity to return to the Opportunity Zone as soon as possible.

PROGRESS LINE: The dashed line connecting the X to the O, reflecting I AM's progress on I AM's Improvement Plan.

PURPOSE: I AM's SOARing journey in alignment with I AM's reason for being.

PZ Problem Zone.

QUADRANTS: A chart divided into four quarters by two lines intersecting each other at right angles.

QUALITY OF LIFE: I AM's satisfaction with I AM's living conditions.

QUEST: I AM's pursuit of living a better life story.

QUICK START: Fast guide of how to use the SOARing Platform.

R Results.

REALITY: That which genuinely exists.

RELATIONSHIPS: I AM's connections with other people, places or things.

REALIZING POTENTIAL: I AM SOARing and becoming all that I AM can become.

RESILIENCE: I AM's ability to adjust to and bounce back from challenging life experiences.

RESISTANCE: I AM's reluctance or refusal to accept or comply with something.

RESPONSE: I AM's reaction to a stimulus.

RESULTS The consequences, effects, or outcomes from I AM's Actions.

S: Situation.

S+AI: SOARing + Artificial Intelligence.

SATISFACTION: The positive energy I AM feels when needs and wants are met.

SE: SOARing Experience.

SELF-ACTUALIZATION: I AM being all that I AM can be.

SELF-ASSESSMENT: I AM's description and evaluation of I AM.

SENSORY AWARENESS: I AM's ability to focus on specific senses like: sight, smell, taste, touch, and hearing.

SIS: The three visual frameworks I AM uses to plan and manage Job #1 and Job #2.

SITUATION: I AM's perception of the set of circumstances Here NOW.

SITUATIONAL AWARENESS: I AM's awareness and understanding of the Here NOW situation with con- sideration for what could evolve in the future.

SKILLS: I AM's having the capacity to do something well.

SMART OBJECTIVES: Objectives that are: Specific, Measurable, Achievable, Relevant and Time-Bound.

SOAR: Acronym of Situation, Objectives, Actions, Results.

SOAR NOW: Situation, Objectives, Actions, Results used at NOW to feel better and to plan the living of a better life story.

SOAR SCORE: I AM's feelings reflected on the NOW Line Feelings Scale.

SOARing: Using the SOAR intentional improvement process to feel better and live a better life story.

SOARing EXPERIENCE (SE): The Situation, Objectives, Actions, Results format that produces and helps manage the Improvement Plan.

SOARing FLOW: The dynamic process of navigating through different growth situations of life.

SOARing FLOWS: The systematic activities directed towards the achievement of specific objectives.

SOARing IMPROVEMENT SYSTEM: The three visual frameworks I AM uses to plan and manage Job #1 and Job #2.

SOARing PROCESS: The SOAR method to reach objectives and navigate life.

SOUL A nonphysical part of I AM that is everything that makes I AM alive instead of dead.

SPACE: A continuous area that is available for use.

SPACE FLOW: The dynamic and continuous movement of space.

SPIRIT: A nonphysical part of I AM that is the spiritual connection between I AM and I AM's chosen god.

SPIRITUALITY: I AM's concern for or sensitivity to things of the spirit or soul, especially as opposed to materialistic concerns.

STATUS QUO: The current situation at NOW.

STIMULUS: A Situation that causes I AM's response.

STRENGTHS: I AM's physical and nonphysical positive qualities.

STRESS: The emotional or physical tension I AM perceives in response to a situation.

SUCCESS: I AM's satisfactory achievement of a desired objective, purpose or aim.

SWOT: Strengths, weaknesses, opportunities & threats analysis of something.

SYNERGY: Two things working together that create better results than the sum of the individual contributions.

TFA CYCLE: A concept showing the interconnection of thinking, feeling and acting.

TALENTS: I AM's having the natural ability to do something well.

TEMPERAMENT: I AM's natural frame of mind.

THOUGHTS: Products of I AM's thinking, like ideas, perceptions and opinions.

THREATS: Conditions perceived as a danger.

THRIVE: To grow vigorously.

TIME: I AM's clock time.

TIME FLOW: I AM's perception and experience of time passing.

TIMELINE: The length of time planned for managing an Improvement Plan from start through Results.

TIME LINE: The horizontal arrow representing the concept of time moving forward.

TOOLBOX: I AM's distinctive attributes.

TOPIC: I AM's focus of attention.

TOPIC CHOICE: I AM's choosing the most-important-now subject in a Choice Cycle and possible SOARing Experience.

TRAITS: I AM's distinguishing characteristics.

UNIVERSE: All of space, time, matter and energy.

VALUES: The moral, social or aesthetic principles I AM uses as guidelines for what is good, desirable or important.

VISION: I AM's long-term visualization of the ideal I AM aspires to create.

VISUAL FRAMEWORK: A pictorial model of the essential supporting structure of something.

VISUAL LEARNING: I AM learning from visual materials.

VISUALIZE: I AM forms a mental picture of a Topic.

WANTS: Topics I AM would like to have.

WEAKNESSES: I AM's physical and nonphysical negative qualities.

WELL-BEING: Positive Energy, Engagement, Meaning, Accomplishments and Positive Relationships.

WISDOM: I AM having knowledge, experience and good judgment.

WOW FACTOR: Improvements to things with a bit of extra pizzazz, to take the good to great.

WWWWWH: Who. What. When. Where. Why. How.

X: I AM.

X BIG PICTURE: I AM on the Big Picture Feelings Platform.

X LOCATION: X placement on the NOW Line reflecting I AM's feelings.

ACKNOWLEDGEMENTS

In creating this work, I draw from an extraordinary body of knowledge that has illuminated the path of human potential, well-being and improvement. I offer special thanks to these guiding trailblazers.

To Abraham Maslow and his profound Hierarchy of Needs, thank you for clarifying the essential stepping stones that shape personal and societal growth.

To Peter Drucker's pioneering concept of Management by Objectives (MBO). He provided invaluable insight into aligning purpose with progress, making it possible to set meaningful goals and measure success with clarity.

I also owe deep personal appreciation to Esther and Jerry Hicks for their many Abraham books, gatherings, cruise seminars and specific guidance through the years. Their Emotional Guidance Scale is a valuable tool that invites each of us to navigate our feelings toward higher positive energy levels with greater alignment and joy.

To Martin E. P. Seligman for your groundbreaking work in establishing the positive psychology movement and defining well-being, particularly through your book Flourish. You have redefined how we understand and pursue a fulfilling life.

Finally, thanks to AI for creating new tools to help I AM improve I AM's life story and for helping the world be a better place to thrive.

These contributions have helped shape this work and my understanding of the limitless potential for human growth. We are at the leading edge of something extraordinary.

Let's go S.O.A.R.

Made in the USA
Coppell, TX
27 December 2024

43562180R10125